COMPARATIVE LEGISLATIVE REFORMS AND INNOVATIONS

Comparative Legislative Reforms and Innovations

Edited by
ABDO I. BAAKLINI
and
JAMES J. HEAPHEY

COMPARATIVE DEVELOPMENT STUDIES CENTER
GRADUATE SCHOOL OF PUBLIC AFFAIRS
STATE UNIVERSITY OF NEW YORK AT ALBANY
ALBANY, 1977

First published in 1977 by
Comparative Development Studies Center
Graduate School of Public Affairs
State University of New York at Albany

Printed and made in the United States of America

Library of Congress Cataloging in Publication Data
Main entry under title:

Comparative legislative reforms and innovations.

Includes bibliographical references.
1. Legislative bodies—Addresses, essays, lectures.
2. Legislative bodies—United States—States—Addresses, essays, lectures.
3. United States. Congress—Addresses, essays, lectures.
I. Baaklini, Abdo I. II. Heaphey, James J., 1930–
III. New York (State). State University, Albany.
Graduate School of Public Affairs. Comparative Development Studies Center.
JF501.C65 328'.3'0973 77-4249
ISBN 0-87395-805-5

Acknowledgement

An edited volume owes its existence primarily to the various authors who contributed to it. This is as much true in this case as any. The authors' willingness to revise their articles to answer questions of concern to the present volume is deeply appreciated. We would also like to express our thanks to Professor Malcolm Jewell who took the time to read the manuscript and provide us with his penetrating criticism and evaluation. Joseph Whorton and Alia Abdul-Wahab of the Comparative Development Studies Center deserve our thanks, the first for his editorial work and the second for her editorial work and the preparation of the index of this volume. Ms. Jeanine Gendron and Mrs. Sophia Caranikas saw to it that the manuscript reached the press in readable shape. Finally, our thanks for the superb editorial work of the State University of New York Press.

Contents

Preface

The coming decade is most likely going to be the decade of legislative reforms. After over half a century of continuous executive growth and aggrandizement, a change in direction in favor of the legislature is crystallizing on the horizon. Watergate and its aftermath are the watershed of this transformation.

For the last five years the Comparative Development Studies Center of the State University of New York at Albany has been actively involved, nationally and internationally, in efforts aimed at legislative reforms and innovations. At the national level it has worked very closely with the National Legislative Conference and with a number of state legislatures on issues such as interference in and openness of the legislative process; modern information needs and electronic data banks of legislatures; legislative fiscal review and program evaluation; science, technology, and the legislative process; and structural and procedural changes to meet the emerging needs of legislatures.

At the international level, the Comparative Development Studies Center, through a major institutional grant from United States Agency for International Development (AID), has undertaken research and technical assistance programs in legislative areas in countries as diverse from each other as Brazil, Costa Rica, Lebanon, Ethiopia, Ghana, Ireland, Netherlands, Jordan, Israel, and Korea. The studies involved research on the legislative process, legislative reforms, how legislatures undertake their functions as institutions and the roles they play in their political settings.

The CDSC involvement in legislative reforms is characterized by a specific approach and methodology. As an academic research institution, the Center follows neither the advocacy approach nor the private enterprise consultancy approach. We do not have a model of what legislative reforms should be (in contrast to the Citizens' Conference or the Common Cause) nor do we claim that legislative reform is a technical problem for the specialists or experts to determine. As social scientists with a phenomenological orientation, legislative reforms are seen as the conscious interaction of legislators, opinion leaders, scholars and other concerned citizens. The purpose of this interaction is to bring about changes in the legislative structures, procedures, equipment and approaches for the purpose of strengthening the legislature as an institution. As social scientists we describe this interaction and the outcome it produces and analyze it in terms of the goals and objectives that it was supposed to achieve.

For the past five years the Comparative Development Studies Center has sponsored three international conferences on legislative development and has organized several panels on the same topics in the context of the annual conferences of the American Society for Public Administration, Society for International Development, and the triennial meeting of the International Political Science Association. The first international conference sponsored by the Center took place in Cyprus in 1972 and resulted in the establishment of the Research Committee on Legislative Development of the International Political Science Association.

The second international conference on legislative development was held at the State University of New York at Albany in January 1975. This conference was cosponsored by the Brazilian Congress and dealt with two interrelated topics; legislative reforms and the role of legislatures in contemporary societies. In September 1976 the CDSC, in cooperation with the Institute of Public Administration of Ireland, held its third international conference in Dublin on the theme of Legislatures and Human Rights.

The present volume brings together the research work of a number of scholars on the theme of legislative reforms and innovations. Two other volumes are also under preparation; one dealing with the roles of legislatures in contemporary societies and the other volume discusses the roles of legislatures in protecting human rights. Most of the papers in this volume were presented at the second international conference held in Albany. Others were presented at the annual meetings of the American Political Science Association or other professional gatherings. However, to provide comparability and consistency all the papers were rewritten to answer certain essential questions that were considered important for the scholars and practitioners in the field of legislative administration.

Abdo I. Baaklini
Albany, N.Y.
September, 1977

List of Contributors

Abdo I. Baaklini

Professor Abdo Baaklini is the Associate Director of the Comparative Development Studies Center and is Assistant Professor at the Department of Public Administration of the State University of New York at Albany. Professor Baaklini directs a national and an international program of technical assistance to legislatures in the U.S.A. and in a number of developing countries. He has numerous articles and books on legislatures, their roles and their administrative and research needs.

Professor Baaklini received his B.A. and M.A. in Public Administration at the American University in Beirut and his Ph.D. in Political Science at the State University of New York at Albany.

Norman Beckman

Norman Beckman is the Acting Director of the Congressional Research Service of the Library of Congress and an Adjunct Professor at George Washington University and the Virginia Polytechnic Institute—State University. Dr. Beckman received a doctorate in Public Law and Government from Columbia University in 1957 and a Masters in Public Administration from Syracuse University in 1952. His publications include numerous articles on urban development, public administration and congressional information needs. He is the main author of *Senate Documents or "Toward a National Growth Policy: Federal and State Development" in 1972, 1973 and 1974.*

Edgar G. Crane, Jr.

Edgar G. Crane, Jr. directed the project on Legislative Program Performance Review at the Comparative Development Studies Center, State University of New York at Albany. He brings to this work a combination of training in the tools of program review and diverse experience in legislative settings. He has directed the National Legislative Conference and has served the legislatures of California, New York, Illinois and Kentucky in research, committee, and leadership staff capacities. He holds the doctorate in Public Administration from the Graduate School of Public Affairs, State University of New York at Albany. At SUNYA he has directed a number of projects at the Comparative Development Studies Center, been an associate of the Ford Foundation Project for Productivity Research in State Government, and served as policy analyst for the School of Social Welfare. Currently he is associated with the New York State Legislative Commission on Expenditure Review.

Erik Damgaard

Erik Damgaard is Associate Professor at the Institute of Political Science, University of Aarhus, Denmark. He has published a number of articles on Danish legislative politics and is author of a forthcoming book on the Danish Parliament.

Keith E. Hamm

Keith E. Hamm received his M.A. from Florida Atlantic University and is presently completing his Ph.D. at the University of Wisconsin-Milwaukee.

James J. Heaphey

James J. Heaphey is Director of the Comparative Development Studies Center, State University of New York at Albany, and Professor of Public Administration. He is the author of *Spatial Dimensions of Development Administration* and of numerous articles in professional journals. He is currently directing a worldwide research project on the role of legislatures in development, in addition to conducting several research projects on organizational aspects of American state legislatures.

Ronald D. Hedlund

Ronald D. Hedlund is an Associate Professor of Political Science at the University of Wisconsin-Milwaukee where his teaching and research interests include legislative process, legislator behavior, and research methods. Professor Hedlund received his Ph.D. in political science from the University of Iowa in 1967. Since 1974 his interests have focused on developing ways to measure legislative performance in the Wisconsin legislature and on the effects of factors like rules changes, procedural innovation, and leadership style on legislative performance. He has authored many articles in political science publications about legislatures and legislators.

R. B. Jain

Dr. R. B. Jain is Associate Professor in Political Science at the University of Delhi. A specialist in Public Administration, Comparative Politics and World Order, he is author of *Contemporary Issues in Indian Administration*, 1974 and of several articles in the field of Comparative Administration and World Order.

Dr. Jain served as a visiting Fulbright Fellow at the School of Foreign Service, Georgetown University, 1975–76.

John R. Johannes

John R. Johannes received his B.S. degree from Marquette University in 1966 and his Ph.D. from Harvard University in 1970. He currently is Associate Professor of Political Science at Marquette. A specialist in American legislative-executive relations, he is the author of several scholarly articles on the U.S. Congress. He is the author of a monograph, *Policy Innovation in Congress*, and of articles in *Public Policy*, *Western Political Quar-*

terly, *Review of Politics*, *Journal of Communications*, *Intellect*, and *Moral Values in Contemporary Life*. Professor Johannes teaches courses on the Presidency, Congress, and Political Parties and Interest Groups.

Khaled Kayali

Professor Khaled Kayali was born in Palestine and was reared in Syria before coming to the United States. He received a B.A. and M.A. in government at Texas Tech University and earned an M.A. and Ph.D. from the University of Maryland at College Park in 1975. He taught at Texas Tech University and the University of Maryland before joining Shippensburg State College where he is teaching as well as working closely with local officials in south-central Pennsylvania through the college's Center for Local and State Government.

Richard I. Nunez

Richard I. Nunez, admitted to practice before the Federal and New York State courts, holds a Ph.D. and J.D. He is Associate Professor of Public Administration in the Department of Public Administration of the Graduate School of Public Affairs, State University of New York at Albany. He has published articles in professional law journals and public administration journals. He served as a member of the New York State Bar Association Committee on Administrative Law.

Joseph W. Whorton

Joseph W. Whorton has had eight years administrative experience at the local level as both an Assistant City Manager and as Director of a public housing authority. In addition, he has consulted with numerous public agencies on information systems, reporting procedures and program analysis. He currently holds teaching appointments at Russell Sage College and State University of New York at Albany and is staff consultant to the Public Executive Project, SUNYA.

John Abbott Worthley

John Abbott Worthley is Director of the Institute of Public Affairs and Associate Professor of Public Administration at Briarcliff College. He formerly was a program officer and assistant professor with the Comparative Development Studies Center of State University of New York at Albany where he continues as a consultant and visiting professor. Mr. Worthley has worked with many legislatures and is the author of *Public Administration and Legislatures* and of *Comparative Legislative Information Systems.* He has published articles in several journals and is an Adjunct Professor at Long Island University and at Russell Sage College.

Introduction

Legislative Reforms and Public Administration

ABDO I. BAAKLINI

Legislative reforms have been, in recent years, the preoccupation of politicians, journalists, and concerned citizen groups. After over half a century of continuous executive growth and aggrandizement, a change favoring the strengthening of legislatures has begun to crystallize. In the American context, Watergate and its aftermath may be viewed as the watershed for these new developments.

With the exception of legislative reforms at the US Congress and recently some state legislatures, social science literature has been oblivious of the efforts of legislatures around the world to equip themselves with the capabilities to enable them to function in the modern world. The literature on legislative reforms is sporadic and fleeting. Often it takes the form of an obscure monograph, or an internal committee proceeding, or a report by an advocacy group interested in changing the legislature in a particular direction. Such literature as exists is characterized by an advocacy and efficiency orientation. The advocacy approach can have a moral-ethical or a political orientation. The moral-ethical orientation literature conceives of legislative reform as an instrument to attain goals and objectives that the reformer conceives to be moral and ethical. It concentrates on such matters as openness of committee deliberations, campaign financing acts, elimination of conflict of interests, and other similar activities. The political orientation literature examines legislative reform in terms of power shifts; it focuses on such matters as the seniority system and its amendments, the leadership staff and prerogatives, and the jurisdiction of certain committees. The efficiency approach is characterized by a conscious attempt at rationalizing the legislative process and purifying it from political meddling.

Neither the advocacy nor the efficiency orientation can provide a proper conception of legislative reforms as phenomena. Furthermore, neither literature has penetrated academic circles and therefore has not contributed to nor benefitted from our theoretical knowledge about organizations and organizational and political behavior. An exchange of information is vitally necessary and efforts to bring it about are overdue.

This volume attempts to view legislative reforms from the perspective of those political actors who initiated the reforms or who are affected by them. In addition, the work tries to utilize public administration theory, particularly organization theory in the study of these reforms. The volume also compares legislative reforms in the United States with those overseas. Some of the reforms and innovations are compared across legislatures, others are compared longitudinally within the same legislature. Finally, the volume seeks to answer a number of questions. What are some of the reforms and innovations that are taking place? Why are these reforms being instituted? What are the implications of these reforms for the power distribution between the legislature and other political institutions in society, for the power distribution within the legislature, and for the ability of the legislature to meet the new challenges it is facing?

The Relevance of Theories of Public Administration to Legislative Reforms

Recent legislative reforms and innovations draw to a large extent on the findings of those who study public administration. The various authors in this volume, therefore, have consciously attempted to review the legislative reforms against the background of certain formulations derived from public administration theories. Thus, it is relevant to the relationship between public administration theory and the study of legislatures. To understand the problems that public administration may face in its involvement with legislatures and to appreciate the kind of issues and questions it has to consider, a brief review of public administration theories concerning its involvement with the executive will be illuminating.

Ever since the need for administrative machinery to conduct governmental business was first recognized, Americans have expressed fear and wariness about bureaucracies. They have always fully recognized that bureaucracies, while necessary for the efficient realization of public goals, are apt to become power centers themselves, if they are unchecked and uncontrolled. Public-administration theory has held that to maintain the essence of the democratic form of government, bureaucracies must be kept under constant control and surveillance.

Public administration theory has consisted largely of attempts to build justifications and rationales to reassure the doubtful and the wary that bureaucracies will remain obedient, efficient instruments for the realization of goals that have been selected by a democratic political process. Public bureaucracies have expanded only when the system had no option but to resort to organizations. Thus bureaucracies have been accepted only in crisis situations and after their dangers have been eliminated, either through procedural and structural controls or through elaborate theoretical reinterpretation of the essentials of democratic societies and the place of bureaucracies in these societies. Woodrow Wilson is generally acknowledged by the public administration discipline as the first to warn against the possible danger of bureaucracies and the need in a democratic society to keep them under control.[1] Realizing that public administration is interconnected with politics in the sense that it may lead to the usurpation of power without proper popular control, Wilson warned that bureaucracies should always be popularly controlled.[2] The Scientific Management Movement (SMM) expressed similar concern that public administration might usurp power without proper popular control. The way the movement unfolded in public administration was, in a sense, a response to Wilson's call for a science of public administration. While SMM was primarily concerned with calling for cooperation between labor and management and the employment of certain scientific principles to increase production, when it considered public administration it confirmed two basic points: first, public administration should remain a tool separate from politics; and second, the purpose of that tool was to maximize rationality to achieve ends decided politically. The SMM also provided a whole set of structural and procedural instruments to insure that whatever power was wielded by the administration was properly controlled and that responsibility was ultimately insured.

During the thirties the politics-administration dichotomy persisted, thus perpetuating the belief that public administration was a tool, and politics the master. The basic innovation during that period was the appearance of the Human Relations Movement (HRM) with its concern for irrational human behavior in organizations. The HRM, under the leadership of Mayo, developed a humanistic dimension concerned with the fate of man in organizational society, but, the movement's basic contribution to public administration was that it tried to arm the manager with new insights and knowledge to enable him to control and reduce the irrational element in organizations. In this sense, it was an extension of the Scientific Management Movement. Under both the SMM and the HRM, public administration remained separate from politics, a tool for increasing the rational and efficient for achievement of politically desired goals. Politics remained the master and the guardian against the usurpation of power by the administration.

The Second World War produced two important public administration changes in the US. The politics-administration dichotomy was challenged and efficiency and rationality were reexamined. The new perspective revealed that public administration was engaged in policy-making and that efficiency and rationality had become ends in themselves rather than means.

As before, proponents of a strong bureaucracy argued that the difference between bureaucracy in a democracy and bureaucracy in a dictatorship is in the primacy given to politics. In a democracy bureaucracies do engage in political choices but they are ultimately controlled by political institutions. "The largest check on arbitrary power" says Appleby, "is in the fact that we have *political* government." [3] To him the characteristics of democratic administration were first politics, second responsibility, and third authority.[4] In a similar vein, F. M. Marx,[5] Thompson,[6] and others asserted that political control over the bureaucracy was a precondition necessary for a democratic government.

Perhaps the best illustration of the attempts to reconstruct public administration theory to justify the role that the bureaucracies came to play after World War II is the literature on "public interest" and the roles bureaucracies play in determining public interest. In his classic work on public interest, Schubert distinguished three different orientations in public administration with regard to public interest: the rationalists, the idealists, and the realists.[7]

The rationalists are those who adhere to the policy-administration dichotomy. For them, public administration is a tool to serve the political decision-makers, meaning here the legislature. The idealist looks upon the public administrator as a decision-maker directly involved in the determination of the public interest within the constraints laid down by the political decision-makers. This determination of public interest, Redford insists, should be done "within the framework of institutional organization and process,"[8] because ". . . the ideals of democratic government also demand that the administrator shall not try to take the full responsibility for the manipulation of interests."[9]

The third group, the realists, acknowledge the political role of the bureaucracy. Following the theory of group politics as originally proposed by Bentley[10] and later elaborated by Truman,[11] the realists assert that if bureaucracy is to function properly it requires a democratic society and that it should be open to group politics. A nonpolitical bureaucracy, it was argued, can become an obedient instrument in the hand of a dictator while an open, politically oriented bureaucracy is the best guarantee for democracy. To assert that bureaucracy plays a political role does not, however, mean that it has arbitrary power over the citizen.

Finally, to insure that bureaucracies would adhere to the role assigned them, public administration theory devised an elaborate set of structures, procedures, and norms within which a civil servant was supposed to act. In fact, the bulk of public administration literature dealt with structural, procedural, and normative issues. Questions of hierarchy, division of labor, communications, authority, recruitment, examinations, tenure, compensations, neutrality, political rights, union activities, accountability, responsibility, professional and ethical standards, and a host of other issues were all discussed, and appropriate institutions were devised to deal with these issues.

Public Administration and Legislatures

Recently public administration has moved to a new area. From a preoccupation with the executive branch of government, public administration is now showing interest in the organization of the legislative branch. While this involvement is considered overdue by some, it may be termed premature and dangerous by others. In any case there are many questions that need to be resolved, both in theory and practice, if public administration is to become a constructive instrument for legislative development.

Public administration as used here refers to an intellectual discipline in social science which is represented by scholars, academic institutions, professional associations, and their product in terms of research, publications, teaching, and training. Thus defined, public administration involvement can take different forms. This involvement is discussed under three headings—empirical, normative, and theoretical.

Empirical

The most obvious and least controversial type of involvement is empirical. By this is meant the need of the discipline to know what exists in terms of the present administrative phenomenon in legislatures and to make it known to scholars, students, legislators, legislative staff, and concerned citizens.[12] This is a process or research, reporting, publication, and teaching. Our present knowledge of the legislative bureaucratic phenomenon is practically nonexistent. What publications as do exist are scanty and mostly written from a moralistic, journalistic, or political reformist perspective. Redman, for example, found two basic misconceptions in the literature. First, it pictures the legislative-executive relations as a zero-sum-game where the executive continuously gains in power while the legislature continuously loses; and second, it portrays Congress only in terms of the elected membership and fails to consider the role of the legislative staff.[13]

Systematic information on various aspects of the legislative bureaucratic phenomenon has yet to be gathered. We need to know the characteristics and behavior of the legislative staff, their motivation, conduct, and orientation towards their work and towards the public and the institution within which they work. We also need to know the institutional arrangement of the legislative bureaucracy, the relationship of the various parts to each other, and the work each part performs. What is the system of authority and influence, the communication system, and the information base of the legislative bureaucrats, and what is the ecology of the legislative bureaucracy, that is, its relationship to the legislature and to its various parts, such as the leadership, committees, political parties, and the rank-and-file legislator. We need to examine the relationship of this bureacuracy to the rest of the political system, such as the executive and its bureaucracy, interest groups, lobbyists, and others. In other words, we need to increase our knowledge of legislatures as functioning institutions and of the role legislative bureaucracies play in this process.

To be able to generate such knowledge we need a community of scholars, students, and concerned public officials and citizens so that our academic institutional capacities and our professional associations can be mobilized to allocate resources for such a purpose. Here several problems exist. Even though empirical involvement is the least controversial, it faces opposition. First of all, public administrators themselves, through their historical association with the executive and their normative commitment toward bureaucratic-legal rationality, feel that either they have nothing to offer to legislatures or that in order to maximize their executive bureaucratic value they should not offer anything, even if they could.

Second, academic examination of legislatures has historically been the domain of political scientists. There is rarely any political science department without some courses taught about legislatures; political scientists have constantly been involved with legislatures, particularly at times of legislative reform; and they have produced practically all the academic literature on legislatures. They view any involvement of public administration in legislative studies as an encroachment on their preserve.

Third, legislators, who have had a rather tense relationship with social science (basically political science), are wary in dealing with any new academic field. From a legislative perspective, social scientists have frequently engaged in moralistic delinquent preaching based on shortsightedness and lack of information. Legislators are likely, therefore, to view the public administration empirical involvement with suspicion.

Normative Involvement

Public administration is an applied science. Its relationship to the other social sciences is similar to that between technology and the natural sciences. Therefore the legitimacy of its claim for involvement in legislatures is based less on its empirical research than on its practical advice to bureaucrats. It is this normative orientation that made public administration appealing to the executive and to the general citizenry. Public administration had a set of answers, principles, and guidelines when it approached the executive offering to help. Can public administration develop a normative orientation towards legislative involvement and, if so, what are its elements and what are its theoretical bases? For example, how would the field answer the following: What is legislative development as far as public administration is concerned? Is it the ability of the legislature to reach decisions in accordance with bureaucratic rationality? If yes, why should bureaucratic rationality be more important and better than political rationality?

To suggest that public administration is simply an instrument concerned with factual objective questions misses the point. For public administration to assert that it can train staff to act as objective researchers in the legislature would probably be worthless in terms of its effect on legislative decision-making. Legislators around the world are skeptical of those who claim they can do research that is not influenced by values. Furthermore legislators want assistance in getting their ideas advanced. They have been elected to further the causes they espouse, so for them, staff service is assistance in pursuing those causes. Viewing the problem at a more concrete level, we can see that any attempts at legislative organizational reform have their own political implications that cannot be justified in terms of the "tool" and the "rational-legal" orientations of public administration.

By defining the structure and the process of decision-making, we would not simply be acting to achieve the same values more efficiently and effectively (as it is claimed in the executive bureaucracy), we would be defining what values are sought and considered, and this is clearly not a bureaucratic right, nor are bureaucracies qualified to do this. Questions such as timing of sessions, structures of committees, procedures of bills, functions and power of leaders, activities and functions of committees or individual members, political ethics, facilities, equipment, and staff available for legislators are all issues with political implications that shape the values as they are defined.

Even in cases where the values to be realized are apparently identifiable, public administration might find itself engaging in value choices. The issue of legislative staffing, for instance, which is closer to the public administration domain than other issues, is loaded with value choices. Should legislatures employ a career, neutral legislative staff, hierarchically controlled as in the executive, or a political staff? To whom should the staff report, to the leadership, committee chairmen, or to the members at large? Should the staff be concerned with matters related to the institution as a whole, such as bill consideration, or should it be involved in assisting the legislator as politician in getting elected? What are the rights and duties of the staff vis-à-vis the legislature and the public? It is clear that each choice involves the promotion of one group's interest over another. Who is, therefore, to decide which group interest is to be promoted? In a collegial body such as the legislature, who is the chief legislator? All legislators are elected and all of them have an equal mandate from the people to represent the whole nation or, in the case of state legislatures, the whole state. Which political right can public administration identify with?

As a practical solution, it has been suggested that public administration should align itself with the leadership. But is there one leadership in the legislature? What are the rights of the opposition or the back benchers of the majority party? How does the legislative bureaucracy define the public interest? How can the legislators and the people be sure they control legislative bureaucratic power?

Theoretical Involvement

While normative involvement challenges the field to answer "what should be" questions, theoretical involvement concerns, the justification for normative involvement and whatever recommendations it produces and the maintenance of a theoretical consistency on the role of bureaucracies in democratic societies.

Public administration has not as yet developed a set of normative prescriptions towards legislative reforms. The reason may be that it has not been sufficiently involved in the study of legislatures, or that, if public administration is to maintain its theoretical consistency (as a tool for rational-legal decisions to achieve politically desired ends), it cannot adopt a legislative normative posture, at least not at this time. Perhaps the absence of a normative orientation is an advantage in the sense that legislators do not feel threatened by the presence of the administrative "experts" around them. On the other hand, such an absence may be conceived as a disadvantage, since it can lead many of those who are involved and interested in legislative reforms to believe that public administration has sold out to the politically influential legislators who are at the base of legislative weakness and corruption. The question becomes, then, how can public administration maintain its theoretical consistency and yet demonstrate its utility?

In view of the growth of public bureaucracies in the executive branch, and the power they have come to wield, it would be naive to accept the thesis that bureaucracies are simply tools for the advancement of rational-legal decision-making. Nonetheless, executive bureaucracies have tenuously managed to justify their existence theoretically and practically. Can legislative bureaucracies do the same?

The most important theoretical question is whether the growth of a legislative bureaucracy will cause it to supplant the elected legislature as the institution of political control over the executive bureaucracy. If it will, what is the difference between the executive bureaucracy controlling itself (by means of a central inspection, auditors, and controllers) and its being controlled by a legislative bureaucracy? Is it likely that the executive and legislative bureaucracies will come to have a common orientation and consequently less control, that they will tend to work together against "political" interference? And, finally, what happens to the theoretical foundation of public administration in a democratic state in which it is postulated that bureaucrats do not determine values but implement them? In other words, can public administration theories claim that values can be rationally and legally determined? The practical implications of these questions and their answers are far-reaching.

In view of the pervasiveness of the bureaucratic phenomena and the domination of the rational-legal mode of thinking over political thinking, what are the guarantees that a legislative bureaucracy would not suffocate the political realm and that the last enclave of charismatic leadership would not be turned into another bureaucracy, status-oriented and committed to already existing rules and procedures. How many legislators would dare to oppose a bureaucratic solution and risk the accusation of corruption or political favoritism? Can legislative bureaucracies respect the legislator's right to know? Legislators come from all walks of life. Many have left very important and lucrative positions in the private sector in order to join the only institution where charisma can survive and where they can participate not in what *was* or *is* but what *should* be. Would the bureaucratization of the legislature discourage such charismatic leaders from running for election?

A number of questions concerning the legislative staff need to be answered. It has been suggested that to maintain political responsiveness, legislative staff should enjoy only a temporary appointment and should keep their values, feelings, and opinions subservient to the political master. Assuming for the moment that such a political master can be identified, what about the civil and human rights of the legislative staff? To maintain neutrality and secrecy civil servants in the executive branch, extracted tenure rights, security, and space for self-realization through administrative action. What about the security, self-actualization, and self-aggrandizement of legislative staff? How can a legislative staff member be expected to forfeit his rights as a citizen or as a human being, especially when he is operating in such an ambiguous structure as a legislature? Since a legislative staff member can operate freely in the legislator's zone of indifference and, in many cases, can filter the constituency influence before it reaches the legislator, he is likely to fill this power vacuum regardless of exhortations to remain loyal and subservient.[14]

Finally, how representative of and politically responsive to the people is a legislature that has been isolated by a legislative bureaucracy? How can the individual citizen be assured that the legislature will not become just another government department where it does not matter who gets elected, since the influence of the legislative bureaucratic machinery is likely to remain the same?

Unfortunately, the history of public administration, even in the executive branch, does not provide an encouraging precedent. Although bureaucracies are considered necessary in modern government, there is some consensus, at least among the rank and file in the United States, against their oppressiveness, irresponsiveness, and adherence to precedent and the status quo. A legislative bureaucracy based on the executive model seems likely to cut the last link between the people and their only representative institution. The argument that more experts placed in the legislature would lead to better decisions is not that persuasive. If a democracy is supposed to reflect the values of the ruled, then why should all our institutions be dominated by "experts?" Where is the role of the people? How can the individual citizen be assured that somewhere in the structure of power there is somebody who thinks the way he does? How can the individual citizen be involved and avoid drifting into apathy? Or have we decided that apathy is what we need?

As this volume illustrates, public administration is now recognizing a need for involvement with legislative organizations. It is just beginning to grapple with the theoretical implication of this involvement. However, it is still far from having devised the institutions and mechanisms for carrying out whatever involvement it plans to undertake. In a sense public administration cannot devise institutions and mechanisms without deciding on the nature of its involvement, and this cannot happen before the questions about empirical and theoretical involvement have been satisfactorily answered.

The Experience of Legislatures

This volume is divided into three parts, the first of which contains three articles and dealing with innovations at the US Congress. The four articles of the second part consider legislative reforms and innovations at the state level in the United States. The third part examines legislative reforms in four overseas legislatures.

The Experience of the US Congress

The thesis of the first article, by John R. Johannes, is that the Congress's ability to initiate and influence legislation and to oversee the executive bureaucracy depends on its ability to obtain needed information. One method of obtaining such information is through the statutory reporting requirement, and while this requirement is not recent, its use has significantly increased in recent years. Statutory reporting may take a variety of forms; study and recommend reporting, post facto reporting, and advance notification reporting. Such reports originate in various agencies of the executive including the president. Congress normally uses information from such reports as a means to control and oversee the executive, as part of the legislative compromise, for congressional committees, for symbolic purposes, and finally for partisan reasons. The author found that if the reports are to be effective, they should be received on time, must be read, and should be available for distribution. A report's usefulness depends on the way it is written and the quality of information it contains. This depends on time and availability of staff resources. The author concludes with a number of recommendations for improving the reporting procedure.

Khaled M. Kayali's chapter analyses the development, growth, and functions of the staff attached to the House Committee on Appropriations. If, as Johannes argued, the Congress is receiving more information, particularly via statutory reporting, then the need for a competent staff to analyze and report this information to the committee members becomes evident. Kayali's article vividly illustrates the dilemma lawmakers face when they wish to increase their information without loosing their ability to act independently and authoritatively as elected political representatives. The committee had to decide not whether to have more or less staff, but what kind of staff, where to locate them, how to control them, and how long to retain them. Kayali suggests that the House Committee on Appropriations chooses to employ, in addition to its permanent staff, a temporary staff, the General Accounting Office, and the Congressional Research Service. Furthermore, the committee usually defines the area of jurisdiction of both the permanent and temporary committee staff in order to limit the danger of the legislative staff bureaucracy usurping the decision-making power of the committee.

Norman Beckman's article describes and analyses the work of the Congressional Research Service since the 1970 Legislative Reorganization Act. The article highlights the complexities and conflicting demands facing the CRS from the perspective of the CRS management and staff. The problems relate to which managerial and administrative alternatives that the CRS should adopt in meeting its mandate of providing the congressional committees with policy analysis. Is it necessary, for example, to set up a separate research staff to provide in-depth services? What is the relationship between the jurisdictions of the congressional committees involved and the subject specializations of each of the existing CRS divisions? How can one recommend or advise without indulging in advocacy? What priorities should CRS adopt in scheduling its work? There are many similar administrative and managerial questions, with respect to other CRS functions.

In cooperation with other institutions (such as Brookings), the CRS has supported a number of public policy seminars for both congressmen and their staffs, has acquired an automated information capability with a number of socioeconomic data sets, and has developed cooperative relations with the General Accounting Office and the Office of Technology Assessment of the Congress. Its future plans call for a better liaison with scholarly community and development of a capability to conduct or commission public opinion surveys. It hopes to strengthen CRS relationship with committees by encouraging CRS staff to spend some time working with committees and by coordinating its work with the newly established congressional budget office. Beckman's article provides a fine illustration of the administrative and organizational dimension of the legislative process.

The Experience of the US State Legislatures

Part 2 of this volume deals with recent legislative reforms and innovations at the US state level. The experience of the fifty states in legislative reforms provides an invaluable source for comparative studies. The states vary in size, population, and socioeconomic conditions, and their legislative traditions and histories reflect these variations. In the past quarter century most bold legislative innovations have taken place at the state level. The experience of the states is, therefore, extremely valuable for social scientists, since it comes closest to control experiment conditions. More importantly, the variety and richness of the states' experience can be particularly informative and useful for many developing countries.

Thanks to the efforts of several professional organizations set up by various legislatures and concerned citizens, a factual inventory of trends is possible. These reforms include topics such as duration of legislative sessions, restrictions on subject matter that can be considered during sessions, presession activities, size of legislature and terms of office, compensation, number and jurisdiction of committees, facilities for legislators and their staff, introduction of new equipment and technologies to facilitate the legislative process, and finally the mushrooming of legislative staff services.[15]

The four articles in this part zero in on significant, specific innovations at the state level. Edgar G. Crane focuses on the experience of the states in adopting capabilities to undertake program review and evaluation functions. After reviewing the structural arrangement and program review activities of selected legislatures, Crane tries to measure the impact of the various alternatives. Adopting a number of indices Crane reaches some tentative conclusions regarding the relative impact of the approaches with regard to the legislature's ability to augment its policy function vis-à-vis the executive. Crane concludes his study by raising two questions: what is the relationship between the program review staff and the legislators and what communication systems are appropriate to insure that program review products are properly communicated to policy makers. He demonstrates that the way these two questions are answered determine to a large extent the impact of program review studies on policy formulation.

John A. Worthley's article examines the expanding use of modern information technologies by state legislatures and compares the various structural arrangements legislatures use to meet internal and external needs. He finds that state legislatures appeared to resist using computers "until mechanisms for controlling the impact were established," but that, computer usage appears to strengthen the legislature's policy-making capacity and role vis-à-vis the executive. In a sense, Worthley's article attempts to answer some of the questions regarding the need to study the impact of legislative reforms. He concludes by calling for additional studies to determine the impact of computers on the legislatures' output. A major problem, however, is how one can determine and measure what legislatures produce.[16]

Ronald D. Hedlund and Keith E. Hamm face the issue of measuring the impact of specific legislative reforms frontally. Relying on a system functional approach, the authors assess the impact of procedural changes in the Wisconsin Assembly on that body's decision-making effectiveness. These procedural changes give the Rules Committee "the power to make any

My article on Brazil deals with the recent comprehensive reform in the Chamber of Deputies. This differs from other experiences because it was comprehensive, rather than incremental, in nature, and it was developed and implemented in a comparatively short period of time. Since the reforms are very recent, the article can only describe them and try to analyze the political motives behind them. It appears that the legislature used the reforms to insure its survival under a military-dominated regime and to rehabilitate its public image. Available data suggest that their short-term impact has been to facilitate those executive programs which stress law and order and rapid economic growth. From the legislative perspective the long-term goals of these reforms are to strengthen the legislature's information base and its management and to improve its public image so that it can eventually participate effectively in policy choices and in curbing executive power. In-depth interviews with various legislators and legislative staff in Brazil tend to support this second hypothesis.

Erik Damgaard analyzes reforms and innovations in the Danish Folketinget, most of which came about for pragmatic reasons and were incremental in nature. Damgaard discusses the changes in terms of their contribution to time saving, work reduction, and specialization. Some adjusted existing structures and procedures, such as longer sessions, full-time legislators, increased work load, increased staff resources, and more specialized committees, but they also include new structures and functions, such as the abolition of bicameralism in 1953, the establishment of an ombudsman institution elected by the legislature, participation in joint executive commissions, and the introduction of questioning and general debate on ministerial policies and actions. Evaluating the reforms in terms of the objectives of the reformers, those who called for a "strong government" model and those who called for a "strong parliament" model, the author finds the reforms fall short of either model. Some innovations favored one model; some the other. Nonetheless the reforms undoubtedly did strengthen the political system, both the executive and the legislature, which has helped it to meet increasing demands. Damgaard's findings, as well as those in the other articles in this section, support the proposition that the strengthening of the legislature does not necessarily mean the weakening of the executive; rather it leads towards the strengthening of the whole political system.

The last article, dealing with legislative reforms in Lebanon, places the legislature within the total political system and suggests that political conflict in Lebanon revolves around certain reforms in the legislature. There are macrosystem reforms which include the question of sectarianism and the distribution of parliamentary seats among the various sects in Lebanon, the relationship of the legislature to political parties, and finally the relationship of the legislature to the executive. Procedural reforms include methods of bill introduction and provisions for delegated Legislation. Organizational reforms include the structuring and strengthening of the committee system, the addition of competent legislative staff, and the provision of needed information. These various reforms are analyzed in terms of the political objectives of the various groups pushing for them.

Legislative Reforms in Comparative Perspective

Who originates legislative reforms, why legislative reforms take place, and what their impact is are questions that permeate this volume. In answering these questions it is possible to distinguish two patterns, one characterizing the US federal and state experience and the other the experience of legislatures in developing countries. The two patterns overlap at various points. In all cases, for example, the driving reason for legislative reforms is political. Administrative or efficiency considerations are secondary. Having said that, however, there is a distinct difference between the way this political need is manifested in the US and the way it appears elsewhere.

Legislatures in the West developed as a result of certain historical circumstances and in accordance with their own logic. The functions they performed and the rationality within which they performed were appropriately suited to the philosophies prevalent in those times. Eloquence, oratory, and rhetoric were qualities highly cherished for a successful member of Parliament in nineteenth-century England. What we now call organizational inefficiency or irrationality was tolerated and sometimes valued as conducive to political rationality and democratic values. In the last half century, however, socioeconomic changes, population growth and movement, science and technology, the emergence of the welfare state and changes in policies have tremendously increased the complexity and diversity of policy problems.[17] Rejuvenation of legislative institutions became a concern of politicians, journalists and scholars.[18]

While the scholarly literature on legislative development is still scanty and somewhat contradictory, certain common discerned assumptions exist. These concern the decline of legislatures, the obstacles to legislative reform, legislative-executive rivalry, and the dichotomy between political rationality and organizational rationality.

Decline of Legislatures

The first assumption of the advocates of legislative reforms is that legislatures have declined in power and that something should be done to rectify the imbalance between the executive and the legislature. While almost all agree that decline exists, its nature, its extent, and the proposed remedies have remained widely disputed. Whether this decline is in absolute power, in efficiency, in public esteem, or in power relative to the executive is not usually spelled out.[19] There is a concensus, however, that complex technological societies and the role governments play in these societies require new political and administrative machineries and the application of modern information technologies.

A number of approaches have been suggested to strengthen legislatures. There are those who have advocated basic procedural and structural changes so that the legislature may again perform its historical and constitutional functions and again counterbalance the executive.[20] Others have accepted the shift in the power to the executive as inevitable and have advocated an adjustment in the legislature's functions to fit the new reality.[21] Still others have advocated a total restructuring of political institutions, including the executive, the legislature, and political parties.[22]

All reformers recognize that legislative organization and procedures need such changes as increased professional staff to improve information assessment, restructured committees, abolition of the seniority system; change in the time and frequency of sessions, abolition of late sittings, creation of specialized committees to consider policy and administrative problems, increased opportunity for backbenchers to participate, provision of research and staff facilities for committees, limitations on floor speech-time, revised bill-passing procedures, and so forth.

Although the "decline of parliament" theme may be relevant to the historical experience of some Western legislatures, its application to developing countries is not so clear. Formal legislative bodies are a fairly recent phenomenon in developing non-Western countries. In formerly colonial countries, the legislatures have just started to evolve. In some cases, they are performing functions that were previously performed by other institutions. It is perhaps more appropriate in this context therefore, to talk of a period of uncertainty where legislatures in developing countries are groping for a role that fits the political, social, cultural and economic conditions of those countries.

Obstacles to Legislative Reforms

A number of obstacles to legislative reform in Western countries appear to have no relevance for developing countries. The claim that traditional parliamentary procedures should not be changed because they act as a source of parliamentary strength is an example.[23] The appeal to a glorious past to justify obsolete procedures is unlikely to happen in developing countries. They are not hindered by what Bernard Crick calls a "decline in constitutional thought," or by stubborn nostalgia for procedural "tradition," or by "the glories of Parliament." [24] Procedural norms, while important in the legislatures of the developing countries, have not yet become so institutionalized and inflexible as to prevent procedural innovations.

It has been argued that legislative reform in developing countries must await the emergence of "politically mature institutions," [25] where a politically mature institution was defined in Huntingtonian variables of adaptability, complexity, autonomy, and coherency.[26] The implication here is that one starts with a developed legislative institution and then improves it. Legislative reform, in these terms, results from legislative development rather than vice-versa. As the case of Brazil illustrates, however, the trend in many developing countries is the opposite; legislative reforms are conceived as instruments to legislative development rather than as by-products of legislative institutionalization.

The correspondence between legislative structures and processes and the out-look of the age in the West has contributed to legislative survival and development. If legislatures in developing countries are to survive and develop, they must reflect the needs and ideologies of development. In many developing countries the political elite is committed to organizational developmental values, and thus an organizationally structured legislative institution is preferable to a more archaic structure that developed over time. Here rational-legal patterns have predominated in legislative reform. Legislative development has been introduced as a way to achieve institutional "maturity."

Legislative-Executive Rivalry

Implied in the literature on the "decline of Parliament" is the assumption of legislative-executive rivalry. As a result, legislative development proposals tend to echo the implication that strengthening the legislature necessarily weakens the executive, or at least is a counterbalancing movement. While the history of some Western countries, particularly the US may justify such an assumption, the experience of many developing countries does not. Some have even argued that with increased functional specificity and structural differentiation, the historical institutional rivalry between Congress and the Executive is no longer an accurate description of the legislative-executive relationship. "What the separation of powers means today is a separation of policy subsystems rather than a separation of political institutions and powers." [27]

The only function of "Congress," as a total institution, is to ratify and legitimize the decisions reached by the policy subsystems. It is quite likely that the subsystems may develop working relationships and a vested interest in the decisions thus reached, which extend beyond the concern and interest of Congress as a total institution. "Indeed, once agreements have been reached in a policy subsystem, those who have participated in the negotiations may have a vested interest in withholding information from other potential participants." [28]

If institutional rivalry is a less-than-adequate description of the relationship between Congress and the Executive in the US, a presidential system which is theoretically based on a separation of the executive and the legislature, it is even less likely to describe developing societies or societies where the parliamentary-cabinet form of government is common. In many developing countries homogeneity among the ruling political elite cuts across institutional barriers. Where there are close, personal relationships among the elite and weak institutional traditions, one can hardly talk of institutional rivalry as an overriding source of conflict. The frequent dissolution, disbandment, or suspension of legislatures in developing societies is less an institutional struggle than an elite political struggle. Quite frequently legislatures have been complacent about or even participated in executive actions aimed at their demise. Often legislators who have been unable to control political trends detrimental to their class interest have appealed to the military against the very institution which they represent. Brazil in 1964 is a case in point.

Executives in developing countries work better with legislatures that conceive of their role as complementary to rather than adversary to the executive. Legislatures who are supposed "to propose nothing, to oppose everything, and to turn out the government," [29] infrequently end on a collision course with the executive. Political conditions in developing societies tend to favor a complementary legislative-executive relationship, so the legislatures seek to structure themselves along rational-legal lines similar to executive departments. This rational-legal approach provides them with a legitimacy accepted and favored by the executive and it tends to minimize the executive-legislative friction.

Developing societies, therefore, do not wish to strenghen the legislature out of a traditional Western desire to offset the executive power. They want the legislature to play a constructive complementary role, so reform proposals have been aimed at such supporting processes as mobilizing support, airing grievances, improving communication mechanisms, and so forth. The reforms enable the legislature to participate in debates on important political matters pertaining to the government's general policies and provide members working in committees the right forum for the less partisan task of scrutinizing the administration; they are not intended to embarrass the government or to obstruct its work.[30]

The executive-legislative institutional dichotomy characteristic of the literature fails to account for the decision-making process even in the United States, where the separation of the two institutions is supposedly most complete. It is, perhaps, a legacy of eighteenth-century jurisprudence, a misconception resulting from the reifications of principles set out in the Federalist papers. In the developing countries, where the tradition of separation of powers is not relevant, legislative development proposals have tended to stress complementarity between legislature and executive. The survival of the legislature is thought to be enhanced by its ability to perform functions considered essential to the system. For this reason it favors a rational-legal style of conducting its business.

Political Rationality vs. Organizational Rationality

Critics of legislative reform have maintained that while the organization and procedures of legislatures may appear to be obsolete and irrational from an organizational point of view, they are rational and meaningful if viewed from a political perspective.[31] One observer noted:

> At issue fundamentally are differing concepts of rationality: Congress is structured to maximize "functional rationality"—a rationality which emphasizes "the coordination of action with reference to a definite goal." The end of most would-be reformers emphasize "substantial" rationality or "thoughts" which reveal intelligent insight into the inter-relations of events in a given situation.[32]

Edward Schneier then goes on to argue that, as politicians, Congressmen would prefer "functional rationality." Procedural and organizational reform is therefore unwarranted, since it may upset the political rules of the game.

A corollary to this distinction between political and organizational rationality is the assertion that because legislative reforms are primarily political in nature, organizational rationality has little relevance to such reforms.

While political considerations are important for the legislator in developing countries, "efficiency" is usually the justification for legislative reform. The distinction between political and organizational justification works in favor of the latter.[33] A look at the accusations usually levied against politicians by the intellectuals, journalists, and army officers shows to what extent these groups value organizational rationality.[34]

We conclude therefore that legislative reforms in developing countries need an appropriate political climate to be carried out. They also need an acceptable justification (in terms of organizational rationality) before they can legitimately become political issues. The attempts at the "improvement in present office efficiency, better organization of, and increase in, staff for legislative reference service, and the development of centralized expertise and manpower to deal with constituent problems" [35] are primarily political issues, but they are also organizational-technical questions requiring organizational-technical answers.

The distinction between "political" and "organizational" rationalities is conceptually viable. Empirically, however, they are not necessarily separate or contradictory. Legislative development, particularly in developing societies where the distinction between the two rationalities is not even admitted, tend to capitalize on organizational rationality to fit the paradigm which the political elite uses to evaluate the work of the political institutions.

Notes

1. Woodrow Wilson, "The Study of Public Administration," in Dwight Waldo (ed.) *Ideas and Issues in Public Administration* (New York: McGraw-Hill Book Co., 1953), p. 71.

2. *Ibid.*, p. 72.

3. Paul H. Appleby, *Big Democracy* (New York/ Alfred A. Knopf, 1945), p. 129.

4. *Ibid.*, p. 340.

5. Fritz Morstein Marx, *The Administrative State* (Chicago: The University of Chicago Press, 1957), p. 187.

6. Victor A. Thompson, "Bureaucracy in a Democratic Society," in *Public Administration and Democracy*, Martin Roscoe (ed.) (Syracuse: Syracuse University Press, 1965), p. 210–211.

7. Glendon A. Shubert, *The Public Interest* (Illinois: The Free Press of Glencoe, 1960).

8. Emmette S. Redford, "The Protection of the Public Interest With Special Reference to Administrative Regulation," *American Political Science Review* 48 (1954):1110.

9. Emmette S. Redford, *Ideal and Practice in Public Administration* (University of Alabama: University of Alabama Press, 1958), p. 233.

10. Arthur Bentley, *The Process of Government*, 1949 ed. (Bloomington, Indiana: Principia Press, 1908).

11. David Truman, *The Governmental Process* (New York: Alfred Knopf, 1951).

12. See Edgar C. Crane and John A. Worthley, "Organizational Dimensions of Legislatures," CDSC, 1975; also Abdo I. Baaklini and James J. Heaphey, *Legislative Institution Building in Brazil, Costa Rica, and Lebanon* (Beverly Hills: Sage Publications, Professional Paper Series, 1976).

13. Eric Redman, *The Dance of Legislation* (New York: Simon and Schuster, 1973), pp. 16–17.

14. See James J. Heaphey, in Heaphey and Balutis, *Legislative Staffing: A Comparative Perspective* (Beverly Hills: Sage Publications, 1975).

15. For an elaboration on these reforms, see the following references:

> 1. Council of State Governments, *The Book of the States 1970–71, 1972–1973, 1974–1975.* (Lexington, KY: The Council of State Governments, 1970).
> 2. Citizens Conference on State Legislatures, *The Sometimes Governments* (New York: Bantam, 1971).
> 3. Donald G. Herzberg and Alan Rosenthal, eds., *Strengthening the States: Essays on Legislative Reform*, (New York: Anchor, 1972).
> 4. Council of State Governments, *American State Legislatures in Mid-Twentieth Century* (Chicago: The Council of State Governments, 1971).
> 5. Citizens Conference on State Legislatures, *Compilation of Recommendations Pertaining to Legislative Improvement in the 50 States* (Kansas City: The Conference, April 1976).
> 6. Donald Herzberg and Jess Unruh, *Essays on the State Legislative Process* (New York: Holt, Rinehart and Winston, 1970).

16. See John Grumm, *A Paradigm for the Comparative Analysis of Legislative Systems* (Beverly Hills: Sage Publications, 1973).

17. For an exposition of the impact of these changes on the work of the legislatures in the US, see The Council of State Governments, *Mr. President . . . Mr. Speaker: Report of the Committee on Organization of Legislative Services of the National Legislative Conference* (Chicago, 1963); see also Kenneth Kofmehl, *Professional Staff of Congress* (West Lafayette: Purdue University Studies, 1962).

18. For details of how these various groups view legislative reform in the US, see Roger Davidson, David Kovenock, and Michael O'Leary, *Congress in Crisis: Politics and Congressional Reform*, second printing (Belmont: Wadsworth Publishing Company, 1968), Chapters 2 and 3.

19. Wheare, Kenneth C., *Legislatures*, second edition (Oxford: Oxford University Press, 1968), pp. 148–149.

20. This group was said to advocate the Literary Theory in Roger Davidson, David Kovenock, and Michael O'Leary, *Congress in Crisis*, pp. 17–25.

21. This is called the Executive-Force Theory by Davidson, Kovenock, and O'Leary, *Congress in Crisis*, pp. 25–31.

Bernard Crick has been advocating the same adjustment for the British Parliament. He argues that Parliament must spend less time considering pending legislation and more time on educational function regarding the broader policies of government, since it will never have the power to unseat the government. See Bernard Crick, *The Reform of Parliament* (Garden City: Doubleday and Company, Inc., 1965), Chapter IX.

Summarizing the literature on the reform of the British Parliament, J. H. Robertson advocates "a radical transformation of the working relationship between Parliament and the Executive, and systematic changes in Parliamentary organizations and Procedures," *Reform of the British Government* (London: Chatto and Windus, Charles Knight, 1971), p. 160.

22. Davidson, Kovenock and O'Leary, *Congress in Crisis*, pp. 31–34.

23. Strathearn Gordon, *Our Parliament* (London: Cassell, 1964), pp. 88–101.

24. Bernard Crick, *The Reform of Parliament*, p. 153.

25. James A. Robinson, "Staffing the Legislature" in Allan Kornberg and Lloyd Musolf (eds.), *Legislatures in Developmental Perspective* (Durham: Duke University Press, 1970), pp. 368–369.

26. Samuel Patterson, "Congressional Committee Professional Staffings," in Kornberg and Musolf (eds.), *Legislatures in Developmental Perspective*, p. 393; Samuel Huntington, "Political Development and Political Decay," *World Politics* 17 (April 1965): 386–430.

27. Edward Schneier, "The Intelligence of Congress: Information and Public Policy Patterns," *The American Academy of Political and Social Sciences* 387 (January 1970): 17.

28. *Ibid.*

29. Sir Ivor Jennings, *Parliament* (Cambridge: Cambridge University Press, 1957), p. 167.

30. Robertson, *Reform of the British Government*, p. 168, 169.

31. Edward Schneier, "The Intelligence of Congress."

32. *Ibid.*, p. 15. The quotation is taken from Karl Mannheim, *Man and Society in an Age of Reconstruction* (New York: Harcourt, Brace, 1940), pp. 51–57.

33. Adbo I. Baaklini, "Comparative Public Administration: The Persistence of an Ideology," *Journal of Comparative Administration* 5, 1 May 1973).

34. The shift from political rationality to organizational rationality has been superbly discussed in: Sheldon S. Wolin, *Politics and Vision*, Chapter 10, which is entitled "The Age of Organization and the Sublimation of Politics," (Boston: Little, Brown and Company, 1960), pp. 352–434.

35. Warren Butler, "Administering Congress: The Role of the Staff," *Public Administration Review*, 26, 1 (March 1966):7.

Part 1

Legislative Reforms and Innovations in the US Congress

Statutory Reporting Requirements:

Information and Influence for Congress

JOHN R. JOHANNES

Of major concern to both members and students of Congress has been the legislature's ability to obtain the information needed to initiate and influence legislation and to oversee the executive bureaucracy. Proposals to deal with this problem are at least as numerous and varied as their proponents.[1] Some involve fundamental changes in Congress's constitutional authority; others offer structural or procedural reforms. Naturally, the most innovative and spectacular recommendations for reform draw the most attention. Many others go unnoticed.

One truly unspectacular technique increasingly employed by Congress to oversee the executive, generate legislative proposals, and generally keep itself informed has been the statutory reporting requirement: a provision *in law* requiring the president, a department, agency, commission, part of the judiciary, or other government-related institution to report to the Congress on decisions, activities, findings, plans, budgets, and so on. Three points of interest about these reporting requirements warrant notice. First, these are formal, legally mandated reporting duties, not merely requests. Second, except for literature on the "legislative veto," [2] they have been virtually ignored by scholars [3]—though not by some members of Congress.[4] And third, despite much political science textbook speculation to the contrary, they seem to work!

Incidence of Statutory Reporting Requirements

Nowhere in the literature is there a quantitative record of Congress's reliance on reports. But from documents issued by the clerks of the House of Representatives, the incidence of reporting requirements over time can be traced (see figure 1).[5] It should be stressed that figure 1 charts the number of different statutory reporting requirements in effect during particular Congresses, and not the number of documents arriving or scheduled to arrive on Capitol Hill. Such a count would be impossible.[6] For completeness, figure 1 includes a handful of reports to be made by congressional committees, the General Accounting Office, the Library of Congress, and other agents. Only recently have these numbered over forty in any one year.

The long upward trend of reporting requirements during this century reflects the overall growth of federal programs, while shorter-term variations seem to bear a relationship to the "pace" of government activity. The drop in reporting requirements during the 1920s and the decreasing rate of growth in the 1950s, and the increases during the New Deal and since the sixties correspond roughly to periods of relative inactivity and activity in the creation of new programs. A noticeable increase in reporting occurred following the first two Congresses organized under the 1946 Legislative Reorganization Act, which consolidated committees and charged them to maintain continuous watchfulness over the executive. At least 83 public laws [7] containing 122 reporting requirements were enacted during the Eightieth Congress (1947–48), and 97 laws with 156 provisions were passed during the Eighty-first (1949–50). These figures compare with 70 laws (105 provisions) enacted in the Seventy-ninth Congress. Figure 1, in a sense, can be viewed as a crude measure of Congress's efforts to supervise the executive and to stay abreast of current problems.

Types of Statutory Reporting Requirements

Scrutiny of statutes enacted since 1945 reveals three major categories of reporting requirements.

Figure 1

Reports to be Made to Congress:
Statutory Reporting Requirements in Effect
during First Session of Indicated Congress

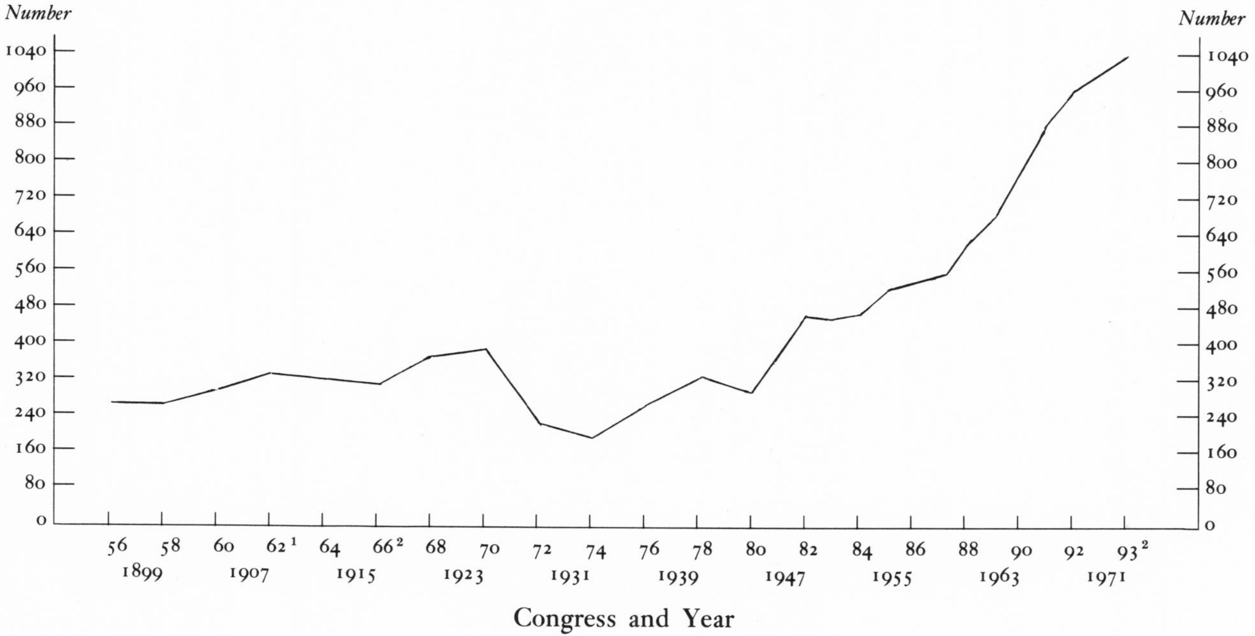

Source: See note 5.
[1] Third Session
[2] Second Session

"Study-And-Recommend" ("Policy-Making") Reporting Requirements

Congress frequently requires the president, agencies, and special commissions to submit findings of studies or program evaluations along with recommendations for legislation. These "policy-making" or "study-and-recommend" reports are of three sorts.[8]

One includes those rather routine requirements that agencies evaluate policies and programs under their jurisdictions and recommend implementing or corrective legislation. Another encompasses the duty to present to Congress various materials in defense of appropriations requests or to furnish cost estimates or feasibility studies to justify construction projects or land purchases. The third kind is the most intriguing. Pursuing ideas and information for new programs and modifications of existing ones, Congress directs the executive or special study commissions to investigate and assess specific issues or general policy areas and to recommend legislation. Examples range from relatively minor matters to those of consequence. The Emergency Insured Student Loan Act of 1969, for example, called for the secretary of HEW to determine:

> . . . whether there are any practices of lending institutions which may result in discrimination against particular classes or categories of students . . . . [He] shall make a report with respect to such discrimination, and his recommendations, to the Congress on or before March 1, 1970.[9]

"Post Facto" Reporting Requirements

In addition to their routine annual reports, government agencies are required to submit other types of "post facto" reports each year, each quarter, or in various contingency situations.[10]

Some reports describe developments related to, or the operation of, specific programs recently added to an agency's responsibilities. For example, a 1968 law charged the director of the Bureau of the Budget to "submit to the Senate and House of Representatives at the end of each calendar quarter . . . a report on the operation" of a section of that law limiting the number of federal employees.[11]

Second, Congress at times requires the president and executive agencies to report when they make determinations or take actions pursuant to delegations of discretionary authority, particularly those which constitute exceptions to policies laid down by statute. For instance, Congress has placed numerous restrictions on foreign and military aid and sales, but it has provided the chief executive with the authority to waive some of them, *provided* he promptly reports such waivers.[12] A slightly different variation can be found in a 1968 statute dealing with interstate travel to incite riots:

> Whenever, in the opinion of the Attorney General . . . , any person shall have violated this chapter, the Department [of Justice] shall proceed as speedily as possible with a prosecution of such person hereunder . . . or in the alternative shall report in writing, to the respective Houses of the Congress, the Department's reason for not so proceeding.[13]

A third variety deals with agency flexibility with respect to appropriations. The Military Construction Authorization Act of 1968, for instance, allowed the secretary of the army to utilize up to $10 million for unauthorized construction made necessary by "unforeseen requirements." [14] Most agencies must report transfers, reprogramming, and so on, of funds. One novel use of these reporting duties occurred in 1969 and 1970 when Congress required the director of the Budget Bureau to report to the president and Congress whenever *Congress's* actions on appropriations bills varied from the president's budget requests.[15]

"*Advance-Notification*" *Reporting Requirements*

Congress also requires notification *before* executive officials act or spend or before a determination becomes binding. Examples range from the trivial to the profound. In 1968 Congress required that literature distributed at the National Visitors Center in Washington, D.C., "shall first be approved by the Architect of the Capitol after consultation with the House Committee on House Administration and the Senate Committee on Rules and Administration." [16] That same year legislators forbade expenditures for acquiring or developing lands on the St. Croix River until sixty days after the secretary of the Interior submitted certain documents to Congress.[17] Congress has forbidden reobligation of funds until the executive has notified the Appropriations Committees; [18] it has required advance reporting of spending, transfers, or contracts; [19] and in 1970 it gave the president authority to raise a congressionally imposed expenditure ceiling *after* he gave written notice to the legislature.[20] Both post facto and advance-notification reporting requirements are found in "legislative veto" provisions, which Congress has turned to with growing frequency of late.

Because of the occasional overlap and the variation in terminology of reporting requirements, precise computation of the frequencies of each type is impossible. But a rough calculation yields the results in table 1. Post facto reports predominate, although to a lesser degree today than during the 1940s. Provisions requiring advance notification are the least numerous, but they have been employed slightly more in recent years than in earlier periods. There has been a marked growth in both absolute and relative frequency of study-and-recommend reports.

Table 1

Relative Frequency of Three Types of Statutory Reporting Requirements Enacted During Six Congresses, 1945–72[1]

	Congress and Dates					
Type of Reporting Requirement	79th 1945–1946 %	80th 1947–1948 %	86th 1959–1960 %	88th 1963–1964 %	90th 1967–1968 %	92nd 1971–1972 %
Post Facto	73	80	63	55	55	50
Policy-Making	21	18	24	25	37	40
Advance Notification	6	2	12	20	8	10
Total Reporting Requirements Enacted	100	100	99	100	100	100
(n)	(105)	(122)	(108)	(130)	(239)	(261)

Source: Figures compiled by author from *Statutes at Large*. See note 7.

[1] Figures refer to individual reporting provisions included in laws enacted during the indicated Congresses. Percentages are rounded.

Whereas during the Seventy-ninth Congress fewer than 3 percent of all public laws called for studies and recommendations, by the Ninety-second one of every ten laws did. This pattern seems to reflect an activist legislative orientation on the part of lawmakers.

Targets of Reporting Requirements

Congress seeks reports from all government units. Table 2 summarizes requirements in effect during the second session of

Table 2

Reports to be Made to Congress: Reporting Requirements in Effect, Second Session, Ninety-Third Congress (1974)

Reporting Agent		Number of Requirements	Percent
President		188	18
(By the President)	91		
(By the Executive Office)	12		
(By cabinet-level departments transmitted by the President	58		
(By independent agencies, boards, etc. transmitted by the President)	27		
Head of Each Department and Agency[1]		9	1
Eleven Cabinet-level Departments, Made Directly to Congress		503	48
Forty-four Independent Agencies, Made Directly to Congress		164	16
Judicial Branch		10	1
Legislative Branch		66	6
Thirty-two Semi-independent Boards, Commissions, and Related Agencies		44	4
Sixty-six Federally Chartered Private Corporations		71	7
Total		1055	101[2]

Source: US Congress, House of Representatives, *Reports to Be Made to Congress*, H. Doc. 93–199, 93d Cong., 2d sess., 1974.

[1] Counted only once for each entry.

[2] Due to rounding.

the Ninety-third Congress (1974). Nearly half of all reports come to Congress directly from executive departments and agencies, with sizeable numbers from the president and independent agencies. Eight percent originate in agencies but are transmitted by the president. These generally deal with matters of importance,[21] and it is likely that that is why they are to be sent via the White House.

Table 3, focusing on agents which account for about three-fourths of all reports, shows that some departments carry greater reporting burdens than others and that such burdens vary over the years. Increasingly, Congress has turned to the

Table 3

Statutory Reporting Requirements in Effect During First Session of Indicated Congress, by Reporting Agent, 56th–93d Congresses

Congress and Year	Total No. Reporting Requirements	Number of Reports to be Made Directly or Through the President by:												
		President	Defense & Military Depart.	State	Agric.	Interior	Justice	Treasury	Commerce	Labor	HEW	HUD	Trans.	General Accting. Office
56(1899)	275	9	44	13	8	45	15	52	*a*	*a*	*a*	*a*	*a*	*a*
60(1907)	269	3	50	9	10	46	13	37	*a*	*a*	*a*	*a*	*a*	*a*
64(1915)	321	14	78	6	16	37	12	42	*a*	*a*	*a*	*a*	*a*	*a*
68(1927)	367	14	76	6	25	41	14	39	15	15	*a*	*a*	*a*	*a*
72(1931)	228	19	66	1	6	14	5	19	4	2	*a*	*a*	*a*	10
76(1939)	249	15	56	0	12	23	5	17	5	3	*a*	*a*	*a*	14
80(1947)	283	21	59	8	10	26	8	15	7	2	*a*	*a*	*a*	16
82(1951)	445	29	107	21	12	34	11	15	24	7	*a*	*a*	*a*	22
84(1955)	446	33	105	15	12	34	18	25	26	9	7	*a*	*a*	21
86(1959)	532	37	137	27	11	43	21	24	30	9	15	*a*	*a*	17
88(1963)	615	41	151	54	9	63	20	18	28	12	20	*a*	*a*	17
89(1965)	654	41	135	49	8	79	21	21	36	12	28	*a*	*a*	17
90(1967)	753	76	159	47	11	85	23	15	46	12	40	12	*a*	18
91(1969)	874	94	173	54	20	93	22	15	27	12	67	26	35	26
92(1971)	958	114	200	55	22	93	22	15	29	19	56	22	47	37
93(1973)	958	91	*b*	*b*	*b*	*b*	*b*	*b*	*b*	*b*	*b*	*b*	*b*	43

Source: See note 5.

[a] These departments not yet established in these years.

[b] Change in format of Clerk's report prevents accurate comparison.

president for all types of reports.[22] Presidential reporting duties usually deal with major policies and programs, often questions of foreign and defense policy, government operations, or new domestic issues. The trend was exaggerated during the late 1960s, probably due to Congress's desire to hold the chief executive responsible for the domestic programs enacted in those years, the concentration of power and decision-making in the White House, and a burgeoning congressional concern with the president's foreign policies.

Most departments have experienced changes in reporting responsibilities. Such fluctuations indicate the shifting of programs into and out of departments and Congress's varying concern with different programs. In at least one sense, the distribution of reporting requirements within the government indicates "where the action is" at any given time.

Congressional Purposes in Requiring Reports

Why do congressmen require reports? Answers were sought in the printed hearings, reports, and debates, and in interviews conducted with congressional and executive personnel during July 1973.[23] Six categories emerge.

1. Information. All reporting requirements are intended to generate information, but the kinds and specific intentions vary. Routine post facto reports are required primarily to have a record of agency activities. Normally the data in such reports are already known or readily available; often, however, they are not available as a package. Nonroutine reports are mandated in order to gather and collate special information that might not otherwise be collected. According to several staff members, the necessity of requiring reports by statute varies from committee to committee and agency to agency. Sometimes informal communication, such as a phone call, is sufficient. Formal but nonstatutory requests are also used; however, to make the sending of data automatic, and especially to add emphasis or signify importance, committees turn to statutory means.

Many policy-making reporting requirements are inserted into bills to generate data on new issues which Congress, on its own, would be unable (or able only with difficulty) to amass. In this sense, reporting requirements are an attempt to have the executive do Congress's "leg work" for it. Calls for legislative recommendations usually are serious, even though legislators expect only modest results.

2. Control of Administration and Oversight of Bureaucracy. Oversight and control are prime goals of reporting requirements. Reporting provisions, especially those calling for advance notifications, are inserted into bills in order to trigger the "law of anticipated reactions"—making executives think twice before acting. Another oversight use is to give a "hot foot" to executive agencies and to let them know that someone is watching or that action is expected. These requirements frequently are loosely worded, in contrast to the explicit language regularly found in study-and-recommend provisions. Interestingly, a greater proportion of executive than congressional officials cited the hot foot as a purpose of mandating reports. Another goal is to discover an agency's plans before it acts to implement policies enacted by Congress. Requirements for evaluations of programs and proposals for improvement not only help assure that executive officials keep on their toes but also protect Congress. If something goes wrong with a program and the administrators fail to catch it, legislators can lay all the blame on them not only for having missed the problem but also for failing to follow congressional directives.

A few reporting requirements have been enacted to "get even" with agencies or to embarrass the administration by forcing them to reveal program weaknesses, identify policy gaps, or to submit unpopular or inadequate legislative solutions. Statutory reporting requirements may be used to attack executive official secrecy by creating opportunities to probe for secrets.[24]

3. Legislative Compromise. Reporting requirements provide an escape route from legislative logjams. Policy-making reports often are enacted to reconcile differences over whether or not a new policy should be initiated or how extensive it should be: "a way of avoiding having to act," said a Senate committee staff member. Other types are also useful to avoid deadlocks. To meet White House objections to the 1974 Foreign Aid Authorization Act (PL 93–189), for example, the conference committee required the president *to report* whether any non-African nation was using US aid to support military activities in its African territories, rather than requiring him to suspend aid to Portugal if he determined that it was so using the aid (as was the bill's original stipulation).

4. Committee Jurisdiction. Reports sometimes are called for by a committee or subcommittee to claim, reaffirm, or clarify jurisdiction over a program or policy area that overlaps several committees. Jurisdictional intentions become explicit when reports are required to be made directly to committees, rather than to the whole House or Senate, as is the custom. Explicitly requiring reports to be made directly to committees is a growing phenomenon,[25] even though it would appear to violate House rules and is somewhat of an affront to the Speaker.

A plurality of direct-to-committee reports go to the Appropriations Committees, which is consistent with their budgetary and oversight responsibilities. The House and Senate Space and Armed Services Committees and the Senate Foreign Relations panel receive numerous reports as well. These committees are the sources of annual authorization legislation for the Defense and State Departments, the Space Agency, and the National Science Foundation. If they wish to match the Appropriations Committees' influence over these agencies' policies, operations, and attention, they must develop the expertise that the Appropriations panels have accumulated. Requiring reports may be a means to that end.

5. Symbolism. Reporting provisions are included in legislation for their symbolic value. Mandating a report expresses formal congressional concern, while offering and winning acceptance of amendments to require reports affords individuals opportunities for personal involvement, publicity, satisfaction, or consolation for the defeat of substantive proposals. Said one Senate aide, "it's better than nothing." Occasionally congressmen have proposed reporting requirements as a gesture to their constituents or interest groups.

6. Partisanship. Partisan interests may be related to the imposition of reporting duties on the executive. Minority party members, for example, have proposed reporting requirements to express their party's interest in programs assembled by the majority. However, the relationship between party and reporting requirements on the aggregate level is unclear. Two hypotheses come to mind. First, it might be supposed that congressional use of reporting requirements would be greater during periods of divided government than when one party controlled both the presidency and Congress. Second, given the Republicans' reputed interest in sound administration and their distrust of executive-dominated government, it might be theorized that they would employ the reporting device more than Democrats. Data in table 4, though limited, provide no support for the second hypothesis and very little for the first.

Table 4

Use of Statutory Reporting Requirements, 1945–1972 by Party Control of Congress and Presidency

Congress and Years	Number of Public Laws	Public Laws with Reporting Requirements	Percent[1]	Number of Reporting Provisions
	Republican Congress; Republican President			
83rd (1953–54)	781	85	10.9	142
	Republican Congress; Democratic President			
80th (1947–48)	906	83	9.2	122
	Democratic Congress; Republican President			
84th (1955–56)	1028	104	10.1	155
85th (1957–58)	936	73	7.8	139
86th (1959–60)	800	66	8.3	108
91st (1969–70)	695	108	15.5	317
92nd (1971–72)	607	104	17.1	261
Average[1]	813	91	11.2	196
	Democratic Congress; Democratic President			
79th (1945–46)	734	70	9.5	105
81st (1949–50)	921	97	10.5	156
82nd (1951–52)	594	45	7.6	80
87th (1961–62)	885	66	7.5	118
88th (1963–64)	666	76	11.4	130
89th (1965–66)	810	112	13.8	232
90th (1967–68)	640	85	13.4	239
Average[1]	750	79	10.5	152

Source: Tabulated by author from *Statutes At Large*. Totals exclude reports from General Accounting Office and other congressional agents. See note 7.

[1] Averages and percentages rounded.

(If one examines only study-and-recommend provisions, however, there seems to be some support for the first.) Only in recent situations of split government (1969–72) does partisanship appear to be associated with increased use of reporting—and that relationship may be spurious. Rather than partisanship, what seems to stand out is Congress's *institutional* search for information and control, particularly in the last decade.

Uses and Usefulness of Statutory Reporting Requirements: The Congressional View

Disagreement and equivocation emerge when scholars discuss the effectiveness of reporting requirements, probably because so little has been done to evaluate them.[26] Based on interviews and the results of very recent studies by the General Accounting Office and the Congressional Research Service, reporting requirements do seem to have considerable value. Probably more often than not they do meet the expectations of congressmen. This judgment, of course, must be qualified by recognizing the enormous variety of intentions and expectations, the varying quality of reports, and the uses to which they are put—all of which depend on individual members of Congress.

Effectiveness of Reports

Among the uses of reports, perhaps the most important is educational: the transmission of executive data and policy judgments to congressmen and staff. Not surprisingly, executive officials emphasized communication of their viewpoints more often than did congressional personnel, who stressed the purely informational and factual side of reporting. Several officials pointed out the utility of reports for courts, state and local governments, the public, and interest groups.

Reports are seen as reference works and storehouses of information. Legislation, hearings, committee studies and reports, speeches, and, generally, support for preexisting policy positions were all mentioned as benefitting from reports, although both this and the CRS study found that reports are not used as often or as much as they might be to prepare for hearings.

On their arrival, some reports—especially the advance-notification variety—serve to flag issues or alert members to impending actions. Normally, those who originally sought the reporting requirements and who are most knowledgeable on the subjects in question are the ones most anxiously awaiting the reports.

As a means of providing new legislative proposals, policy-making reports are marginally successful. An in-depth study of some sixty such provisions enacted during the Eighty-ninth, Ninetieth, and Ninety-first Congresses found that: (1) there was almost total formal compliance from the executive (studies were undertaken, reports submitted, and recommendations made); (2) most recommendations were general, corrective (of program weaknesses), technical, relatively minor, repetitious of earlier proposals, negative, or nonlegislative.[27] There were, however, some important exceptions. Not all recommendations made by the executive were actively pushed. In some cases, when recommendations were included in reports, the reporting requirement could be credited only with speeding up what appeared to be their inevitable appearance. Frequently recommendations called for more study or cautioned against unwarranted haste.

Even lacking major legislative recommendations, the intentions of Congress in requiring studies are often met. The executive is, to use the words of one House committee staff member, prodded to "look at something they might not be interested in" and to hasten its deliberations. Needed information is supplied, sometimes surreptitiously, as executives team up with congressional allies against agency heads or the White House. Congressmen use the findings of studies and data in reports to develop their own legislative proposals. In the process, studies and reports contribute to the milieu that surrounds most legislative breakthroughs. In the words of a House Ways and Means Committee aide, they are "the best and most feasible way to inform ourselves."

Finally, reports are seen as helping Congress perform its oversight functions, if only by making the executive aware of congressional interest and presence. The degree to which this works varies. For example, there is some doubt about whether requiring notification of presidential foreign policy decisions has actually deterred the president. The Congressional Research Service (CRS) concluded that such reporting "has not proved to be very effective in bringing about greater Presidential attention to congressional guidelines." [28] At lower levels, effectiveness would be greater.

Conditions For Effectiveness

At least five factors determine the degree of usefulness of reporting requirements and of the reports.

1. Timely Receipt of Reports. Virtually all required reports are sent, although they come in several forms. Most study-and-recommend and post facto reports are made available in published form; notifications generally are typewritten or mimeographed. A crucial problem is that reports are normally late. According to one House staff member, if it deals with a matter of some urgency, "what good does a late report do us?" The CRS studies suggested that "the speeding up of reports is perhaps the single most important step the executive branch can take to make its reports useful to Congress." [29] Lateness is caused by: unclear or unrealistic deadlines; heavy agency workloads; insufficient funding; a tendency of those preparing reports to view the due date as their deadline, thus overlooking the clearance process in the agency and in the Office of Management and Budget; lack of concern; and deliberate noncompliance.

2. Reports Must Be Read. Although executive officials tend to think that reports are not read, or only given cursory review, it seems almost certain that today—if not twenty years ago—the vast majority are read by staffs. (If nothing else, the growth in staffs since World War II has produced this one positive result.) One House International Relations Committee aide categorically stated that *all* reports to his committee are read—usually carefully. A few, however, undoubtedly go unread by the committees to which they are sent.

3. Availability and Distribution. Some reports are not fully utilized because potentially interested committees and members do not automatically receive copies, even though they may share jurisdiction over the programs covered by the documents.[30] Accessibility is particularly difficult when the report comes to the Hill as a typewritten letter or when its dissemination is limited by security classification.[31]

4. Quality. Opinions concerning the quality of reports were mixed. "Some reports are excellent," said a congressman in a typical comment, "but some are a piece of garbage." The majority of officials insisted that many reports were packed with usable information and were quite good. The CRS reached the same conclusion, but it added that of the foreign-policy-related reports it studied, "many, perhaps even most, . . . did not contain enough information to assist Congress effectively in reviewing how legislation and programs were being carried out or how funds were being spent." [32]

An objective assessment on the quality of reports is impossible for an outsider to make. Even members of Congress and their staffs find it hard to tell whether a report is accurate. Quality seems to depend on the agency doing the report, its aims, and degree of its interest; the nature of the subject matter; the specificity of the reporting requirement; and the interest of the congressmen and staffs who await the report.

Reports prepared by independent agencies and special study commissions apparently are more thorough and innovative, and hence potentially more useful, than those produced by executive departments. But such commissions are costly, slow, and impractical for most reporting. When the interests of an agency, bureau, or individual in charge of a report coincide with the interests of those who required the report, the results normally are of a higher quality and more useful than when there are differences of opinion and opposing interests. When the reporting requirement is perceived by the executive to be important, it usually results in a better job. When not, according to a deputy assistant secretary whose implication was clear, "you can always find someone to write a report." Clearly, White House and Office of Management and Budget interest in or sympathy with a reporting requirement is beneficial. The CRS found that certain aspects of US foreign operations, such as economic aid, are more fully and accurately covered by reports than others (military assistance), in part because of secrecy classification. Congress and its foreign affairs committees feel that they are not being well served by reports in foreign and defense policy, if recent legislation is any indication.[33]

Normally, the more technical and factual the information sought, the better the report. Annual reports are frequently aimed at the public rather than at Congress, and they are conceived of as an introduction to or survey of agency activities. Many congressional officials interviewed feel that reports, especially annual documents, are too self-promotional. "Agencies aren't going to tell you what they're doing wrong," said one House staff member; "they only tell you what they want to know."[34]

The language of the reporting requirement itself is of great consequence—and it was given major attention by the Congressional Research Service's studies.[35] When Congress does not specifically indicate what it wants, agencies are free to define issues and supply information as they choose, potentially frustrating the purposes of requiring reports. Precision, however, is difficult when the committees are unsure of their information needs or of the best way to realize them. Even to ask questions, after all, implies prior knowledge.

The degree of congressional interest in a report affects its quality. The greater a committee's (or member's) interest and knowledge in a given policy area, the more likely the committee will specify the information sought, make the reporting duty explicit, and attach a deadline—and the less likely it is to leave loopholes. And, over time, the more expert a committee is with respect to a given program, the more likely the agency will know what the committee wants. Often, with new programs, the reporting requirements are loosely worded, precisely because of the newness and relative unfamiliarity.[36] Interested committees, members, and staffs are more likely to keep in touch with the executive while the report is being prepared. Such informal contacts can clear up doubts about what is wanted and can spur executive interest. Sometimes, too, congressional concern can lead members and staff to force an agency to produce a high caliber document by means of some sort of threat. One member of the House Appropriations Committee remarked that when a report is sloppy, "we make them eat it" and "get tough" at the hearings. An aide to a senator said that "if a study is ___, I get on the phone and start asking questions." Much of the "threat," however, depends on the staff's ability to challenge the facts in a report—an ability few staff members claimed.

5. *Time and Staff Resources.* Two key factors restricting the use of reports were summed up by a pair of House committee staff members; "Yes, the reports come back to us, but the problem is that we just don't have the time or staff to give them the consideration they should get." "The staff is swamped with reports." Scholars have long recognized that Congress may be limited as much by a deluge as by a scarcity of information,[37] and the sheer number of reports arriving on the Hill each year somewhat confirms their thesis. Some of these reports were required years ago and may have no current importance. Others deal with contemporary issues of secondary concern and are consulted "if time permits." These documents, according to a Senate aide, were probably instigated by "some staff guy" who is gone when the report arrives. "So the report goes on the shelf and is forgotten." Although Congress on many occasions has acted to improve, modify, or repeal hundreds of reporting requirements,[38] there probably remain many obsolete or at least marginally valuable and overlapping reporting provisions.

Uses and Usefulness of Reporting Requirements: The Executive View

Contrary to the pessimistic views held on Capitol Hill, requiring reports does have an impact on the bureaucracy and administration. From the executive's perspective, reporting can provide numerous benefits. Reporting requirements generate within agencies a degree of awareness of problems and of congressional interest that might not otherwise exist. Several administrators interviewed quickly pointed out constructive changes in regulations and procedures that were direct products of reporting requirements. On occasion, having to file a report makes it easier for administrators to probe programs that have become sacred cows and to undertake studies for which they lacked legal authority, funds, or White House permission. Major reports, particularly the study-and-recommend variety, can serve as historical or reference documents. One Housing and Urban Development Department official stated that, though "I can't believe they (congressmen) read them, I do, and so do others here." Some reports are used to prepare for hearings. Reports can be a morale booster under some circumstances. When a new reporting provision is put on the books, said another HUD executive, "someone nine floors down working on the matter all of a sudden gets to write a document on his efforts." Reporting can help "educate" congressmen and staffs, and it can establish, formalize, and strengthen communications between executive and congressional centers of interest. Reporting duties are used in interagency jurisdictional squabbles and sometimes to protect a department against a study by "outsiders" (a commission). And they often can substitute for concrete executive action. For these and other reasons, it is not uncommon to find supposedly reluctant executives from all ranks welcoming or even soliciting some reporting requirements.

On the negative side, the most frequently heard complaints focused on routine reports. Some typical comments: "Having to file reports is a pain." "They're drudgery." "A burden." Other complaints deal with the costs, the drain on staff resources, and the energy that must be expended in the clearance process. A high Office of Management and Budget official indicated that his agency opposes the proliferation of reports. "They take a lot of time from some important people who could be doing more important things." As a result OMB has been making an effort to cut back on the number of reports Congress requires each year and to improve the reporting system across the board.[39]

When reports are made, they can become instruments of congressional attacks on agencies, either because the reports are poorly done or because they reveal practices and decisions with which congressional committees or factions disagree. This puts executives in a delicate position. To tell the truth (and show that flaws exist) invites criticism; to "fudge" a report to cover up problems may lead to something worse. From the administrator's point of view, reporting, especially advance notifications, is sometimes seen as a limit on necessary discretion and as an unwarranted intrusion on his or her responsibilities.

Strengthening the Reporting System

Several methods have been or could be tried to assure that reports arrive on time. For some years, Congress required that the executive keep it "fully and currently informed" on certain programs. This language all but dropped out of usage during the 1960s, but it reappeared several times in the Ninety-second Congress. The Congressional Research Service, however, found the "fully and currently" provisions as applied to foreign affairs to be ineffective in producing more information in a more timely manner.[40] On the executive side, installing or improving existing flagging systems to alert responsible officials of impending deadlines would be useful. Since many statutes calling for reports fail to include clear deadlines, a firm yet *realistic* date should be specified whenever possible.

To cope with the problem of quality, several devices could be tried. Requiring fewer reports might relieve both the pressure and the sense of futility and overwork felt by many executives. Thus a continuing inventory and analysis of existing reporting provisions under its jurisdiction should be undertaken by each committee to follow up the periodic efforts of the General Accounting Office and the House Committee on Government Operations.[41] A means of discouraging superfluous reporting duties would be beneficial. Perhaps a rule specifying that a price tag be attached to each proposed reporting provision might inhibit the tendency to "make them report."

Congress must be clearer as to its needs, and the language of requirements should be more complete and specific. Toward this end, the 1974 Congressional Budget and Impoundment Control Act charged the General Accounting Office to "assist committees in developing their information needs, including such needs expressed in legislative requirements . . ." and to "make recommendations to the Congress and committees for changes and improvements in their reporting requirements."[42] Language requiring the executive to list alternative solutions to problems, along with analyses of each solution, could prove useful, but it might raise questions of executive privilege.[43] Another problem, uncovered in reading reports, is that the executive often lists a series of straw-man alternatives; but such tactics can be caught and criticized.

Congressional interest in reports could be made more explicit to the agencies preparing them. If that fails to guarantee a thorough job, Congress and its committees might develop a way to grade the quality of reports. But since committee members and staffs are often incapable of judging accuracy and completeness, the only agents available are the Congressional Research Service and the General Accounting Office, both of which have quietly become more directly involved with reporting in recent years. Fortified with such analyses, committees could complain often and loudly about poor reports.

If the number of reports is not reduced, increasing congressional staffs could help.[44] Indeed, if anything stands out from this research, it is that the burden of making use of reports falls squarely on staffs which already feel overloaded. Because most interested aides are often too busy to give proper attention to reports, a call for larger staffs and, perhaps, a division of labor on staffs to allow one or more aides to devote their efforts to monitoring and reading reports (in connection with other oversight duties) may be in order.

To solve the occasional but serious problem of security classification, the CRS has suggested that at least one unclassified version of sensitive reports be released when the executive finds a need to send a secret document to the Hill for committee eyes only. Such a system was incorporated into a 1972 statute requiring the transmittal of international agreements to Congress.[45]

Lastly, a means is needed to guarantee that every committee and each congressman at least know of the existence of all reports. (Currently, most, but not all, reports are listed in the *Congressional Record* upon their receipt.) This could be done by establishing a central monitoring system in each House. Now, the clerk of the House prepares an annual list of reporting requirements in effect for the following year, but it is based on agency records and organized according to agency reporting duties. What may be needed instead is a system which would: (1) keep track of reports scheduled to arrive and inquire about those that are late; (2) prepare a monthly document listing the arrival and nonarrival of reports due that month, together with a short summary or index (rather than merely the titles that now appear in the *Record*) of each report; (3) organize the list around congressional needs or committee structure; and (4) publish the document, making sure that each committee, each senator and representative, and the CRS and GAO receives a copy.[46] It should be noted that the 1974 Budget and Impoundment Control Act gave the task of monitoring reporting requirements to the GAO. As of this writing, however, the details of how that office will implement this duty have not yet been published.

Implications

Congress and the Executive. Having to research, prepare, and clear increasing numbers of reports cannot but affect executive staffing and operations. A noted authority on the presidency, for example, has suggested that one reason for the swelling of the White House Office and the Executive Office of the President is congressional insistence on presidential reporting to Congress.[47] The pressures on departments and agencies would be no less acute.

More inter- and Intra-agency squabbles are likely to be triggered or exacerbated as reporting requirements proliferate, particularly when they are used by executives to gain leverage against superiors or against other agencies. Executive recalcitrance and resentment, leading to tension between legislators and executives, may accompany the imposition of reporting requirements designed to limit executive discretion without providing concrete congressional guidance. This is already the case in, for example, energy policy and aspects of foreign policy. Reporting duties imposed with less than sincere congressional interest weaken executive respect for Congress, in turn causing legislators to accuse administrators of lack of cooperation. Such developments can undercut the positive results that reporting has achieved, and they do no good for the day-to-day interbranch relations so vital in a system predicated upon sharing of powers and information. If the use of reporting requirements were accompanied by a greater congressional resolve to employ them conscientiously, perhaps inroads could be made into negative executive attitudes and into the executive's penchant for secrecy and manipulation of information. Lack of cooperation on informal requests is one thing; violation of statutory provisions mandating the release of data is another.

Policy Functions: Legislation and Oversight. Statutory requirements calling for studies and legislative recommendations from the executive are designed to bolster the law-making capacity of Congress. Some lead to new legislation, either directly (via presidential-executive proposals and data) or indirectly (through the incubation of policy ideas). Thus at least study-and-recommend reporting provisions constitute a viable tool for congressional initiation of legislation; [48] and their successful use provides some evidence that Congress has means to serve as a partner in policy innovation, even when presidents are active.

Similarly, the growing tendency to require reports of all kinds testifies to congressional concern for proper policy implementation. Formal reports are no panacea. But by gathering data, creating opportunities for more informal communication, making administrators aware of problems, and affording them occasions for preoversight evaluations of their agencies and bureaus, reports do strengthen congressional oversight. The system of reporting is an institutionalization of an oversight technique which places a presumption of activism on the shoulders of those congressmen in positions to receive reports on behalf of the House and Senate.

Internal Congressional Politics. For members and committees of Congress, regular contact with, information from, and jurisdiction over executive agencies are ingredients of power. Since statutory reporting requirements facilitate contact, produce information, and support claims of jurisdiction, legislators who do not have ready access to reports are disadvantaged vis-a-vis those who do. Making reports more available to potentially interested members might spread access to and influence over a given agency or program to more members. That could, of course, lead to more intercommittee rivalry.

Since members usually are too busy to read all but very important reports, the task devolves upon staffs. Staff influence, and perhaps staff size, will rise if the number of—or reliance on—reports increases. If a greater number of reports go unread and unused, it may produce more executive skepticism or cynicism.

Congress and Representation. Insofar as some reporting requirements are enacted explicitly to inform constituents, interest groups, or the general public, reports contribute to Congress's educational and representational functions. Elite opinion has been jogged more than once by the results of required studies, and outsiders both use and help prepare reports. Constituents can be shown that their man in Washington is working on matters of interest to them.

Conclusion

Statutory reporting requirements are a tool employed to help Congress meet both its internal and external needs and strengthen its position vis-a-vis the executive. Clearly, they are *only* a tool, and their effectiveness depends on individual members and staffs and on other formal and informal techniques they use in connection with reports. The increased incidence of reporting requirements reveals a congressional dependence for information on the executive that is implicit in the American system of separation of powers. The pattern of reporting provisions and the degree to which they accomplish their goals suggest that the formal legislative procedures so often overlooked by students of legislative behavior deserve more attention. Not all important developments in legislatures need be "reforms" or "innovations." Some are quiet mutations. But slow change, gradual improvement, and partial success are not unknown to Congress precisely because it is a *real* legislature, with many competitors, a broad spectrum of members, and numerous jobs to do. It needs all the help it can get.

Notes

1. See, among others, Joseph S. Clark, *Congress: The Sapless Branch*, Colophon Books, Rev. ed. (New York: Harper & Row, 1964); Clark, *Congressional Reform: Problems and Prospects* (New York: Thomas Y. Crowell Co., 1965); Richard Bolling, *House Out of Order* (New York: E. P. Dutton & Co., Inc., 1966); Alfred deGrazia (ed.), *Congress: The First Branch of Government*, Anchor Books (Garden City, N.Y.: Doubleday & Co., Inc., 1967); Stephen K. Bailey, *Congress in the Seventies* (New York: St. Martin's Press, 1970).

2. "Legislative veto" refers to the congressional practice which requires the executive to notify Congress of certain decisions or actions before or after they are made or taken while reserving to Congress the power to negate or veto the decisions within a specified time period. For elaboration and references, see Joseph P. Harris, *Congressional Control of Administration,* Anchor Books (Garden City, N.Y.: Doubleday & Company, Inc., 1964), chap. 8; and John S. Saloma, III, *Congress and the New Politics* (Boston: Little, Brown and Company, 1969), pp. 139–145.

3. The sole exception is J. Malcolm Smith and Cornelius P. Cotter's study of "emergency" and national security statutes enacted between 1933 and 1956: "Administrative Accountability: Reporting to Congress," *Western Political Quarterly* 10 (June 1957): 405–15.

4. During the Ninety-first Congress the House Foreign Affairs and Senate Foreign Relations Committees commissioned the Foreign Affairs Division of the Congressional Research Service to undertake an evaluation of reports to Congress in the foreign affairs area. The resulting studies have been invaluable: (1) Senate Committee on Foreign Relations, *Reporting Requirements in Legislation on Foreign Relations,* Committee Print, 91st Cong., 2d sess., 1970; (2) House Committee on Foreign Affairs and Senate Committee on Foreign Relations, *Required Reports to Congress in the Foreign Affairs Field,* Joint Committee Print, 93rd Cong., 1st sess., 1973 (hereafter cited as *Required Reports*); and (3) *Improving the Reporting Requirement System in the Foreign Affairs Field,* Joint Committee Print, 93rd Cong., 2d sess., 1974 (hereafter cited as *Improving the Reporting Requirement System*).

In March 1972 the chairman of the House Government Operations Committee, repeating a practice of earlier years, requested the General Accounting Office to study reports submitted to Congress by executive agencies and to make appropriate recommendations for improvements. The study was made and proved fruitful: Comptroller General of the United States, *Usefulness to the Congress of Reports Submitted by the Executive Branch,* Report to the House Committee on Government Operations, B-115398, October, 1973 (hereafter cited as *Usefulness of Reports*).

Finally, in the Congressional Budget and Impoundment Control Act of 1974 (PL 93–344; 88 *Stat.* 297), Congress amended the 1970 Legislative Reorganization Act (PL 91–510; 84 *Stat.* 1140) to require the comptroller general to assist Congress in its information needs generally and in its reporting system specifically. See the discussion below.

5. With slight variations, the documents are entitled "Reports to be Made to Congress," and they are usually issued annually in January. Data in this study are from: H. Docs. 56–19, 58–3, 60–486, 62–990, 64–394, 66–366, 68–96, 70–83, 72–44, 74–77, 76–42, 78–38, 80–32, 82–27, 83–25, 84–24, 85–24, 86–23, 87–23, 88–23, 89–23, 90–23, 91–31, 92–21, 93–21, and 93–199.

6. Many reports are or may be made more than once each year. Others need be made only if particular actions are taken or if certain contingencies occur. About a dozen reporting requirements in effect for each Congress call for reports from the heads of *all* agencies, but each of these is counted by the clerk of the House, and here, only

once. Consistent with the clerk's report, figure 1 does count as two, three, or four those requirements which explicitly call for reports from specifically identified—and so listed—reporters such as the secretaries of defense, army, navy, and air force. Such multiple requirements total about two to three dozen annually.

7. In addition, Congress passed two concurrent resolutions requesting studies. These resolutions are exceptions, for Congress rarely uses concurrent resolutions to request reports. The figures in the text and in the tables dealing with reports *enacted* were counted by the author after an extensive search of the *Statutes at Large*. Heavy reliance was placed on the index to the *Statutes*, which is not altogether thorough. Moreover, a great deal of subjective judgment had to be made in including or excluding certain provisions and in categorizing them, especially when they were repetitions or minor alterations of earlier requirements, or when they required multiple reporters or reports. Therefore, the count in any one Congress may vary slightly from what someone else might find. But the method of counting was consistent throughout, resulting in totals that reliably reflect the changes and trends over time. Whatever inaccuracy exists is one of undercounting.

8. For purposes of classification, a policy-making or study-and-recommend reporting requirement is identified as any required report that must include "recommendations" (or the equivalent).

9. 83 *Stat.* 142. See also 82 *Stat.* 36, 270; 83 *Stat.* 852; 84 *Stat.* 1876.

10. Congress sometimes requires the secretary of agriculture to file with Congress maps and legal descriptions of areas Congress designates as parts of the National Forest or Park systems. When filed, the documents carry the force of law. Such papers are not considered reports in this study, nor are they indexed in the *Statutes at Large*. For examples, see 82 *Stat.* 51; 86 *Stat.* 38, 48, 505, 578, 792, 811, 918.

11. 82 *Stat.* 271, 479; 81 *Stat.* 522. Disposal of equipment and transfers of government property to state or local governments or private enterprise are usually subject to reporting as well. See 81 *Stat.* 443; 82 *Stat.* 1131.

12. 81 *Stat.* 937; 84 *Stat.* 6–10, 1943, 2055. See also 82 *Stat.* 48.

13. 82 *Stat.* 76.

14. 81 *Stat.* 282. NASA has been subject to similar restrictions. See 84 *Stat.* 369.

15. 83 *Stat.* 82; 84 *Stat.* 405.

16. 82 *Stat.* 46.

17. Plans for new wild and scenic rivers could not become effective until ninety days after they had been forwarded to the Hill. 82 *Stat.* 908–09.

18. 82 *Stat.* 1137.

19. 84 *Stat.* 369, 371, 911–12.

20. 84 *Stat.* 405.

21. But some do not. For instance, President Nixon was charged to transmit a report by the Father Marquette Tercentenary Celebration Commission and a Department of Transportation report on an awards program for suggestions and inventions. US House of Representatives, *Reports to be Made to Congress*, H. Doc. 93–21, 93rd Cong., 1st sess., 1973, pp. 9–12.

22. The numbers in table 3 understate the role of the White House, since (until 1973) the clerk of the House tallied reports according to their originating source, not the final transmitter. The military leads all executive agencies in reporting duties, but this is somewhat misleading, since: (1) many identical reporting requirements apply to each of the services; (2) the Defense Department is subject to more contingency reporting duties than any other agency, and many may not actually result in reports; and (3) as a percentage of all reporting requirements, those applying to the Pentagon have been

decreasing. (Many DoD reports deal with nonmilitary operations of the Corps of Engineers.)

23. The interviews were unstructured, anonymity was guaranteed; and, with a few exceptions, no notes were taken during the interviews. A transcript, according to the memory of the writer, was made immediately following the interview. Interviews were conducted with: three congressmen; five House and nine Senate committee staff members; two aides to congressmen and three to senators; three members of the Congressional Research Service; one official of the Office of Management and Budget; and fifteen executive and independent agency administrators at various levels.

24. Leon Sigal argues that sensitive matters (the World War II Manhattan Project and the bombing of Cambodia in 1969–70) bearing heavy classification restrictions are not always truly secret—that the word does get around Washington via informal processes. Congressmen and staffs who would like to challenge or at least expose or investigate such secret policies are inhibited. Requiring official reports on these activities, however, affords would-be investigators a "handle" on the matter of concern—and perhaps an excuse for holding a hearing or at least for forcing the executive to widen the circle of insiders on the particular issue. "Informal Communication Between the Bureaucracy and Congress," paper delivered at the Annual Meeting of the American Political Science Association, Chicago, August, 1974.

25. For instance, in laws passed during the Eightieth Congress, there were provisions ordering 39 reports to be made specifically to committees. Under laws enacted during the Eighty-sixth, committees were to receive 71 reports. That figure jumped to 116 during the Ninetieth.

26. For example, see Smith and Cotter, "Administrative Accountability," pp. 405–06; William J. Keefe and Morris S. Ogul, *The American Legislative Process: Congress and the States* (Englewood Cliffs, N.J.: Prentice-Hall, Inc., 1973), p. 423; Roland Young, *The American Congress* (New York: Harper & Row, Publishers, 1958), p. 183; George B. Galloway, *The Legislative Process in Congress* (New York: Thomas Y. Crowell Company, 1955), p. 614; and Harris, *Congressional Control*, pp. 259, 264–65.

Reports from national or presidential study commissions constitute a minor exception. In his study of presidential commissions (which usually report to Congress), Thomas Wolanin found that they had an important, though marginal, impact in public policy and that they had an educational value. "The Impact of Presidential Advisory Commissions, 1945–1968," paper delivered at the Annual Meeting of the American Political Science Association, Washington, D.C., Sept., 1972. George T. Sulzner found national study commissions and presumably their reports to be quite valuable. "The Policy Process and the Uses of National Government Study Commissions," *Western Political Quarterly* 24 (Sept. 1971): 438–48.

27. John R. Johannes, "Study and Recommend: Statutory Reporting Requirements as a Technique of Legislative Initiation," *Western Political Quarterly*, xxix (Dec., 1976), 589–596.

28. *Required Reports*, p. 11.

29. *Ibid.*, p. 12; *Improving the Reporting Requirement System*, p. 2.

30. *Required Reports*, pp. 21–23.

31. *Ibid.*, pp. 13–14.

32. *Ibid.*, p. 15.

33. Public Law 92–226 (86 *Stat.* 27) not only required the president to sign and publish in the *Federal Register* certain reports, but it stated:

> No committee or officer of either House of Congress shall be denied any requested information relating to any finding or determination which the President is

> required to report to the Congress . . . under any provision of this Act [and others] . . . even though such report has not yet been transmitted to . . . Congress . . . . Any Federal department, agency, or independent establishment shall furnish any information requested by [the foreign relations committees] relating to any such activity or responsibility [spelled out in the Act.]

34. The same is true of informal reports. See Kenneth Kofmehl, *Professional Staffs of Congress* (West Lafayette, Ind.: Purdue University Press, 1962), p. 157.

35. *Required Reports*, pp. 17–19; *Improving the Reporting Requirement System*, p. 3.

36. See Charles R. Dechert, "Availability of Information for Congressional Operations," in DeGrazia, *Congress: The First Branch*, p. 161.

37. *Ibid.*, p. 160; and Kenneth Janda, "Information Systems for Congress," *ibid.*, p. 414. See also Saloma, *Congress and the New Politics*, chap. 7.

38. 45 *Stat.* 986; 60 *Stat.* 866; 65 *Stat.* 701; 68 *Stat.* 966; 74 *Stat.* 245; 79 *Stat.* 1310; and PL 93–608.

39. OMB Circular A–44, Transmittal Memorandum No. 1, 1970.

40. *Required Reports*, p. 10.

41. See note 4. By surveying executive agencies and interviewing congressional committees, the GAO developed a list of reports that were modified, consolidated, or eliminated—at a savings of about $200,000—by PL 93–608. Many reports deemed expendable by one source were felt to be important by another.

42. PL 93–344.

43. See, for example, the 1972 amendments to the 1968 Gas Pipeline Safety Act, 86 *Stat.* 616.

44. Interestingly, the CRS recommended that each piece of major legislation contain a reporting requirement calling for periodic statements by the executive on how the law is being carried out. While potentially useful, such requirements might prove counterproductive, since they would generate hundreds of new reports. See the discussion below. *Required Reports*, p. 3. The GAO proposed that legislation include specific requirements that agencies evaluate their programs. House Select Committee on Committees, *Committee Organization in the House, Panel Discussion*, 93rd Cong., 1st sess., 1973, vol. 2, pt. 2, p. 344. Under the 1974 Budget and Impoundment Control Act, the GAO was required to help Congress "eliminate duplicative or unneeded reporting."

45. *Required Reports*, pp. 15–16. See 86 *Stat.* 619.

46. For elaboration on some of these, and for other suggestions, see the two CRS studies, *Required Reports* and *Improving the Reporting Requirement System*, and the GAO's *Usefulness of Reports.*

47. Thomas Cronin, "The Swelling of the Presidency," in Stanley Bach and George T. Sulzner (eds.), *Perspectives on the Presidency* (Lexington, Mass.: D.C. Heath and Company, 1974), pp. 179–89.

48. For one discussion of legislative initiation, see John R. Johannes, *Policy Innovation in Congress* (Morristown, N.J.: General Learning Press, 1972).

Patterns of Congressional Staffing:

The House Committee on Appropriations

KHALED M. KAYALI

The importance of standing congressional committee staffs to the proper function of committee affairs has been sparingly discussed in several literary works.[1] The literature to date involves general observations of staffing behavior, but never a detailed study of specific committees. The nature of these literary discussions can be described as a dialogue over controversies, which surround such areas as methods of appointment, qualifications of appointees, length of tenure, majority and minority staff, and the political loyalty of staffs. Two general themes prevail: one, that recruiting practices often neglect professional considerations; and two, that most committees are understaffed.

This chapter takes a somewhat different approach to the study of congressional staffing behavior by looking at the staffing patterns of a single House committee, the Committee on Appropriations. While there is no attempt to arrive at generalizations, this study nonetheless provides general insights on the experience of other committees in the House in the field of legislative staffing. The Appropriations Committee has developed a sophisticated staffing system which includes a limited permanent staff and the extensive use of external and nonpermanent staff resources.

As one of three "major" House committees, the Committee on Appropriations holds a position of great influence in the legislative process. The committee is not involved in lawmaking per se, but rather is charged with the responsibility of funding programs authorized by the House. As the active fiscal control agent in the House, the committee is involved in a complex and demanding set of roles. Specifically, the committee sets appropriation levels within the limits of federal revenues; it oversees the executive branch through review and approval of the federal budget; and finally, it represents the House in negotiations with the Senate as joint conference participants.

Given the complex nature of its task, the committee must possess strong staff capability in order for its members to have sufficient information to act on the matters which come before it. The focus of this paper is on the strategies adopted by the committee to equip itself with adequate staff help, while at the same time preventing the emergence of a legislative staff bureaucracy that may impair the committee's independence.

Developments in Committee Staffing

External as well as internal congressional factors have heightened the importance of committee staffs. The need for additional staff is primarily the result of four important developments in the American political system. These are: (1) changes in the relative influence of the system's institutional structure, (2) increased influence of both the federal government and technology, (3) the growing potential threat of unenlightened opposition,[2] and more recently (4) junior and minority congressmen requesting their own committee staff, largely for reasons of equality.[3]

Changes in the relative influence of the system's institutional structure has placed a demand on the legislative branch to staff its committees. This institutional arrangement, which has enjoyed a tradition of stability due to its secularized and differentiated structures, has been threatened by the increased influence of the president and the executive bureaucracy, which arises out of a dependency on the president and executive bureaucracy for information and knowledge regarding public policy.

In addition, the increased role of the national government in the lives of its people and in the affairs of foreign countries has increased dramatically the volume of demands for action, placing additional demands on Congress to strengthen its internal resources.[4] Indeed, in the past when the nation was young and the exercise of power by the federal government was limited, the need for staff to assist congressmen was not as acute. In reality, "the detailed development of governmental functions was largely a state and local matter." [5] Subsequently, as the nation has matured and as the national government has become increasingly involved in domestic and foreign affairs, and as its activities have continued to take scientific and technical forms, the need for sufficient and competent committee staffs has become apparent.

A third causal factor, the potential harm of unenlightened opposition, has also directed attention to the need for adequate staffing. Unlike the first two factors, which were external in nature, this factor is an internal one. Unaware of certain facts surrounding an issue, congressmen will attempt to oppose programs for no other reason than to show that they were carrying out their duties. This behavior is cited by Senator Hubert Humphrey:

> Faced with an impressive case by the Administration, and unarmed with counter facts and arguments, even a conscientious Senator sometimes vacillates between giving a grudging consent and opposing for the sake of opposing.[6]

Finally, junior and minority congressmen have joined together in voting for additional staff employees out of a desire to achieve equality as members of Congress.

Demands for Reform

The changes in the relative influence of the system's institutional structure, the growing role of the national government as well as that of technology, and the potential threat of uninformed congressmen, stimulated critics both within and outside Congress to take measures to insure the continued influential role of the legislature. To maintain the differentiated political structure and to insure sound and independent judgment,

Congress could no longer depend on information supplied by the executive branch. In the words of Gladys M. Kammerer,

> These critics deemed it essential that Congress empower itself to obtain its own independent staff services and that it pay adequately for them.[7]

Similar concerns have continued to be aired. Reflecting the several sources of the problem, Speaker of the House Carl Albert indicated a general concern when he told members of the House Select Committee on Committees in 1973 that if the House committees are to function effectively, they must "have sufficient and capable professional staff. . . ."[8] The vice-chairman of the Select Committee cited a problem of inadequate oversight by certain committees. Referring to an executive agency report sent to a congressional committee, he said:

> The report comes up, but nobody pays any attention to it, and we don't have the followthrough and the oversight in the committee as to how that program is working. I think that is one of our great weaknesses here.[9]

Another congressman blamed a part of the problem on the organization of Congress. Representative Mike McCormack told his colleagues:

> A serious consequence of the fragmentation of jurisdiction is the fact that no committee can justify a staff of adequate size having expertise in energy matters. Since the energy problem is primarily a technological one and requires detailed analyses of short, medium, and long range aspects, we need staff members who are top flight scientists, engineers, economists, working together in an integrated team for a single committee. This staffing does not exist in the House today.[10]

Still another representative, Peter W. Rodino, blamed part of the problem on a lack of personal recognition and job security for the skillful, professional, committee staff employee. Consequently, he advocated the establishment of a congressional civil service to attract and retain qualified personnel.[11] While these demands for reform indicate a general need for improving staff resources, today's staffing practices, regardless of their inadequacies, are an improvement over past practices.

Early Staffing Practices

Institutional procedures to staff congressional committees were slow in coming. At the end of the Civil War the total number of clerks employed by House committees was only eight.

Evidence indicates that during the nation's formative years committee chairmen were obliged to keep their own records.[12] According to Lauros G. McConachie, the Committee on the Defeat of General St. Clair paid a clerk $150 in 1793 and a like sum to another clerk in 1796.[13] Subsequent proposals to employ two clerks for all the committees in the years 1803, 1815, and 1817 were rejected. By 1840, upon the insistence of chairmen, Congress finally agreed to allow some assistance on a per diem and hourly basis "by special resolutions adopted by each house every session."[14] The first two committees allowed to employ clerks on a full-time basis, in 1856, were the House Ways and Means Committee and the Senate Finance Committee. By 1900 appropriation acts began to specify special funds for clerks of standing committees. The first comprehensive legislative pay bill providing funds for congressmen's staffs as well as committee staffs was not enacted, however, until 1924. And in 1946 the Legislative Reorganization Act instituted the first comprehensive system by which each standing committee of Congress was authorized to employ four staff members and six clerks. Certain committees, such as the House Committee on Appropriations, were exempt from the limitation on their number. Although the Legislative Reorganization Act specified that employment of clerical staffs be on a professional, nonpolitical basis, as of 1951 this norm did not seem to be followed uniformly by all committees.[15]

Recent Staffing Developments

In 1970 Congress passed the Legislative Reorganization Act in which it enlarged the staffs of standing committees to six and continued to exempt the Appropriations Committee from limitations on the number of staff. In addition, Congress reiterated its rule for employment of the staffs on a permanent basis and without consideration as to political affiliation:

> The professional staff members of each standing committee . . . shall be appointed on a permanent basis, without regard to political affiliation and solely on the basis of fitness to perform . . .[16]

In order to insure the continuous professional capabilities of its committee staffs, Congress also allowed the standing committees of both the Senate and House to obtain needed special training for their staffs, subject to approval by the Committee on Rules and Administration or the Committee on House Administration, as the case might be.[17]

Finally, in 1975 two committees in the House, the Appropriations Committee and the Rules Committee, acted to allow each committee member to employ one "associate staffer" who would be paid out of the committee staff budget. This staff employee is to be housed in the congressman's office but is to work on committee matters.[18] This act may have been promulgated by the 20 May 1975 order of the House Administration Committee, which allowed "each Member of the House of Representatives, the Resident Commissioner from Puerto Rico, and the Delegates from the District of Columbia, the Virgin Islands, and Guam . . ." to spend a $22,500 additional annual sum on office clerks.[19] Since both committees are exempt from the rules of the House regarding staffing practices, it would seem logical to conclude that their act may have been motivated by that of the House Administration Committee.

In regard to the House Appropriations Committee, while Congress does not limit the number of its permanent staff, it does limit the budget of the Committee's temporary staff. This is, however, subject to modification without much difficulty. In essence the committee is free to control the size and activities of its permanent staff, and it has relative freedom over the size of its temporary staff. Ironically, today Congress is encouraging the committee to increase its permanent staff, and the committee itself is the reluctant one.[20] Although the committee is slowly increasing its permanent staff, the intent is to avoid creating a large internal bureaucracy.

Problems in Committee Staffing

Congress is essentially a representative body, while the federal bureaucracy is largely a distributive one. Consequently the limited number of congressmen must act with authority on a limitless number of subjects, while the federal bureaucracy can increase its size with the increasing volume of public policy output. While the federal bureaucracy can physically expand itself, Congress cannot do so without changing the Constitution. * Representation is limited today to 435 representatives, 100 senators, and 4 delegates. Since representation, by definition, implies limitation of size, the only method by which Congress can increase its ability to respond to increased demands is by employing staff assistance.

A large staff could eventually establish its own norms and thus escape the control of Congress, yet informed opinion is not in agreement on this point. Representative Rodiono evidently does not fear the possibility of a bureaucratic structure which might develop as a consequence of his proposal to establish a congressional civil service.

Professor Kenneth Kofmehl would discourage the development of staff bureaucracy by limiting the size of the permanent staff by a statute: ". . . I maintain that the statutory quota for permanent professional staffs should be kept relatively small, not being more than doubled or tripled. . . ." [21] On the other hand, Professor John S. Saloma does not foresee the development of such bureaucracy. "The more fundamental question," according to him, "is one of need." [22] Professor Saloma believes that the general system would not permit a large permanent staff to become harmful:

> I have the highest regard for the ability of Congressmen to adapt to such a situation. I don't foresee . . . the danger of the techniques taking over your job or the administrator's job. The sanction of the electorate, the connection between the Congressman and the voter and the connection between the administrator and the President or the cabinet secretary is strong enough, that the real danger is one of not having an adequate dialogue between the

* The size of the Senate is limited by the Constitution, and the House is limited by its own statute.

> Executive and Congress because of the absence of staff rather than the admitted problems of management. . . .[23]

For fear of developing an internal staff bureaucracy, chairmen of the House Committee on Appropriations have traditionally exhibited a reluctance to employ a large permanent staff. The last chairman, Representative Clarence Cannon, favored a small permanent staff but encouraged the hiring of temporary staff.[24] The present chairman, Representative George Mahon, favors a larger permanent staff, but he cautiously warns against an excessively large one. In 1965 he told his colleagues:

> I think we are somewhat understaffed and have been for years . . . I think we will increase our staff as we go along, and should, but I would like to say unequivocally that a real large staff is not the answer to our problems.[25]

More recently he gave specific reasons as to why he opposes a large permanent staff. His remarks tend to support the contention that man's ability to deal with information is inversely related to his capacity to gather it: [26]

> Since 1964 the number doubled from 17 to 34 in 1973. . . . It is my view that gradual and careful increases in staff are far preferable to massive infusions of new people.
>
> Massive staffs for congressional committees could bring with them many significant problems. Bureaucracies, as we all know, tend to develop their own personalities, points of view, rivalries—sometimes petty and debilitating. Neither should it be forgotten that they bring with them coordinating, personnel, and other management problems that would ultimately fall to Members to resolve. In terms of assistance in decision-making, they could very well result in contributing little more than adding another point of view that Members must again ultimately sort out and compare with a cupboard full of opinions pressed on them from other quarters.[27]

Thus, according to Chairman Mahon, the staff could be a *source* of cumbersome problems with which committee members must deal.

An important aspect in the utilization of committee staffs involves the division of power and control in Congress. According to Representative Sam Gibbons, giving more staff to congressmen may weaken the powers of committee chairmen.[28] Indeed, staff assignment is a source of power. Although Carl D. Perkins, chairman of the House Committee on Education and Labor, favors having a well-staffed minority, he acknowledges that the minority staff of his committee "frequently is working against the majority's legislative goals. . . ." [29] While staff assignment is a source of power, a strong chairman does not need as much staff assistance as a weak one.[30] And the issue of power and control could be the most overriding influence in the House's behavior over staffing practices. Representative Paul S. Sarbanes echoes this concern:

> So the question of staff control at the committee or subcommittee level is related to a number of other questions. What is the relationship to be between committee decisionmaking and subcommittee decisionmaking, and what is the relationship to be between the committee chairmen and the subcommittee chairmen who often in fact may not be on the same team or necessarily in agreement with one another? The fight over staff control is only the surface reflection of what may be a much more fundamental difference over how *power* is to be shared and who is to exercise it.[31]

In fact, in spite of testimony by members of Congress and the academic community, the ultimate deciding factor in staffing behavior may be political considerations involving issues over power and control—as may have been the case in the Senate's June 1975 vote to give each senator a maximum of three staff employees to work on committee matters.[32] Senator Robert J. Dole described the Senate's debate on this measure as a "battle between the 'haves' and the 'have nots,' " and he argued that equal state representation had been absent from the Senate due to inequality in staff resources.[33] In the House, Congressman William L. Dickson of Alabama told his colleagues:

> I don't think that the majority or the minority should mandate the hiring of staff or deny staffing by binding its own group to impose its will on the will of the majority of the House.[34]

Another problem in committee staffing is primarily a theoretical one, concerning the proper role of Congress as a legislative authority rather than an administrative one. Representative John W. Davis was concerned with this problem when he warned that in its attempt to continuously react to developments in the executive branch, Congress could eventually lose its role as a legislative body:

> The organization of Congress should be primarily shaped in relation to the constructive functions of the Congress as a legislative body, rather than in relation to historical functions of the Executive branch as an operating arm of the government, or to the funding and reviewing function of Congress.[35]

According to Davis, the legislative role of Congress would be concerned with "defining what is legal and illegal, what is lawful and criminal, or what should be inhibited and what encouraged [sic]." [36]

These problems, inherent in large permanent staffs, can be seen as having affected congressional practices in staffing the House Committee on Appropriations. The chairman of this committee has sought to strengthen external staff resources and to deemphasize the role of the internal permanent staff. Analysis of the function and utilization of both external and internal staff resources presents an interesting example of organization which is politically viable while promoting effective and efficient support services.

Staffing in the House Appropriations Committee

The Appropriations Committee is encouraging information input by strengthening the role of the temporary staff. The committee also emphasizes the role of other external sources of information such as the General Accounting Office and the Congressional Research Service. But in spite of the numerous information sources, the Congress is ironically in an unenviable position from which it must continuously ask for information. Indeed, an argument may be made that although the power of the purse resides in Congress, it is ultimately easier for governmental agencies to get their annual budgets approved than for Congress to get certain information from those agencies. *

The committee realizes, however, that it is not at a disadvantage because of the *legal* structure of the political institutions. Indeed the Supreme Court decided in *Kendall v. United States* that the executive officers "are subject to the control of the law." [37] The executive agencies remain under the supervision and direction of the legislative branch. Congress is at a disadvantage, however, because of extralegal developments such as bureaucratic procedures, a large maze of information to be analyzed in a short period of time, and ever-growing bureaucratic structures. Thus, regardless of legal norms setting structural relationships between the executive bureaucracy and other governmental units, bureaucratic officials often act as "though they were in business for themselves." [38] The executive is at an advantage because, among other things, Congress must rely on data that the executive collects. Indeed, private studies often rely on information prepared by agencies of the executive branch. The agencies are the sources of information because they often create as well as collect it.

> When one samples the reports prepared by Congressional committees or the Legislative Reference Service of the Library of Congress, one notes that many, if not most of the data in the papers are drawn from sources in the executive branch of the government.[39]

According to James A. Robinson, Congress itself is now out of functional balance vis à vis the executive. Congress does not now initiate, but generally acts to legitimize, executive decisions and proposals.[40]

The leadership of the committee views its internal resources as an adequate means of acquiring sufficient information and expertise while avoiding the threat of creating a new bureaucracy:

* This is true in spite of the Statutory Reporting Requirement which the Congress uses to obtain information from various executive agencies. See the chapter by Johannes in this volume.

> It is my feeling that while it might be appropriate for committee staffs to grow only gradually, their impact could be measurably strengthened through ready access to powerful analytical and information resources *outside the House of Representatives itself.* The emphasis of the 1970 Reorganization Act on strengthening the CRS and GAO seems more promising to me than lodging enormous staffs in the committees of the House. I do believe, however, we must take care not to assign these institutions responsibilities that might get them tangled and managed—politically.[41]

The committee's resources include its limited number of permanent staff, its skilled temporary staff, and other sources of information such as the General Accounting Office, the Congressional Research Service, and other special reports. Discussion of staffs will follow, but first let us examine the extent to which the committee relies on its other sources of information.

External Sources of Information

General Accounting Office. The Appropriations Committee uses the services of the General Accounting Office in two capacities. The committee uses GAO studies which are sent to Congress and to the committee as well. The committee may also request GAO to undertake special studies and investigations such as defense systems (table 1). Recently, in addition to these studies and special requests, GAO's capabilities have been extended to management surveys as well. Certain areas which might be of interest to the committee are condensed by GAO in special documents entitled "Significant Audit Findings" and sent to the committee. These compilations are a valuable source of information for the committee. Chairman George Mahon commented on the importance of these publications during the 1965 hearings on the organization of Congress:

> It is a report of "significant findings" whatever it might be. One volume is in the area of defense and one volume is in the area of non-defense. . . . They help us. *They help direct the attention of the Committee* to areas of their regular audit reports that might be especially important to us.[42]

Table 1

Examples of GAO Special Studies Requested by the Committee

Study of circumstances surrounding proposed acquisition of twelve Boeing 707/720B or DC-8 fan-jet aircraft to loan to the navy.
Analysis of the Army's Advanced Attack Helicopter Evaluation and Material Needs.
Review of army program to modernize ammunition plants.
Investigation of possible use of funds appropriated for the Peace Corps for purpose of lobbying.
Review of effectiveness of leasing and rental guarantee housing programs in Europe for military dependents.
Review of adequacy of standard barracks developed by military services.
Study of the viability and economic trade-offs of alternate methods of providing family housing overseas for military personnel.
Study of circumstances surrounding construction of postal bulk mail-handling facilities.

Source: Committee Memo., p. 7.

More recently the chairman described how these reports can bring about some corrective efforts through different means:

> This compilation is designed to identify problem areas in an individual agency which might have applicability to other organizations. These findings relate to matters which are felt to require corrective action either by the Committee's efforts, through legislation, or through administrative efforts.[43]

While it is difficult to assign a man-year equivalent to the GAO efforts, the following table provides some evidence of the committee's reliance on GAO's studies.

According to a 1973 statement by the clerk of the committee, the committee studied the possibility of utilizing the services of GAO in securing rapid studies on issues arising out of the hearings themselves, but which were not evident before the hearings. Such studies would then be used by the committee in conducting hearings. To date "very few" such studies have been conducted.[44]

Congressional Research Service. The Congressional Research Service prepares papers and obtains information for the staff of

Table 2

Number of References to GAO Studies in Annual Appropriation Hearings 1962–1971

Year	References
1962 (87th Cong., 2nd Sess)	68
1963	126
1964	113
1965	88
1966	na
1967	na
1968	649
1969	727
1970	701
1971	722

Sources: For 1962–1965, *Hearings on the Reorganization of Congress*, 1965, pt. 2, p. 1652; for 1968–1971, *Committee Organization in the House, Hearings*, 1973, I, pt. 2, p. 639.

the committee upon request. The Legislative Reorganization Act of 1970 authorized CRS to aid committees of Congress by providing them with research and analytical services. The reliance of the committee on this service, however, is considerably less than its reliance on GAO. Indeed, the temporary staff may find this service more helpful than the permanent staff. According to a committee staff member, the permanent staff in its daily functions rarely comes in contact with the Congressional Research Service.* [45]

Special Reports. In addition, the staff often requests special reports from agency budget officers on matters pertinent to subcommittee hearings. Individual members of the committee receive informal reports and memoranda from private groups and individuals. A special group may want to protest the method by which some agency is administering a certain program. Such complaints provide congressmen with the opportu-

* For a full explanation of the function of the Congressional Research Service, see the chapter by Beckman in this volume.

nity of questioning executive agencies. While these special reports are rarely resorted to, they do, nevertheless, direct the attention of the committee members to areas of interest and they are generally of high quality.

Internal Sources of Information

The Temporary Staff. The temporary staff of the Appropriations Committee, which is larger than the permanent one, provides a valuable service to the committee, and it constitutes a major internal resources in the support of the committee's activities. The value of the studies this staff makes is not measured by the number of times they are cited in annual appropriation hearings, but is evident by the fact that these studies are made upon the request of the committee itself.[46]

Until very recently, the committee spent on the temporary staff an amount comparable to that spent on the permanent staff.[47] The 1975 fiscal appropriation for the temporary staff was $1,875,000.

The temporary staff is known officially as the "Surveys and Investigations Staff." Its individual members are referred to as "investigators" and are headed by a "director" who is assisted by a first and second "assistant director." The temporary staff, like the permanent staff, is supported by several "clerical assistants." The director, who is an experienced administrator, and his two assistants come from the Federal Bureau of Investigation and are paid by the committee for the duration of their stay. Each is first employed for two years in an apprenticeship capacity and then one year as director. After three years they return to the bureau.

Most of the temporary staff is recruited from the bureau. For example, the *Congressional Record* shows that the committee employed 46 investigators for the least-busy six-month period from 1 July to 21 December, 1972. Forty of the investigators came from the Federal Bureau of Investigation. The other six came from the following agencies: the Naval Audit Service, the National Aeronautics and Space Administration, the Defense Contract Audit Agency, and the Department of Agriculture. Taking into account the heavy work-load period, the average number of these investigators is approximately 60. During the 92nd Congress 105 individuals comprised the investigative team; they were on loan from nineteen different governmental agencies, and they spent a total of 1,160 man-months in the conduct of their studies. This is equivalent to approximately 97 man-years.

The staff works on specific assignments directed by the chairman with the approval of the ranking minority member.[48] During the 92nd Congress the investigative staff conducted eighty studies for the committee. These studies, which were concerned with various agency operations and programs, were incorporated into seventy-two reports and eight memoranda and were used for the purpose of budget examination.[49]

In the past the committee has consistently utilized the services of government experts on an *ad hoc* basis for investigatory purposes but without placing the investigators on the committee's payroll. In such instances the investigator continued to receive a salary from his respective governmental agency, and his agency was eventually reimbursed for his services to the committee.

In addition to the investigative staff, the committee now has the benefit of technical assistance provided for under section 232 of the Legislative Reorganization Act of 1970. The fiscal and budgetary data processing system established under the act has provided for the committee a qualified system accountant and a computer specialist to help the committee in its efforts to cooperate with the establishment of a computer system for the legislative branch. Finally, the staff of the committee receives from federal agencies, upon request, special analyses and information in addition to the budget justification materials.

The Permanent Staff. The permanent staff of the Appropriations Committee works directly with committee members.[50] Literary discussions of this staff often stress the investigative function of its members but neglect its valuable administrative function.[51] As will be seen, the thirty-four members of the staff constitute a truly permanent professional staff with adequate qualifications.

Members of the permanent staff are referred to officially as "staff assistants" but are known in the committee as clerks.

They are headed by a permanent staff member with the title "clerk and staff director," who is in fact an administrative director of the staff and who works most directly with the chairman of the committee. Three of the staff assistants are assigned to the full committee, two to the minority, and the other twenty-nine are assigned unequally among the thirteen subcommittees according to work load (table 3). In addition, each chairman and ranking minority member of the thirteen subcommittees is entitled to a staff person to use as desired. As indicated earlier, each committee member, excluding chairmen and ranking minority members, are now assigned one "associate staffer" to work for the congressman on committee matters. While these staff personnel do not occupy a space in the committee offices, and while they do not sit in on subcommittee hearings, they are, nevertheless, paid out of the committee payroll. Because of

Table 3

Distribution of Staff Assignments Among the Various Subcommittees 1973

Clerks	Assignment
3	Agriculture-Environmental and Consumer Protection
5	Defense
2	District of Columbia—Legislative
1	Foreign Operations
3	HUD-Space-Science-Veterans
2	Interior
3	Labor-HEW
1	Military Construction
3	Public Works-AEC
2	State-Justice-Commerce-Judiciary
2	Transportation
2	Treasury-Postal Service-General Government
3	Full Committee
2	Minority
34	Total

Source: The clerk and staff director of the House Committee on Appropriations, May 1973. Since this table was provided by the clerk, the total has increased to thirty-nine, as a result of the following changes: Agri-Env. two, Defense six, Labor-HEW four, and Minority six, July 1975.

their detachment from the direct activities of those staff employees who work with the committee chairmen and who are housed in committee offices, they are excluded from the discussion below.

Staff appointments are made with attention paid to educational and administrative backgrounds. According to the clerk:

> The type of degrees held by the staff of the Committee on Appropriations vary widely, but are heavily flavored with business administration, economics, political science and accounting . . . three staff members hold law degrees.

Of the thirty-four staff members, all but one have bachelors degrees. Eight have masters degrees, another nine have done graduate work, and two have done doctoral work. This is in addition to the three who have law degrees.

Prior to being appointed to the staff of the committee, members of the staff have had various administrative experience, and the majority have had experience in the budget offices of the various departments and agencies of the executive branch. Several staff members have had investigative and administrative experience with the Federal Bureau of Investigation or the General Accounting Office. Several have come from program organizations in the executive branch; two have had experience with state budget offices; and one has had experience in banking. Thus recruitment for the staff of the committee is made primarily from the executive branch. The agencies from which they were appointed to the committee are listed in table 4.

Staff members are appointed on a permanent basis without regard to political affiliation. As pointed out earlier, the number of the permanent staff in 1964 stood at seventeen. Today the overwhelming majority of these have remained on the staff, and nine have been in their positions a minimum of fifteen years (table 5). Considering their educational background and experience, the permanent staff is a capable, professional body qualified to support members of the committee with relevant analysis, administrative capacity, and the ability to readily pinpoint sources of needed information. Furthermore, it must be pointed out that their continued tenure provides a continuity which is

Table 4

Clerks' Assignments Immediately Prior to Appointment to the Committee Staff

Clerks	Agency
4	Department of Agriculture, Office of Budget and Finance
2	Small Business Administration
2	General Accounting Office
4	Department of Defense
2	Federal Bureau of Investigation
1	Congressional Research Service
2	State budget offices
3	Department of Housing and Urban Development
1	Treasury Department
3	Office of Management and Budget
2	General Services Administration
1	Central Intelligence Agency
1	Interior Department
2	Department of Health, Education and Welfare
4	Other
34	Total

Source: The clerk and staff director of the House Committee on Appropriations, May 1973.

Table 5

Tenure on the Staff of the Committee May 1973

Clerks	Years
6	Over 20 years
3	15 to 20 years
4	10 to 15 years
7	5 to 10 years
14	1 to 5 years
34	Total

Source: The clerk and staff director of the House Committee on Appropriations, May 1973.

essential for their administrative duties and the committee's oversight function.

Behavior of the Permanent Staff

In order to understand fully the duties of the permanent staff, one must look at the staff's function. One will find that the staff work is more than investigative in nature; the staff actually aggregates information, examines budget justifications of different agencies, seeks out weaknesses in program and management areas, interacts with personnel of executive agencies, visits offices of agencies whether in the District of Columbia or overseas, communicates with its counterpart in the Senate, helps in writing bills, settles the final arrangements for taking the bill to the floor of the House, and sometimes assists in writing speeches for committee members, supposedly on matters relating to the work of the committee itself.

Of course, although a staff member may perform more than one of the above functions, he is by no means a generalist.[52] He is first and foremost supposed to fulfill his supporting role of oversight by analyzing budget justifications. Assessing the staff member's role, the clerk of the committee stated:

> The most valuable contribution that can be made by staff is providing assistance to Committee Members in the examination of budget estimates with the objective of helping secure economy, efficiency, and responsiveness in government programs.

Certain job specializations are evident, however, especially with respect to the clerk of the committee and the ranking staff members of the individual subcommittees. The clerk functions in an administrative capacity to coordinate the general work of the committee. Working closely with the chairman in the committee office, H-218 in the Capitol, which is adjacent to the office of the chairman; the clerk helps him prepare for the presentation of motions on the floor of the House; and when necessary he locates for the chairman members of the committee who will be on conference committees with the Senate. The clerk exhibits a vast knowledge of the rules of Congress and the structure and functions of the executive agencies, as well as the heavy work load of the committee. Inasmuch as the clerk is a qualified administrator, he is a strong arm of the chairman and thus supports the role of the chairman as a congressional leader.

A ranking subcommittee staff member described himself primarily as a coordinator, who spends most of his time talking with people inside and outside of government, recommends witnesses for the committee, deals with his counterpart in the Senate, and coordinates staff work. Of course not all ranking staff members of every subcommittee fall into this category. Nevertheless, one's investigative role is inversely related to the work load of his subcommittee.[53] During the hearings the ranking clerk sits to the left of the chairman, ready in case he is needed. Most budget analysis and preparation of suggested questions are integrated, however, by other members of the subcommittee staff.

The committee clerks who were interviewed enthusiastically view their activities as supporting the congressmen's role of oversight. They express an intense interest in and a vast knowledge of the topics of the hearings; they assume the responsibility of informing most committee members of suggested lines of questioning, even if they have to do so during the time of the hearings. They exhibit a keen awareness of the intricacies of preparing a budget, because at some point before they were appointed to their present position they themselves prepared agency budgets. And they are aware of how agencies "cover soft spots and loopholes." [54] Their skills and interest often result in producing new areas of interest that cannot be covered in the time allotted for the hearings. After one particular hearing an enthusiastic clerk told another, "we will never have time to ask them all the questions we need to ask them." He continued by saying, "Did you hear what he said? Why didn't he say that before today?" But there was yet another day of hearings to come and another opportunity to face the officials of the agency.

The relationship of the staff to the executive agencies, however, is not antagonistic; rather it is a cooperative effort.[55] They interact most often with the budget officials of the various agencies rather than with the agency head or his assistant. The clerk of the committee describes this interaction as follows:

> Because of the unending flow of information of a fiscal nature that is required for the functioning of the appropriations process, staff members of the House Appropriations Committee share a bond of trust and respect with agency budget officers. Contacts are continuous and in many instances problems are experienced on the same subject.

Members of the committee staff and the budget officers of the various executive agencies annually hold a Budget Officers Conference, the latest meeting of which took place in May 1975.[56] The conference is informal; during the meeting participating members exchange views on various area problems in their mutual budgetary process. For example, during a meeting on 13 and 14 April, 1973, two members of the committee staff addressed the group on "the subject of impoundment legislation and the activities and recommendations of the Joint Committee on Budget Control."

Important aspects relevant to understanding the role of the permanent staff employees are the degree to which they rely on information already prepared for them, and the degree to which they prepare their own studies and analyses. Permanent staff members are basically engaged in the examination of budget estimates—a process which begins as soon as the president sends his budget to Congress. They prepare the estimates for their subcommittee members, acquire other pertinent information to prepare possible questions, and assist in carrying out the subcommittee hearings. Their collective efforts in study and investigation comprise, to a considerable extent, a coordination effort. Their output, which is based on many sources of data and which covers a vast number of programs—many of which are technical in nature—must be presented to the congressmen in a relatively comprehensible form. This basic complexity of the area with which they deal renders a major portion of their function coordinating in nature. Accordingly, their limited number prevents them from handling many of the studies and investigations necessary to the committee's work. The clerk of the committee described the role of the staff as follows:

> Analyzing information and programs and suggesting lines of questioning for subcommittee members is the principal responsi-

bility of staff members. The study of agency justifications is an important part of this process. With respect to gathering information, the relatively small size of the staff and level of responsibility has resulted in the practice of calling in other sources for the gathering of information.

Of the various sources of information, the permanent staff relies most heavily on studies conducted by the surveys and investigations staff, General Accounting Office, and the Congressional Research Service.

Communication Among Staff Employees and with Members of the Committee

Members of the permanent staff, although assigned to the chairman, work in close cooperation with the chairmen of the subcommittees. There is little interaction between staff members of the various subcommittees. There is, however, cooperation between those subcommittees which share subject matter of some similarity. An example would be the Defense and Military Construction Subcommittees, as well as the State-Justice and Foreign Operations Subcommittees. The clerk describes the staff's interactions as follows:

> There is no regular schedule for staff meetings largely because of the demands on time. However, there is good staff communication centered around the full Committee offices and the Clerk of the Committee undertakes to keep staff advised of developments of mutual interest. A private intercom system between all Subcommittee and full Committee offices promotes ready communication.

Members of the subcommittee staffs, especially the ranking clerks, remain on one subcommittee by developing rapport with its chairman. This behavior is favored by the various chairmen, who expect their staff to anticipate and carry out their responsibilities without being told to do so. One ranking clerk has been on the same subcommittee for twenty-five years, another for nineteen years. According to the clerk, movement of staff members among the several subcommittees is limited to the new appointees. The subcommittee chairman holds a considerable influence over his staff members. Although according to the Legislative Reorganization Act of 1970 termination of staff members is subject to full committee decision, the dissatisfaction of a subcommittee chairman with a staff member could result in his removal from the staff.

Summary and Conclusions

This chapter has attempted to explain the staffing procedures of the House Committee on Appropriations. The contention was made that the committee uses its internal resources in a manner which emphasizes its sources of information input and minimizes a conceived potential threat of a dominant permanent staff.

A considerable amount of information input comes from the General Accounting Office and the committee's temporary staff. In recent years citations attributed to GAO during committee hearings have risen considerably (table 2). During 1965 and 1973 hearings on the organization of Congress, Chairman George Mahon placed considerable emphasis on his committee's use of GAO resources. To a greater extent the committee also relies on its temporary investigative staff. The individual investigators work solely for the committee and contribute a total of ninety-seven man-years through their investigations. This figure represents approximately three times the thirty-three man-years contributed by the permanent staff in 1972. The role of this staff is purely investigative.

The permanent staff is a professional one, recruited according to professional qualifications and experience and largely without political considerations. The staff's role is basically an investigative one, but skewed somewhat toward administration and integration. Some division of labor exists among the various staff members, with the ranking subcommittee clerk assuming a coordinating role. Furthermore, this study revealed that clerks remain on the staff of the same subcommittee over a long period of time by developing rapport with the subcommittee chairman. This practice may also be attributed to the chairmen's desire to maintain a staff which is constantly informed of the programs and the managerial behavior of their respective agencies and programs.

Two major interrelated explanations have been cited in support of the above contention. The legislative branch has an inherent need for staff because the limited number of elected congressmen are necessarily representatives rather than technical experts, and two, the committee does not suffer from a lack of information, but rather from the means to digest all this information in the limited time involved in appropriation procedures. The executive branch can increase the number of its agencies and officials according to need, but Congress is limited by Constitutional provisions. The official in the executive branch is not elected, however, the congressman is and is supposed to act in an independent manner. A congressman's authority can conceivably be threatened by a large, internal, informed bureaucracy. The possibility of controlling it would surely be questionable. The committee's present chairman, as well as its previous chairman, pointed out this danger. While searching for an investigative organization to replace the dismantled Bureau of Efficiency, Chairman Cannon in 1943 cited two difficulties associated with a large permanent staff:

> [one], through its intimate association with the members of the Committee would slowly but surely increase its salaries, its personnel, and its jurisdiction until it became in effect a Frankenstein which could not be controlled or dislodged, and, second the establishment of an organization amenable to political manipulation which could be used for partisan purposes.[57]

In other words, additional permanent staff in the name of reform may not be progress.

Chairman Mahon told the Committee on the Organization of Congress in 1965 that the problem before his committee was not as much a staffing problem as it was a need for some means to assimilate the large input of information:

> I have no hesitancy in saying that in my judgment the problem facing Congress in this general connection is not so much one of getting more information as it is of doing more about the information and knowledge we have. And it is also a question of the members of the committee finding the time to fully assimilate the information and put it to use.[58]

Thus, the committee faces the problem of staffing by emphasizing information input and minimizing the dangers of a large bureaucracy. Theoretically the problem could best be solved by maximizing the congressman's skills and knowledge. An informed and hard-working congressman is able to utilize the information the staff provides best.[59] Thus when federal judges, for example, are appointed they are already equipped with the knowledge and the skills to function with the smallest possible staff. Similarly a skillful, knowledgeable legislator usually depends less on staff than does a weak one. Congressmen, however, are seldom elected because they qualify for a specific legislative area.[60] Finally, to assume that a certain number of permanent staff could meet the total needs of congressmen is to get involved in a value judgment that may not necessarily coincide with reality.[61]

Making sure that each congressman develops an interest and specialization in his favorite policy area and maximizing the input of legislature-controlled external sources of information may be the best answer. This would insure the preservation of independently elected legislators while strengthening the role of congressional oversight.

The progress of the Office of Technology Assessment and the work of the newly established House Commission on Information and Facilities may help point the direction which the House wishes to follow in its future reform efforts. This commission is charged

> with the function of conducting a thorough and complete study of House information resources, including the Congressional Research Service, the General Accounting Office, and the Office of Technology Assessment, and the organizational framework that makes them effective or ineffective.[62]

It should be made clear first that this system is based primarily on democratic principles; second, efficiency and democracy are not necessarily always compatible; and third, representatives are political actors rather than academic scientists. One of the most ardent supporters of liberal additions in the number of permanent staff personnel, Professor Saloma, also supports increased external information and data analysis sources such as a legislature-controlled "Rand Corporation." [63] In short, even a very large permanent staff would not necessarily solve the inherent problem in staffing committees of Congress.

The Appropriations Committee will continue to gradually increase the number of its permanent staff, while emphasizing its temporary staff and other sources of information. This process will continue as long as the committee perceives that its authority is not endangered and so long as it remains free to determine its own staffing procedures.

Author's Note

I wish to thank Professors Franklin L. Burdette and Conley H. Dillon for their comments on an earlier draft of this manuscript.

Information for this chapter was collected through several visits to the office of the House Committee on Appropriations between 1973 and 1975 and to subcommittee hearings as well as visits with some members of the staff. I wish to thank Chairman George Mahon for inviting me to his committee office and for allowing me to observe him as well as his staff at work. Although certain knowledge was derived from observation, most of the information was provided by the clerk in several interviews and by his response to a set of questions submitted to him. I wish to thank the clerk and the other staff members who granted me their valuable time.

Notes

1. One volume which is devoted to a general discussion of staffing practices in Congress is Kenneth Kofmehl, *Professsional Staffs of Congress* (Lafayette: Purdue University Studies, 1962); two excellent articles on the topic provided by Gladys M. Kammerer, "The Record of Congress in Committee Staffing," *The American Political Science Review* 45 (December 1961): 1126–1136, and "The Administration of Congress," *Public Administration Review* 9 (Summer 1949): 175–181; also Lindsy Bogers, "The Staffing of Congress," *Political Science Quarterly* 56 (March 1941): 1–22; Samuel C. Patterson, "The Professional Staffs of Congressional Committees," *Administrative Science Quarterly* 15 (March, 1970): 22–36. Other valuable discussions are found in Bertram M. Gross, *The Legislative Struggle: A Study in Social Combat* (New York: McGraw-Hill Book Company, Inc., 1953), pp. 280–423; George B. Galloway, *The Legislative Process in Congress* (New York: Thomas Y. Crowell Company, 1953); pp. 407–425; Ernest S. Griffith, *Congress: Its Contemporary Role* fourth edition, (New York: New York University Press, 1951); and Richard F. Fenno, Jr., *Congressmen in Committees* (Boston: Little, Brown, and Company, 1973).

2. Ernest S. Griffith also discusses the influence of such factors as increased demands by constituents, reliance upon expertise, the rise of pressure groups, and the erosion of

congressional party responsibility; see his *Congress: Its Contemporary Role*, Chapter 7, pp. 74–99.

3. Discussion of internal congressional factors such as specialization of congressmen, and the increasing number of congressional committees is found in Patterson, "The Professional Staffs of Congressional Committees," pp. 22–23.

4. Certain senators have, as a result, allowed their skilled legislative assistants to act as advocates in their behalf. See Spencer Rich, "Senate Aides Play Key Role in Defense, Diplomacy Battles," *The Washington Post*, 2 June 1975.

5. Griffith, *Congress: Its Contemporary Role*, p. 75. Gross suggests another line of analysis. According to him "the theory of congressional staffing seemed to be that each member of Congress was a statesman capable of handling all legislative problems," *The Legislative Struggle: A Study in Social Combat*, p. 282.

6. Hubert H. Humphrey, "The Senate in Foreign Policy," *Foreign Affairs* 37 (July 1959): 534.

7. Kammerer, "The Record of Congress in Committee Staffing," p. 1126.

8. US Congress, House of Representatives, *Committee Organization in the House, Hearing*, 1973, I, pt. 1, p. 8.

9. *Ibid.*, pp. 33–34; see also Representative John C. Culver's statement, pp. 81–82; also that of Representative Carl D. Perkins, p. 112.

10. *Ibid.*, I, pt. 2, p. 534.

11. *Ibid.*, I, pt. 1, pp. 151, 154.

12. Galloway, *The Legislative Processs in Congress*, p. 410.

13. According to Galloway, *ibid.*.

14. Kofmehl, *Professional Staffs of Congress*, p. 307.

15. Kammerer, "The Record of Congress in Committee Staffing."

16. Legislative Reorganization Act of 1970, Sec. 302(a), 84 *Stat.* 1177 (1970).

17. *Ibid.*, Sec. 304, p. 1178. Prior consent by either of these committees may be attributed to Congress's desire to prevent the use of such practices for political reasons; see Gross, *The Legislative Struggle: A Study in Social Combat*, p. 281.

18. The House Committee on Appropriations acted on 7 May 1975, and the House Rules Committee acted on the following day. According to the former's staff employee, the proximity of the two dates is mere coincidence. The vote of the Appropriations Committee was an unrecorded voice vote, while the Rules Commmittee voted thirteen to three. Of the three voting "No," two were Democrats, Chairman Ray Madden and James J. Delaney, and one was Republican, Delbert L. Latta; based on conversations with two staff employees, one from each committee, 8 July 1975.

19. US Congress, House, *Congressional Record* (Daily Digest), 20 May 1975, p. 4468. The chairmen of committees and subcommittees as well as ranking minority members did not benefit from the increases because they were allowed to employ one "associate staffer" before these rules were adopted.

20. Richard F. Fennno, Jr., *The Power of the Purse: Appropriations Politics in Congress*, (Boston: Little, Brown and Company, 1966), pp. 154–155.

21. US Congress, House of Representatives, *Committee Organization in the House, Panel Discussions*, 1973, II, pt. 1, p. 186.

22. *Ibid.*, pp. 193–194.

23. *Ibid.*, p. 206.

24. Chairman Cannon, who argued against a large permanent staff, cited the threat of establishing a bureaucracy which could build friendship with officials of the agencies and which could evade control by the committee members. See US Congress, House, 82nd Congress, 1st Session, 21 March 1951, *Congressional Record*, 97, p. 2804.

25. US Congress Joint Committee on the Organization of Congress, *Hearings on the*

Organization of Congress, 89th Congress, 1st Session, (Washington: U.S. Government Printing Office, 1965), p. 34.

26. Robert P. Biller, "Adaptation Capacity and Organizational Development" in Frank Marini (ed.), *Toward a New Public Administration* (Scranton: Chandler Publishing Company, 1971), p. 101.

27. *Committee Organization in the House, Hearings*, 1973, I, pt. 2, p. 635.

28. *Ibid.*, p. 341.

29. *Ibid.*, I, pt. 1, p. 111.

30. See Representative Sam Gibbons discussion of the case in the Committee on Ways and Means, *ibid.*, I, pt. 2, p. 351.

31. *Ibid.*, II, pt. 1, p. 207, emphasis added.

32. US Congress, Senate, *Congressional Record* (Daily Digest), 11 June 1975, pp. 10410–10425 ff. and 12 June 1975, pp. S10519–10527. Those who voted for the defeated Senate measure on 11 June "averaged 7.6 years in seniority. Those voting against averaged 13.7 years." In addition "17 of the 18 chairmen of standing committees voted against the change." However, on the following day when a less expensive measure passed the Senate, eleven chairmen voted for it; see Stephen Isaacs, "Staff Rise Rejected by Senate," *The Washington Post*, 12 June 1975; and his "Senate Reverses Itself, Votes Increase in Staff;" *The Washington Post*, 13 June 1975.

33. US Congress, Senate, *Congressional Record*, (Daily Digest), 12 June 1975, p. 10525; see also Stephen Isaacs, "Issue of Equality Was a Key to Senate Vote on Added Staff," *The Washington Post*, 16 June 1975?

34. *Committee Organization in the House, Hearings*, 1973, I, pt. 2, p. 613.

35. *Ibid.*, I, pt. 1, p. 216.

36. *Ibid.*

37. *Kendall v. The United States*, 12 Peters (524).

38. Louis C. Gawthrop, *Bureaucratic Behavior in the Executive Branch: An Analysis of Organizational Change* (New York: The Free Presss, 1969), p. 129.

39. James Robinson, *Congress and Foreign Policy: A Study in Legislative Influence and Initiative* (Homewood: The Dorsey Press, Inc., 1962) p. 192.

40. *Ibid.*, p. 203.

41. Chairman Mahon in *Committee Organization in the House, Hearings*, 1973, I, pt. 2, p. 635.

42. *Hearings on the Reorganization of Congress*, 1965, p. 1638. Emphasis added.

43. *Committee Organization in the House, Hearings*, 1973, I, pt. 2, p. 639.

44. According to a staff employee, in a personal interview 1 July 1975.

45. *Ibid.*.

46. *Ibid.*

47. Since the recent addition of "associate staffers" will be paid out of the same account, the committee will be spending proportionately less on the temporary staff.

48. A memoranda distributed by the staff of the committee on staff resources and information capability, 1973, p. 1.

49. *Ibid.*

50. Since this study was completed, one permanent staff employee has retired and was replaced.

51. As is implicit in Professor Patterson's article "The Professional Staffs of Congressional Committees," this author also discovered that generally the staff employees tend to deemphasize their administrative role.

52. See Professor Patterson's discussion of committee staff specialization in *ibid.*, p. 35.

53. As he becomes more involved in day-to-day activities, the staff employee is less

able to carry out his highly regarded investigative duties. His involvement in day-to-day activities may also be inversely related to his feeling of acquiring status and independence; see Professor Saloma's remarks in *Committee Organization in the House, Panel Discussions*, 1973, II, pt. 1, p. 212.

54. Fenno, *The Power of the Purse: Appropriations Politics in Congress*, p. 323.

55. This supports Aaron Wildavsky's statement on the nature of interaction between appropriations committees and administrative agencies. See his "Toward a Radical Incrementalism," in *Congress, The First Branch of Government*, The American Enterprise Institute, Alfred de Grazia, coordinator, (Washington: The American Enterprise Institute, 1966), p. 131. See also J. Leiper Freeman, *The Political Process: Executive Bureau-Legislative Committeee Relations* (Garden City: Doubleday and Company, Inc., 1955), pp. 6–7.

56. According to a staff employee in an interview, 1 July 1975.

57. US Congress, House, 78th Cong., 1st Sess., 11 February 1943, *Congressional Record*, 80, part 1, p. 887.

58. *Hearings on the Reorganization of Congress*, p. 1653.

59. A congressman is not, nor should he be, elected as an expert. What is important is that he be provided with sufficient information and that he act independently. V. O. Key wrote, "The contribution of the lawmaker in the governmental process is not in the exercise of professional expertness. If he merely mouths what his experts tell him, we lose important values of representative government." See V. O. Key, "Legislative Control," in F. M. Marx (ed.), (New York: Prentice-Hall, Inc., 1946), p. 360.

60. Dean Acheson commits an error in judgment when he claims that judges have small staffs, because they work hard. See his *A Citizen Looks at Congress* (New York: Harper and Brothers, 1956), p. 123.

61. Gross, *The Legislative Struggle: A Study in Social Combat*, p. 421.

62. US Congress, Congressional Record (Daily Digest), 21 May 1975, p. 4489.

63. *Committee Organization in the House, Panel Discussions*, 1973, p. 212.

Use of a Staff Agency by the Congress:

Experiences of the Congressional Research Service under the Legislative Reorganization act of 1970

NORMAN BECKMAN

The mission of the Congressional Research Service is to provide the Congress, and only the Congress, with research and reference assistance on the complete spectrum of public policy issues that Congress must consider. The Service has no monopoly on this function—sharing it with a wide range of resources within the Congress, i.e., members' staffs, professional staffs of committees, policy committees and informal research groups, the General Accounting Office, the Office of Technology Assessment, the new Congressional Budget Office, and such outside resources as the executive departments and agencies, the various interest group organizations located in Washington and elsewhere, and universities and private research organizations.

Following a very brief history and introduction to the Service, this chapter will speak to four questions. What has been done to implement the specific new statutory mandates given the Service in 1970? What has been done to provide additional analytical support to the Congress? What are some of the new directions being considered by the Service? What are the implications for CRS of new proposals to improve Congress's research and information base?

The Congressional Research Service is the largest institution solely devoted to providing public policy research and information assistance to the Congress. It receives and responds to over 240,000 requests a year, which include over 700 assignments for in-depth analytical assistance requiring a significant amount of research manpower. CRS provides factual information, analyses of issues, alternatives to proposals, and evaluation of alternatives without either advocacy or partisan bias. It also observes strict confidentiality of both requests and responses. Its assignments are received from four primary sources—committee staffs, members and their staffs, constituents (received through congressional offices), and specific statutory requirements, such as provision of lists of terminating programs and activities and preparation of the Digest of General Public Bills and Resolutions.

The Service, a relatively autonomous entity within the Library of Congress, has subject matter specialists organizationally located in seven research divisions, which are based on the concept of professional skills. Their division titles—American Law, Economics, Education and Public Welfare, Environment and Natural Resources, Foreign Affairs and National Defense, Government Science Policy Research—indicate the skills and subjects involved. An eighth division, including many of the senior specialists and their support staff, involves a wide range of public policy issues. Requests for factual data, documents and materials, and for information for constituent use which together account for two-thirds of all CRS requests, is the responsibility of a ninth division, Congressional Reference. The acquisition, distribution, and organization of new research materials is provided by the Library Services Division. Together, these two latter divisions constitute approximately 20 percent of the entire staff.

Implementation of New Statutory Responsibilities

As evidence of the growing information needs of Congress, specific provisions were included in the Legislative Reorganization Act of 1970 to strengthen the research capability and scope of responsibilities of the Congressional Research Service. The legislative history of Section 321 of the Legislative Reorganization Act of 1970 indicates that the Congress sought to achieve two principal goals in revising the basic statute of the Service. First, it was clearly intended that the Service's research and analytical support for the committees of Congress should be expanded. The House report on H.R. 17654 speaks of the "massive kind of analysis committees so urgently require," and calls for expansion of the Service's functions and facilities to provide committees with this "massive aid in policy analysis." [1] Second, while sanctioning CRS assistance to committees and members in their representative functions and activities, it intended to make clear, as the House report put it, that "the major function of the Congressional Research Service is to provide assistance to committees and individual Members of the Congress with respect to legislative matters." [2]

To emphasize the priority the Service should give to public policy research, section 321 of the Legislative Reorganization Act of 1970 (Public Law 91-510) changed the institution's name from the Legislative Reference Service to the Congressional Research Service. The intent of this section of the Act was to expand and change the nature of CRS support to congressional committees, emphasize the primary importance of assistance on legislative matters, promote anlaytical and original research, grant the Service greater autonomy within the Library of Congress and render it more directly responsive to the Congress. Several of the Act's provisions are directed to the Service's support of congressional committees: an explicit mandate for policy analysis of legislative proposals, new anticipatory functions—the submission of subject and terminating program lists at the beginning of each new Congress, the preparation of purpose-and-effect memoranda on legislative measures for which forthcoming hearings have been announced—and a directive to maintain continuous liaison with all committees. The continuation of traditional CRS services was authorized as well, including the preparation of briefs and background reports, research and reference materials, digests of bills and other legislative compilations.

Four major new directives to the Service are discussed in detail here: (a) To provide policy analysis and research to assist committees in their legislative function; (b) To submit lists of subjects and policy areas to committees at the opening of each new Congress; (c) To submit to each appropriate committee at the beginning of each Congress a list of programs and activities scheduled to terminate; and (d) To maintain continuous liaison with all committees.

Policy Analysis for Committees

The statute directs that: "(a) Upon request, CRS is to advise and assist all committees and joint committees of Congress in the analysis, appraisal, and evaluation of legislative proposals in order to assist them (1) in determining the advisability of enacting such proposals, (2) in estimating the probable results of such proposals and of alternatives to them, and (3) in evaluating alternative methods for accomplishing the goals of such proposals." [3] It further directs CRS to maintain continuous liaison with committees.

As a result of the mandate of the 1970 Act, over 119,000 man-hours were expended on committee requests for research assistance in fiscal 1975, an increase of more than 180 percent over the man-hour expenditure in fiscal 1971. While numbers are important, one must know what is being counted and its corresponding significance. This, as part of its evaluation and planning effort, the Service now identifies and monitors major committee projects that require analysis, have a direct connection to legislation, and require a significant investment of CRS manpower. During fiscal 1975, 500 such projects were in progress. These projects involved work with 56 committees and subcommittees of the Senate, 65 of the House, and 8 joint committees and subcommittees—a total of 129 committees and subcommittees.

An assessment of the primary end products of major committee projects completed during fiscal 1975 indicated that approximately 23 percent were for congressional documents, 11 percent were contributions to the hearings process, 51 percent provided analytical assistance and background on specific legislative proposals, 11 percent provided an analytical study or report on a legislative issue, and 4 percent provided other types of research support, such as conducting a seminar or preparing a manual.

The following list illustrates the type of work done for committees in recent years:

—Preparation of report and related assistance on Medicare and Medicaid amendments;
—Analysis of the effectiveness of executive branch reports in foreign affairs as an element of congressional oversight;
—Comprehensive analysis of problems of the inner city, including studies of the literature, present programs, and pending legislation;
—Questionnaire survey of agency approaches for implementing Sec. 102(2) (C) of the National Environmental Policy Act;
—Analysis of modern conference committee methods and procedures;
—Provision of analytical and other assistance prior to and during hearings on legislation to extend authorization for the Law Enforcement Assistance Administration;
—Analysis of the present structure of the petroleum industry factors (court decisions, tax law provisions, etc.) that have contributed to that structure, and a review of all relevant factors, including alternative market arrangements, which should be considered in connection with legislation; and
—Assistance in evaluating urban mass transportation and in drafting a bill to establish a Bureau of Transit Statistics.

An earlier analysis of CRS research for committees highlights a number of variables affecting the amount and type of work CRS provides congressional committees.[4] This analysis notes that even with its new mandate, CRS progress is conditioned by factors over which it has little or no control. The basic decisions that determine both the volume and the type of CRS work are made by the committees. A committee's workload may vary from Congress to Congress, session to session, and even week to week, and its need for research and analytical support may fluctuate correspondingly. In addition, the basic character of a committee's jurisdiction may require little, or only sporadic, research support, as is the case of the House Committee on Rules and the Senate Committee on Rules and Administration and the Select Committee on Standards and Conduct.

Furthermore, some committees prefer to employ other research resources—their own staff or an executive agency, for example—as is sometimes the case of the Joint Committee on Atomic Energy.

In spite of these varaibles, the overall pattern has been one of more research time allocated to more committees. A significant number of committees moved from the category of minimal support in fiscal 1971 to categories of larger time expenditures in fiscal 1975. Thirteen committees to which CRS devoted fewer than 1,000 research hours in fiscal 1971 received more than 1,000 hours in fiscal 1975 and, in several cases, considerably more.

A third development within the overall growth pattern relates to those committees that made minimal use of the Service in both fiscal 1971 and fiscal 1975. Seventeen committees called upon the Service for fewer than 500 hours of support in both years. Several committees in this category are not likely to become major customers of CRS because of the nature of their jurisdiction. The Service nevertheless did increase the hours of its support for nine of the seventeen committees in this category.

Lists of Subjects and Policy Areas for Committees

One of the major new responsibilities assigned to the Congressionl Research Service by the Legislative Reorganization Act of 1970 was designed to assist committees with their advance planning. CRS was thus directed to make "available to each committee of the Senate and House of Representatives and each joint committee of the two Houses, at the opening of a new Congress, a list of subjects and policy areas which the committee might profitably analyze in depth. . . ."

For the pilot implementation of this new responsibility, the following procedures were developed and carried out. Late in 1972, in preparation for the 93rd Congress, appropriate CRS staff met with committee staffs and, in some cases, members. *Ad hoc* teams consisting of some 30 percent (144 persons) of the total research staff were formed to work with each congressional committee. Individual teams were composed of individuals knowledgeable in most aspects of a committee's jurisdiction and in many cases included staff from several divisions. The committee was encouraged to discuss their plans and needs for research with the appropriate team and in turn CRS staff suggested additional promising subject areas for the committee to consider. It was also an opportunity to describe the CRS capability in the committee's fields of interest. The resulting lists of subjects and policy areas thus incorporated by both CRS and the committee.

Each committee was given the option of receiving a selected list consisting only of subjects on which the Service could provide assistance, or a comprehensive list, which included, but was not limited to, those subjects on the selected list. The final product, unless specifically requested otherwise by a committee, included a summary list of agreed-upon subjects and policy areas, a one-page description of each subject to explain the reasons for its inclusion and to provide additional sources of information, and, to the extent feasible and desired by the committee, additional materials to supplement and illustrate the one-page treatment.

A total of forty-five lists were prepared with the average list containing eighteen subjects. Lists were not deemed appropriate for eleven nonlegislative committees and these committees were sent explanatory letters.

Committee cooperation in the process was remarkably good. In the judgment of the CRS senior staff who played key roles in discussions with the committees, approximately 55 percent of the committees reacted positively to the process, about 7 percent reacted negatively, and the remainder, while treating CRS people courteously, seemed uninterested, indifferent, or passive.

To obtain more systematic and comprehensive data about the impact of the lists on committee activities, the Service compared the subjects that appeared on each committee's list with those the committee actually took up in one way or another during the first session of the 93rd Congress. Without exception, every committee to which a list was submitted—standing, special, select, and joint—took up at least one of the subjects submitted to them. Overall, House committees took up a frac-tion less than one-half the subjects on their lists, Senate committees took up almost 5 percent more than half, and committees as a whole dealt in one way or another with 48.3 percent of their subjects. Since the data approximates only one-half of the committees' activities for an entire Congress, the figures are relatively encouraging. At the very least, the lists evidently included pertinent issues of interest to the committees. This reflects the Service's attempt to make the lists realistic working documents rather than esoteric or academic products. Committee participation in evolving the lists also contributed to this characteristic.[5]

Terminating Programs

Documentation and current status of legislation has always been a paramount concern of the Congress. One of the first statutory responsibilities of the Service was to compile, process, and transmit information of this kind rapidly and accurately through the Digest of Public General Bills and Resolutions. The Reorganization Act inaugurated new documentation responsibilities by directing CRS to prepare for each congressional committee a list of programs and activities within its jurisdiction scheduled to terminate during each Congress. CRS, in developing its guidelines, assumed that the principal purpose of preparing the lists was to further assist the committees in their advance planning efforts.

Beginning in late 1971, the American Law Division of the Service examined over 4,000 statutes enacted during the preceding decade and by December, 1972 had identified some 730 programs and activities scheduled to terminate during the 93rd and subsequent Congresses. Over half of these programs related to authorization of appropriations, and an additional 23 percent provided general authority for programs operated by executive branch agencies. Other categories included termination of commissions, loan authority, tax authority, reservations of land, pensions, and reporting requirements.

Following identification of terminating programs, the Service prepared summary lists of the 458 programs and activities scheduled to expire during the 93rd Congress and transmitted these, with supplementary descriptive materials, to thirty-two House, Senate, and joint committees of Congress. Each committee packet included basic identifying information and a legislative history on each terminating program within the committee's jurisdiction. For 319 programs terminating during the first session of the 93rd Congress, the Service, insofar as resources permitted, also sent to each committee a more detailed report to aid the committee in reviewing the program.

These more detailed reports were prepared by the CRS subject divisions according to the following directions from the director of CRS:

> A mere list of the expiring programs and activities may not be very meaningful or helpful to a committee. As I indicated in my testimony before the House Appropriations Committee earlier this year, "what is needed in addition is some backup information, perhaps a description of the program, what it has cost, how long it has been in operation, perhaps some evaluation, setting out criticism or favorable comments that have been published about the program, and the like, and that will beef up the information that the committee will have at the beginning of the Congress."
>
> It should therefore be understood that it is the policy of the Service insofar as possible and practicable to transmit to each committee, with each terminating program or activity, a report that will assist the committee in considering and evaluating each program.
>
> Part I will be prepared *for every program and activity scheduled to terminate during the 93rd Congress.* It will consist of basic identifying and descriptive information, not to exceed two or three pages.
>
> Part II, to be prepared only for programs terminating in the 1st session of the 93rd Congress, should contain, to the extent such material is available, the following:
>
> (a) information on the program's operations: purpose, accomplishments, milestones, and other aspects;
>
> (b) Administration policies and interest group positions regarding the program;
>
> (c) summaries of existing major studies and evaluations, particularly alternative legislative proposals;
>
> (d) summaries of basic issues that the committee might have

to consider when reviewing the program for further action; and

(e) bibliography of particularly relevant, available materials.

Although the Service has no obligation under law to prepare terminating program lists at the beginning of the second session of a Congress, several factors persuaded CRS to offer updated lists for the second session of the 93rd Congress. First, the Service wished to accommodate a few committees that responded affirmatively to a question on this subject in the covering letter for the lists delivered at the beginning of the first session. Second, the Service believed that an updated 1974 list reflecting actions taken in 1973 might serve as a useful checklist for some committees. A final consideration was that producing such updated lists would be a relatively simple matter—if background reports were not required—because the program descriptions were stored in a computer that could produce them by subject or by committee of jurisdiction. It was therefore decided to make such simple updated lists available to committees desiring them.

CRS Liaison with Committees

The Legislative Reorganization Act requires CRS to maintain continuous liaison with all committees so that they may better understand and utilize the Service's multidisciplinary research resources and facilitate advance planning. Although separately stated in the 1970 Act, several of the Service's new duties concerning congressional committees are closely related in overall purpose. Because preparation of lists of subjects and policy areas and terminating programs for committees was not required until late 1972, the Service early turned its attention to the general liaison function.

A first step, taken in late 1971, in carrying out this obligation involved an assessment of the existing CRS work relationships with committees. While the informal network of working relationships with both members and staff was found to be extensive, they were not uniform or comprehensive in coverage. The objective of the new liaison effort was described in a memorandum from the director stating in part:

> We have enough information about the intent behind the language to formulate a preliminary description of what these responsibilities should involve. . . . This description is an ideal toward which we ought to work but . . . is not intended as a rigid and inflexible formulation. On the contrary, because each committee is unique to one degree or another, liaison efforts should be applied with the flexibility necessary to accommodate the unique circumstances of each committee, the present state of our relationship with the committee, the degree of liaison the committee will tolerate, the degree of liaison suitable to that committee, and, of course, the available resources of the Service.
>
> Overall, our goal is to establish closer and more continuous contact between the Service and all committees so that we may more effectively assist them in every suitable way and most particularly in the area of policy analysis.
>
> Our liaison efforts with committees should be directed toward: (a) keeping them informed about our present and potential resources for assisting them; (b) acquainting them with Service reports, already prepared or in preparation, of interest to them; (c) informing them about other, non-Service, materials of use to them and of techniques by which the Service can keep them regularly informed about such materials; (d) the preparation and submission of those lists of subjects and policy areas the committees might profitably analyze in depth that we are obligated to supply them, including subjects of emerging interest to them; and (e) preparing and submitting the lists of expiring legislation also required by the Reorganization Act.[6]

Perhaps the major options facing the Service in implementing the liaison function were those of internal organization and rate of implementation. A recent internal memorandum describes the basic organizational issues:

> One of the first questions the Service examined after passage of the 1970 Act was whether it should establish a staff exclusively devoted to committee liaison—that is, personnel whose sole function it would be to maintain communication and contact with committees. After careful consideration, and at the urging of virtually every senior CRS staff with experience in working closely with committees, the Service decided not to adopt this approach, at least during the first few years of operations under the 1970 Act. Until circumstances indicated another course, therefore, we decided to rely upon our senior subject people,

> those who actually do substantive work for committees, for the liaison function.
>
> The Service is aware that other agencies, including the General Accounting Office, employ the exclusive liaison group system, and we know something about their experience with it. We realize that such a system is more amenable to direct control by top management, that liaison with committees requires special talents, and that placing the liaison function upon subject staff inevitably erodes some of their time.
>
> On the other hand, several factors have persuaded us to adopt the course we have taken. Ours was and remains a relatively small organization; we do not feel we can afford to devote positions to this exclusive function, positions better devoted to research. We are not like other agencies in our dealings with Congress and its committees. Ours is a supplementary staff function; we are often an extension of committee staff. This involves a close, day-to-day working relationship between our people and committee staff and Members. Our people sometimes participate in the full range of committee work, from the first ideas about hearings through floor proceedings and conferences between the two Houses on bills. We believe that a bureaucratic layer of professional liaison staff inserted between our subject experts and the committees for whom they work might disrupt these necessarily close relationships. We also feel it would introduce a communication barrier distorting the nuances and subtleties of committee research and analytical needs which are often so important and which only close personal relationships can convey. Finally, our experience indicates that by and large, members and staff of committees much prefer to deal directly with subject experts than with professional liaison people.

While a more formalized network might have been expected to be established by this time, the process to date has been an evolving one. This, in large part, is due to the number of committees and subcommittees involved, approximately 350. The goal continues to be an evolutionary approach designed to build working relationships based upon subject expertise.

Other Innovative Services

The Service's response to congressional needs goes beyond the very ambitious and explicit statutory provisions of the

Legislative Reorganization Act. The legislative history of the Reorganization Act itself directed CRS to experiment with additional ways of providing assistance to Congress:

> Staffs should become proficient in existing analytical techniques and develop new ones as necessary. Both agencies [CRS and GAO] should be encouraged to experiment and to be innovative in carrying out their new as well as their older functions.[7]

The Director of the Congressional Research Service, in his testimony before the Joint Committee on Congressional Operations, identified certain new services not explicitly required by the 1970 Act:

> We sponsor several series of seminars at which outside experts discuss major public policy issues with Members or staff. We have steadily expanded our automation facilities and sought new and promising applications. One of these, for example, provides us, and therefore the Congress, with one of the largest and most up-to-date economic data bases currently available and includes programs for analyzing the economic impact of alternative fiscal and monetary policies. With the encouragement of the Senate Committee on Rules and Administration, CRS is developing an issues briefing system through which we will be able to provide concise updated information about current legislative issues by video screens located in the offices of Members.[8]

The public policy seminars for members and staff, the automated information services, and cooperative efforts with the General Accounting Office and the Office of Technology Assessment are described in more detail below.

Public Policy Seminars

The Service has expanded cooperative arrangements with outside organizations to permit members and their staffs to meet informally with experts on national issues. With the Advanced Study Program of the Brookings Institute, CRS initiated in the fall of 1972 a series of seminars for members of Congress and a separate series for the senior staffs of member and committee offices. In the past three years, eighteen seminars for members have included discussion of such topics as: US relations with China, crime prevention and law enforcement, energy and the environment, national housing programs, consumer protection, media and the government, and the multinational corporation. Thirteen seminars have been held for congressional staff on: food scarcity, agricultural policy, budget reform and control, legislation affecting the status of women, and new trends in strategic weapons policy in the national defense budget. The series has attracted an overall attendance of 386 members and 1,098 congressional staff.

At the request of the Senate Subcommittee on Housing and Urban Affairs, and in conjunction with the National Planning Association and Resources for the Future, Inc., in fiscal 1973 CRS undertook the development and sponsorship of a series of informal seminars on national growth policy. Held at the Library of Congress and featuring speakers with new research findings in various aspects of national growth policy, the seminars have been well attended by congressional staff. The program was continued this year with speakers addressing themselves to such major legislative issues as rural development, housing policy, and community development special revenue sharing.

Additional seminar activities have included four seminars exploring basic tax issues, held for congressional staff in 1973, and presentations by CRS and the Office of Management and Budget in February 1974 to House, Senate, and CRS staff on use of the 1975 budget documents.

Automated Information Services

Increasingly in evidence in any analysis of congressional operations over the past quarter-century is the rising proportion of time spent by members, their staffs, and support groups such as the CRS on matters requiring up-to-date and accurate information. In response to these needs, the Service has identified research procedures with potential for the storage and delivery of information through the application of data processing techniques.[9]

In recent years, the Service has gained access to or has internally developed a number of data files—among which are the three CRS computer files, collectively known as the Legislative Information Display System (LIDS). Included within LIDS are the contents of the printed *Digest of Public General Bills and Resolutions.* Each bill from the 93rd and 94th Congresses is monitored for twenty-two data elements and is directly available to members and committees of Congress by means of the SCORPIO (Subject Content Oriented Retriever for Processing Information On-line) retrieval command system. Examples of elements are bill cosponsor, committee action, identical bills.) Information is retrievable via video screen in several formats (for example, a listing of all bills assigned to a particular committee or all bills relating to a specific subject).

More recently, at the request of the chairman of the Senate Committee on Rules and Administration, the Congressional Research Service has been developing an automated Issue Briefing System. This new service is currently available to all congressional offices. The system is designed to serve the current information needs of members, committees, and their staffs by maintaining concise, easily accessible summaries of many key issues of public policy. The summaries, or Issue Briefs, are provided by means of a computer information storage and retrieval system that can be accessed by video screen terminals. Copies of individual Issue Briefs are also available to both the Senate and House in printed form. Each Issue Brief contains current information on background facts, legislation, congressional hearings, reports, and chronological developments and provides useful references.

Issue Briefs in the file have been selected on the basis of a statistical analysis of information requests received by CRS from members and committees of both Houses and on the recommendations of the chiefs of the various CRS research divisions. The Issues Briefing file now contains about 180 briefs.

The third LIDS component, the bibliographic citation file, is comprised of references to significant current periodical articles, pamphlets, interest group publications, and congressional, executive, and UN documents.

In addition to these programs, the Service currently has rental access to five outside data banks. The New York Times

Information Bank is accessed by a video screen and associated high-speed printer and queries are transmitted by direct telephone line to the data files. The files contain indexes and abstracts of all news articles published in *The New York Times* since 1969 and abstracts from additional selected magazines and newspapers. MEDLINE (MEDLARS-on-line), an automated bibliographic service made available by the National Library of Medicine, contains over 400,000 entries from some 1,200 journals in the medical research and public health fields. Its bibliographic data are retrievable by author or subject. *JURIS* (Justice Retrieval and Inquiry System) maintains the text of six information files, including the *U.S. Code* and public laws from the 93rd and 94th Congresses. Additionally, CRS has access to programs that provide the program grants and expenditures of the Department of Health, Education and Welfare; project and costs of federal support to education and other programs; and provide an econometric model of the national economy, which enables extensive analytical review of the federal budget.

The Office of Technology Assessment and the General Accounting Office

The Technology Assessment Act of 1972 (Public Law 92–484) created an Office of Technology Assessment (OTA) within the legislative branch to provide early indications of the impact of applications of technology and to develop and coordinate information to assist the Congress.

The Act directs CRS to make available to OTA appropriate and feasible services and assistance, including, but not limited to, all those CRS is authorized to provide to the Congress. The director of CRS is an ex officio member of OTA's Technology Assessment Advisory Council.

During the first years of OTA's existence, CRS has provided a wide variety of assistance to the Office. This has included responses to numerous requests for factual information of various kinds, frequent consultations with senior CRS staff about problems in various public policy areas, and the preparation of a comprehensive compilation of possible areas of congressional interest in which technology assessments might be initiated.

The basic working relationship between the General Accounting Office and CRS was described in the report of the Rules Committee on the Legislative Reorganization Act of 1970. It calls for cooperation, while maintaining the independence of the two congressional institutions, as follows:

> The new statutory responsibilities of the GAO and the CRS occasionally result in overlapping activities. We expect these agencies to resolve any problems that may arise in a cooperative fashion, if necessary by consulting with the requesting committee. We also intend that the two agencies shall exchange information freely, collaborate whenever feasible, and in general maintain close liaison with each other. Needless to say, there is no intent to circumscribe or restrain either agency in carrying out any of its present responsibilities or functions.[10]

Most important is cooperation by the two institutions in new public policy areas. CRS staff has been encouraged to contact their GAO counterparts at the early stages of significant research efforts. Recent CRS annual reports identify specific cooperative projects undertaken, with committee concurrence, by the two agencies:

—Review of legislation on munitions imports and exports;
—Analysis of the policy positions taken by the Environmental Protection Agency on the implementtation of the Federal Water Pollution Control Act Amendments;
—Evaluation of environmental impact statements;
—Need for a central energy data bank; and
—Impact of proposed budget cuts on health and education programs.

In addition, the GAO Office of Federal Elections requested that CRS collect, index, and abstract federal and state legislation and federal court litigation affecting election laws within each state. The CRS reports, provided on a regular basis, are subsequently printed by GAO and distributed to members of Congress, state leaders, and interested organizations.

The Past Is Prologue

In the past five years, CRS appropriations requests have placed the highest priority on implementation of new and expanded responsibilities under the 1970 Act. Although the rate of growth has been slower than anticipated, the Service has acquired significant new staff resources, and assistance to committees has grown correspondingly. Now that the Service is moving toward completion of its five-year implementation program, new approaches are being explored to satisfy the research needs of the Congress.

A recent statement by the director of the Service at hearings of the Joint Committee on Congressional Operations on research and information support for the Congress sketches certain of these exploratory efforts:

> The Service has already asked for funds that will permit us to explore the addition of another dimension to our support for Congress: futures research. This relatively new discipline might help us to do a more penetrating job of identifying and analyzing emerging public policy issues, especially of the type suitable for the team approach I mentioned a moment ago. The potential of futures research was endorsed by the House Select Committee on Committees, which recommended that each House Committee establish a subcommittee devoted to this area and to oversight functions.
>
> . . . We also hope to establish closer liaison with the scholarly community, perhaps by a program of temporary assignment of scholars to the Service who could provide tangible assistance on specific projects and who would bring fresh insights to the staff of CRS and the Congress. With this in mind, we have held preliminary discussions with the Woodrow Wilson International Center for Scholars at the Smithsonian Institution, exploring the possibility of having their scholars spend some time with us on mutually agreed-upon assignments, I particularly want to examine how CRS might take advantage of the Civil Service Commission's new Government Affairs Faculty Fellowship Program, which is intended to encourage faculty fellowships in government agencies.

Many Members and committees show increasing interest in the use of public opinion surveys to supplement their informational resources. Although it is probably inappropriate for CRS to conduct such surveys, there are a number of ways in which we might assist Congress in this area. We are going to be examining the availability of survey research information, its values and techniques and its applicability to legislative research.

I have already mentioned our interest in establishing programs that would permit us to attach some of our staff to committees for limited periods so they can learn more about the needs of those organizations.[11]

Other areas currently being explored include the impact on CRS of the new Congressional Budget Office. The legislation establishing that office specifically authorizes CRS to cooperate with the new budget staff and directs it (and other congressional agencies) to "fully coordinate and cooperate in planning and conducting their operations to utilize most effectively the information, services, and capabilities of all congressional agencies in carrying out the various responsibilities assigned to each agency.[12] Since the appointment of the CBO director in early 1975, CRS and CBO staff have had several exchange briefings on the role and services of the two agencies. The Service has received, and responded to, numerous requests for assistance from the CBO staff.

Support for Individual Congressmen

This chapter, while describing implementation of the Legislative Reorganization Act of 1970, has emphasized the policy analysis and committee support roles of CRS. Nevertheless, high priority continues to exist in assisting the individual Congressman and in the allocation of staff and resources within CRS to carry out its responsibility to assist members in not only their capacity as legislators but also in their performance as representatives of their respective states or districts. This responsibility to assist members in their representative functions involves assistance both in providing information requested by constituents and in the preparation of reports, studies, speech drafts, collections of informational materials, etc., which the member himself plans to use in addressing or writing to his constituents.

Within CRS, all incoming inquiries are classified as either "Member" (including those for committee or other official congressional use) or "Constituent." The distinction is made on the basis of who will be the recipient of the services. Very few limits are placed on CRS responsiveness to member/committee inquiries beyond the physical capability to respond, regardless of whether the ultimate purpose they serve is legislative or representative, whereas in the case of constituent requests there are necessarily some restrictions. Principal among these is the limitation that CRS will not do extensive or original research or prepare individually tailored reports, such as student term papers, for constituents.

Future Directions

The recommendations of the House Select Committee on Committees, as modified and adopted by the Committee Reform Amendments of 1974 (H. Res. 988), have had a number of impacts on CRS, as well as on the delivery of research and information services to the Congress generally. Of major long-term significance, the resolution created a House Commission on Information and facilities to study and make recommendations on the information problems of the House of Representatives against the background of the existing institutions and services available to the House. The study is to include, but not be limited to, CRS, GAO, and OTA and the organizational framework that makes them effective or ineffective. The language of the recommendations also mentions "resources outside the Congress for information and their utilization, . . . methods for setting up and organizing the flow of information from and to the executive, . . . experimental or pilot approaches to information problems, such as the creation of mechanisms for outside groups, or for pooling of resources," and "the creation of a congressional staff journal or other process for communication."

Other legislation introduced the Ninety-third and Ninety-fourth Congresses to establish new offices and commissions in the legislative branch would, if enacted, also impact on CRS and its plans for further implementation of the 1970 Legislative Reorganization Act.

Implicit in certain of the proposals for improved congressional decision-making is the search for a "philosopher's stone," a device that will produce the right answers: a "deus ex machina" that will recommend legislation that best achieves the public interest.

The Service, as a staff arm of a policy-mediated and partisan power structure, operates on an entirely different premise. It has no official views regarding which is a better solution to a legislative problem. It attempts to identify choices and to forecast the apparent implications of the alternatives, but it is the individual members and, therefore the Congress, who make the decisions.

These and other proposals will continue to involve CRS and the Congress in carrying out the spirit of the Legislative Reorganization Act of 1970. The CRS mission remains to respond to the research, analytical, and informational demands of Congress. To do so will mean constantly seeking and implementing new and improved ways of fulfilling that mission within the ground rules of confidentiality, nonadvocacy, and nonpartisanship.

Conclusion

This chapter highlights two significant points: (1) that Congress needs additional improved analysis in order to meet the complex challenges of legislation, and (2) that responsibility for research services can be effectively placed in a central staff agency, provided sufficient resources are made available. The responsibility and work load of the CRS are shown to be increasing in direct proportion to the information needs of Congress. Beginning with the Legislative Reorganization Act of 1970, both the role and quantity of service delivered has expanded. The operation of the CRS has been marked both by attention to the specific needs of congressional committees, and by utilization of all available resources to meet those needs. Recent action by Congress points to even greater expansion of the CRS research capability.

The second point has even greater import, particularly for students of the legislative process. The CRS experience demonstrates that Congress can expand the role of a staff agency and still maintain control over it. Congress has made explicit the role of the CRS and the agency has organized itself accordingly. Congress continues to control both the volume and type of research undertaken by the CRS. For its part, the CRS responds basically upon request; it does not initiate its own research projects. By providing mechanisms for the utilization of the research capability of agencies such as the GAO, Congress has seen to it that the CRS is not isolated from kindred research agencies. This technique insures that the CRS will remain an open system and use a multidisciplinary approach so essential to analysis of the complex and diverse nature of its subject matter.

Notes

1. US Congress. Committee on Rules. *Legislative Reorganization Act of 1970; Report to Accompany H.R. 17654.* Washington, U.S. Government Printing Office, 1970. (91st Congress, 2d session. House. Report no. 91–1215), p. 18.

2. *Ibid.*, p. 104.

3. P.L. 91–510, sec. 203(d) (3).

4. "Recent Development of CRS Research and Analytical Work for Committees," in US Congress. Joint Committee on Congressional Operations. *Congressional Research Support and Information Services: a Compendium of Materials.* (Joint Committee Print). Washington, Government Printing Office, 1974, pp. 38–63.

5. *Ibid.*, pp. 5–37.

6. US Congress. Joint Committee on the Library. *Annual Report of the Congressional Research Service of the Library of Congress for Fiscal Year 1971.* (Joint Committee Print). Washington, Government Printing Office, 1972, p. 45.

7. US Congress. Committee on Rules. *Legislative Reorganization Act of 1970*, p. 19.

8. Lester S. Jayson, *Statement before the Joint Committee on Congressional Operations*, 16 May 1974.

9. For additional information on use of computer in CRS, see "Automatic Data Processing in the Congressional Research Service," in US Congress. Joint Committee on Congressional Operations. *Congressional Research Support and Information Services: a Compendium of Materials*, pp. 499–510.

10. US Congress. Committee on Rules. *Legislative Reorganization Act of 1970*, pp. 18–19.

11. Lester S. Jayson, *Statement before the Joint Committee on Congressional Operations*, 16 May 1974.

12. P.L. 93–344, *Congressional Budget and Impoundment Control Act of 1974*.

Part 2

Legislative Reforms and Innovations in the States

Legislatures as a Force for Government Accountability:

The Organizational Challenge of New Tools of Program Review

EDGAR G. CRANE

American legislatures are in the midst of a unique effort to strengthen the function of legislative program control by employing new tools for program review. The success of this effort requires the harnessing of professional expertise as an instrument for making political choices. To meet this need, legislatures are innovating organizational arrangements for the support, conduct, and utilization of program review. This chapter surveys these innovations, discusses their strengths and weaknesses, identifies patterns of state characteristics associated with the various program review approaches, and suggests several key problems which affect every phase of these efforts. Finally, this chapter will briefly explore the implications of these developments for relationships between the legislature and other institutions, for power distribution within the legislature, for the policy functions of the legislature, and for the representative democratic functions of the legislature.

Legislative Program Control: New Tools and Special Conditions Energize a Traditional Function

Legislatures have traditionally performed the function of controlling, and thus legitimizing, the actions of government bureaucracy through powers of the purse, investigation, and education. Baaklini and Heaphey find that "without parliaments, kings could never have developed the vast scope and depth of power that they did." [1]

Max Weber, often identified as a founding father of our perspectives on bureaucracy, has made the classic case for the importance of the legislature vigorously undertaking program review of activities as part of its political function.[2] While the bureaucracy derives its legitimacy from efficiency and effectiveness, this legitimacy rests on the assumption that the legislature, that is, the people's elected representatives, is setting the criteria, inquiring whether they are met, and providing for corrective action. In such matters, a bureaucracy cannot adequately control and criticize itself. Normanton, in his comparative study of government auditing, has observed that the executive depends on the legislature for the feedback required to give it the capability of responding to needs for change.[3] As Baaklini has noted, ". . . even the most resolutely executive government can find some of its most persistent structural problems eased through the efforts of an efficiently functioning legislature." [4]

Yet contemporary legislatures face special challenges in performing this function. It is a commonplace but truthful observation that the industrialization and urbanization of society, together with the communications explosion made possible by new technology, have placed a burden on democratic institutions of government, one to which they have not yet fully responded. Policy-making institutions have in the twentieth century been faced with accelerating requirements to manage and simplify large volumes of information and with a corresponding need for advise and support based on special expertise. New tools of program review provide a basis for meeting this challenge.

Program review plays different roles in different legislative systems. In American legislatures, legislative program review is conceived as a component of legislative oversight. Whereas "review" is an analytic, intelligence, and reporting function, "oversight" is a control function requiring legislative desire, a responsive agency implementation of that desire, and the availability

Figure 1

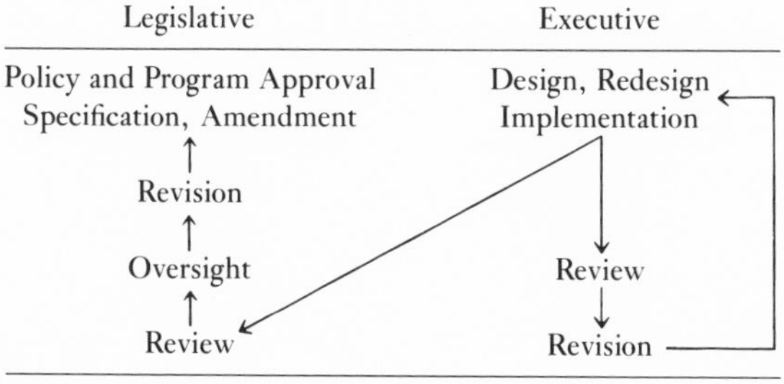

of manageable sanctions. Review is not performed exclusively by the legislative branch. Central executive budget, planning, and management units, or operating agencies may also perform the function. Some of the relationships involved are illustrated in figure 1.

The budgetary cycle is seen in terms of four basic phases: (1) development, planning, and submission; (2) review, revision, and adoption; (3) implementation and control; (4) program review and oversight. In the American system of government an effective budgetary cycle requires that each of these phases be fully performed and linked with each other to produce a cumulative effect over a number of cycles. This requires a conscious intention on the part of the legislature and continuous monitoring of its own activities.

American legislatures currently manifest a surge of emphasis on the "program control" function. They are determined to rectify what Rosenthal found them to consider very inadequate performance in this area.

In the late 1960s, Rutgers' Eagleton Institute of Politics surveyed legislators in six states and asked them to assess the way they exercised their legislative tasks. The results illustrate that legislators perceive a weakness in the way they perform oversight responsibilities.[5] Significantly, each of these state legislatures has since taken some sort of action in the direction of establishing a program review capability.

American participants perceive several factors as influential in the current thrust toward strengthening the legislative control function:

legislatures are clearly one among several avenues for government accountability, and most of the other avenues are currently in some disrepute;

for a decade, a general legislative modernization movement has been changing the institution in many ways which make it more able to exercise program control and more aware of its deficiencies;

there has been a public disillusionment with the myriad new programs of the 1960s;

economic difficulties have intensified concern about resource allocation;

confidence in the presidency and in the executive branch has waned;

new tools of program review have become available to legislatures providing a rational, objective basis for independent legislative action, which legislatures can use successfully to justify action against executive or professional opposition.

The new tools of program review are of special importance, since they make it feasible for the legislature to respond to new circumstances and to act upon its own dissatisfaction. These tools are a powerful extension of traditional compliance and financial audit approaches. Over the past decade they have been emerging from the convergence of developments in accounting, the management sciences, and the social sciences. The most common terms for the activities using these tools are performance auditing and program evaluation.

These tools enable a legislature to obtain independent, objective information on the efficiency and effectiveness of the bureaucracy. They make it possible to specify program objectives, develop indicators and standards by which results can be measured, compare actual performance with promise, and assess alternative ways of achieving those objectives. Since the "state of the art" for these new tools is still developing, severe limitations are still encountered in methodology and in the skills of professions using these tools. As a means of giving themselves the flexibility to work around these limitations in various ways, legislatures have introduced various organizational arrangements for the support, conduct, and utilization of program review.

The Organizational Dimension of Program Review

The experience of the states presents seven organizational options and two alternative products for conducting program review. This wide variation gives legislatures an important degree of flexibility and hence a degree of assurance that, by employing these organizational options singly or in combination, or by creating one as a replacement for another, the legislature can remain in control of the product of program review.

The six organizational options are: post audit agency, special purpose program evaluation agency, fiscal bureau or appropriations staff, standing committee system, general research agency, and hybrid agency.

The two product options for review of program effectiveness are: limited review and intensive review.

At least twenty state legislatures are actively developing capability to use the new tools of program review, and most states have chosen to emphasize one approach. Of interest are the strengths and weaknesses of each of these arrangements.

Some important characteristics are shared by all. With very few exceptions these arrangements serve both houses jointly and are organized on a nonpartisan basis. All provide for complementary but differentiated legislator and staff roles. Some important features do not correspond exclusively to one type of organization, but vary across all types. For example, the professional staff may or may not report to a legislative supervisory committee. Others are in the process of changing. For example, whereas interdisciplinary staffs were introduced via the special purpose agency, they are increasingly characteristic of all program review efforts.

The following discussion reviews trends in the development of each organization and discusses its relationship to the legislature, staffing patterns, and nature of product.

Legislative Audit Agencies. Legislative audit agencies are a major manifestation of the principle that post audit is more appropriately performed by the legislature than by an executive appointee or an elected state auditor. The rapidity with which the idea has been implemented is seen in the fact that in 1951 only three legislatures performed this function whereas by 1972 more than thirty did so.

The emergent emphasis on program and performance auditing is directly related to the transfer of the audit function to legislative supervision. This results from the policy and oversight functions of the legislature. However, a recent survey by the Council of State Governments suggests that legislative audit agencies, while recognizing the importance of performance auditing, have been slow to implement it on any significant scale.[6] This may be associated with the fact that they are staffed primarily by accountants who have traditionally been preoccupied with financial, compliance, and management audits. States in which the legislative auditor has moved farthest toward a performance orientation include Hawaii, Michigan, Maryland, Montana, Kansas, Tennessee, Wisconsin, Georgia, and North Dakota.

A major issue is whether such agencies will be able to convert fast enough to the performance audit and whether it will be as broad in scope as emerging legislative concerns require. Most post audit agencies with the exception of Hawaii, Wisconsin, and Kansas, currently conduct "limited" review. Another issue is whether the value of "independence" from the legislature is achieved at too great a price in terms of reduced utilization and impact. There appear to be significant differences in the practices of legislative auditors in this respect.

Special Purpose Program Evaluation Agency. Legislative program evaluation agencies reflect the most concentrated effort to implement evaluation in a legislative setting. Generally these agencies are joint, nonpartisan, and emphasize the preparation of major formal evaluation reports or performance audits for distribution to the legislature and for public release. Staffs are multidisciplinary and organized on a team basis. Usually these agencies are governed by legislative commissions designed to operate outside the legislative process in the sense that, unlike standing committees, they are not part of the bill flow. The agencies vary considerably, however, in the extent of legislative participation in and utilization of their work, and in the extent to which the commission or staff makes specific recommendations based on their findings. They also vary in the missions assigned by their charter legislation which may include more than program evaluation or performance audit.

New York's Legislative Expenditure Review Commission, established in 1969, was the first such agency. Similar agencies created since are the Illinois Economic and Fiscal Commission and the Connecticut Program Review Committee. Other states moving toward this approach include Massachusetts, Mississippi, Virginia, and Washington. Ohio, Oregon, and Pennsylvania are presently considering the adoption of this approach.

These agencies are most readily adapted to "intensive" program review products. However, a major challenge is whether they can have sufficient impact on legislative decisions and executive programs by bridging the gap between the use of highly technical tools and the political requirements of simplification and relevance; another challenge is whether they can conduct evaluations rapidly enough and in sufficient quantity to meet the legislature's needs on a timely basis.

Legislative Fiscal Agencies and Appropriations Committee Staffs. Legislative fiscal agencies and appropriations committee staffs may also be used to couple performance evaluation with legislative review of the governor's budget. States which have succeeded in incorporating an identifiable evaluation component in legislative fiscal review include joint agencies like the California Legislative Fiscal Analyst, the North Carolina Legislative Fiscal Research Division, the Wisconsin Legislative Fiscal Bureau, and the Appropriations Committees in Michigan, Florida, California, and Illinois legislatures.

There are difficulties in this approach because agencies responsible for review of the governor's budget face such intense daily demands that it may not be possible to sustain evaluation activities.

Partisan appropriations committee staffs rarely become involved in program review studies. New York is an exception, where the budget staff prepares analytic reports on policy issues which incorporate a substantial program review component. A similar approach is taken by nonpartisan staff in California and North Carolina.

A different approach is taken in Texas and Michigan where a distinctive staff unit within the fiscal agency conducts "intensive" program review and evaluation. This kind of unit has the potential of combining the advantages of a special-purpose agency and integration with budget decisions and the legislative process.

Standing Committees. Standing committees in most states are too lightly staffed and too overwhelmed by day-to-day responsibilities to be able to perform the evaluation function well. However, some are seeking to overcome this problem through, for example, the "model health committees," which are operating under the aegis of the Citizens' Conference on State Legislatures in eight states and the education committees of four states working in association with the Eagleton Institute.[7] In addition to the substantive policy committees, government operations committees offer potential for program review and its utilization.

Florida appears to be the state which has placed the greatest reliance upon its standing committee system for program performance review. Leadership, seeking to develop operating capabilities in this area, has encouraged the standing committees by mandating that each conduct at least one evaluation between the 1974 and 1975 legislative sessions. Significant activity is under way in the Florida House Committees on Appropriations and on Health and Rehabilitative Services. In the Senate, the Government Operations Committee is developing a computerized operation for compilation of citizen complaints as an input to program evaluations. The Education Committee is participating in the Eagleton Institute project.

The Florida House Government Operations Committee offers an example of the difficulties of a standing committee maintaining a program review focus. Plans were developed in 1973 to utilize the staff of this committee to: (a) conduct selective evaluations; (b) provide direction and guidance to the legislative auditor, including development of a special multidisciplinary performance group within the auditor's staff; and (c) train staff of other standing committees to do selective evaluations. These plans apparently have not materialized.

Whatever the limitations of standing committees in the conduct of in-depth studies, they are essential "users" of such studies and key vehicles for the direct exercise of legislative program control.

Research Agencies. General legislative research agencies include the traditional legislative council, a legislative committee which, in some states, incorporates the legislative auditor and an audit subcommittee. Together the research and auditing staffs may combine to do what amounts to a program performance review in many of the reports which they prepare for the legislature. In North Dakota, for example, a Joint Legislative Budget and Audit Committee is served by a staff which is part of the Legislative Council. This committee has recently contracted with private audit firms for performance audits not carried out by a separate state auditor. The Indiana Legislative Council houses a Fiscal Research Division which is actively involved in performance audits. In some larger states research agencies conduct highly sophisticated program evaluations. An example would be the California Assembly Office of Research.

There may be two major barriers to the conduct of extensive program review by legislative research agencies—the large number of projects requires that limited resources be spread too thin, and a tendency exists to emphasize development of new legislation rather than review of existing programs. The staffing of most legislative research agencies does not incorporate the specialized analytic skills required for "intensive" program review.

Hybrid Agencies. Hybrid agencies have been developed in recent years to reintegrate staff functions or to take on multiple functions. These structures have implications for the manner in which legislative evaluation is conducted. They suggest the possibility of close and fruitful collaboration among complementary fiscal functions.

In New Jersey, the Joint Legislative Office of Fiscal Affairs features three distinct divisions: budget review, legislative post audit, and legislative program analysis and evaluation. In Maryland, the Legislative Department of Fiscal Services contains divisions of budget review, fiscal analysis (revenue and tax), and post audit. Hybrid agencies such as these possess the advantage of potentially greater central coordination among the fiscal services. A number of the "legislative council" agencies might also fall in the hybrid category. One of the major challenges these hybrid agencies must meet is the increased risk of staff isolation from the legislative process through hierarchical staff organization. The Maryland agency is closely linked to the legislature via the Joint Budget Committee but it does not perform "intensive" review. The New Jersey unit, on the other hand, conducts "intensive" review, but it is not linked to a supervisory committee primarily concerned with its work.

Multiple Approaches. Five states have chosen to go a "multiple approach" route in order to have access to complementary approaches. These states are California, Illinois, Michigan, New York, and Wisconsin. Each state has selected a different combination of two or more options. These are all complex legislatures which use a variety of independent staff agencies. Their biggest problem is setting priorities, establishing a division of labor, and coordinating activities.

Program Review: Two Alternative Products. Analysis of program review studies released from 1970–1975 suggests that it is important to distinguish between two major types of products, the "limited" review and the "intensive" review. Not all agencies perform the latter, but some audit, special-purpose, fiscal, and hybrid agencies do so. The differences between the two products are outlined in table 1 along the following variables: identifying legislative intent, clarifying program objectives, developing indicators, setting standards, collecting data, setting the scope of the study, establishing a research design, utilizing research tools, providing staff capabilities, setting limits of competency, developing conclusions, framing alternatives and making recommendations.

"Limited" Program Review. In this approach, legislative intent is taken very concretely. Highly specific legislative instructions are identified. Objectives for discrete activities are identified. Readily available indicators, measures, standards, and data are taken. Records and documents already available from the agency are the focus of attention. Programs and activities within agencies, not across agencies, are treated. Conclusions and recommendations are drawn in the most concrete, manageable output terms, suspectible to more or less routine follow-up. Suggestions are made for future improvement in program objectives, indicators, measures, standards, and data, but no developmental work is done. Professions are not challenged. Often it is found that there is no basis for reviewing important

Table 1

Program Review: Two Alternative Products

Area	Limited Review	Intensive Review
Legislative Intent	Focus on concrete, specific instructions; narrow interpretation	Search covers a wide variety of written or unwritten, formal or informal sources
Program Objectives	Specified in terms of discrete activities if developed prior to review	If not developed prior to review, developed during review in cooperation with program agency if possible; several levels of objectives may be involved
Indicators	Used if readily available	Developed if not available
Standards	Used if readily available; extensive use of common sense and "reasonable man" view	Adapted from related fields, other states, private sector; or new one developed
Data	Used if readily available from agency records and documents	Generate new data if necessary through surveys; tap unusual data sources
Scope of Study	Conforms to organizational structure; may be restricted to housekeeping, functional and regulatory programs; tangible, proximate outputs	Cuts across organizational structure; may develop a special program structure for focus of study; covers any substantive program and broad impacts
Research Design	Simple statistical samples or descriptive data only	Control groups; experimental design
Research Tools	Heavy reliance on direct observation, investigation	Methods of social sciences, statistics, organizational sciences
Staff	Accountants, management	Social science/public administration
Limits of Competency	Avoid issues with professionals; substitute efficiency for effectiveness indicators	Prepared to challenge professional standards, practices, and opinions
Conclusions and Recommendations	Concrete, manageable, and routine; may cite lack of data for any conclusions on program results	May raise broad policy questions which require further development by other legislative staff

objectives. Traditional accounting tools, and only the simplest research designs are used. More complex program review activity is seen as an executive or university responsibility.

"Intensive" Program Review. In this approach legislative intent is broadly construed and related to other sources of program objectives, such as executive agencies and professions involved with the program. A range of objectives is identified including the broadest objectives of social impact. The option is left open and frequently taken to conduct independent developmental work on definition of objectives, development of measures and standards, generation of new data through surveys and studies, and to base major recommendations on this work. In addition to agency records and documents, extensive interviews are conducted with program clientele. Programs which involve several agencies are studied and interagency program structures are developed for the purpose of conducting the review. Program output is broadly defined to include side effects and impact on society. Cost benefit analyses are supplemented by cost effectiveness analyses which can incorporate a broader range of considerations. In the conduct of research, a variety of tools from the social sciences, economics, statistics, organization sciences, and elsewhere are used. Consideration is given to the development and use of scientific research design or practical adaptations of it as a means of answering questions about program impact of concern to the legislature. Conclusions and recommendations can include some of broad scope, for example, the suggestion of alternative programs to achieve the objectives. These may require substantial effort to develop. Also, more developmental work may be done on improvement of executive systems. Special expertise is brought into the project from outside if necessary to provide the legislature with a legitimate basis for challenging professional practices, standards, and opinion. There is a disposition that some way can be improvised to provide the legislature with a reading on any objective, rather than deferring it to possible future activity by the executive or a university institute.

We claim that these two options are distinguished "without prejudice" for several reasons. First, they do not correspond perfectly to any particular program review operation. Second, each has advantages and disadvantages.

Limited program review appears to satisfy the needs of a legislature for numerous reasons: the pool of available staff who are trained to do this kind of work is much larger; since the skills which have to be used are less diverse, the problems of coordinating a project team are considerably simplified; the product can be produced in less time, with fewer personnel, and/or at less cost; generally, findings and recommendations are readily understandable and subject to implementation; the scope of political conflict likely to be engendered if the legislature pushes for implementation will probably be less; and the methodology is more routine and less subject to criticism.

Intensive program review appears to be harder to staff and manage, more costly and time-consuming, more challenging to implement, and more subject to political conflict and methodological criticism. Nevertheless, it has seemed sufficiently attractive that at least a dozen legislatures are trying to move in this direction.[8]

Only a few legislative agencies as yet have the capability or inclination to conduct intensive program review. Among the auditors, Hawaii has been doing it for years, and Wisconsin and Kansas have recently begun to do it. Among the special purpose agencies, New York and Illinois do it, and Virginia is beginning to do it. Among the budget staffs, Michigan's LPER unit and the Texas Budget Board and evaluation unit are doing it. The program analysis unit of New Jersey's hybrid agency is doing it. No standing committees or research agencies are doing it.

The Legislature and Program Review Success

The preceding discussion identified seven structural patterns entrusted with program reviews and two possible products. While the structure and the product are very important in determining the extent to which the legislature utilizes program review findings, other variables are also important. These include legislative supervision and initiation of program review, degree of specificity of legislative intent and program objectives, and development of a complementary executive information system.

Supervision and Initiation of Program Review. Legislator involvement in the selection of topics and setting of priorities for program review, as well as prior identification of clients for the finished product, are keys to utilization. All program review agencies seek to work with a committee, even if they are not under the formal supervision of one. Legislative auditors, reflecting their tradition of "independence," lack a supervisory committee in fully half of the thirty states where they exist. States with an active audit committee include Colorado, California, Illinois, and Florida.

The boldest steps toward legislator involvement have been taken by special purpose agencies in Connecticut and Massachusetts, where legislators participate actively in the conduct of research and in drafting the report. In these states, program review may come closest to serving as an instrument of legislative political will.

Currently the New York Legislature is facing a different situation. The Legislative Commission on Expenditure Review has set a middle course there, limiting itself to selecting topics. Five years of experience seem to show that, in this complex system, the Commission, which is comprised of the leadership, needs to take a more active management role to assure utilization of reports and a generation of priority topics.[9]

Action at Release of Report. Most legislatures have not developed complete procedures for action on program review findings. Some auditors, Illinois for example, have developed a routine which provides for a formal hearing by the supervisory committee, an opportunity for the program manager to present his views, a formal agreement on action to be taken, and a review and report to the committee by the governor in cases of disagreement. A staff separate from the program review staff serves the supervisory committee in this procedure, as a means of preserving the objectivity of auditors.

In contrast, special purpose staffs in Connecticut and Massachusetts are actively involved in testifying before standing committees and developing materials supporting action in the legislative process on specific measures. These are cases where the program review staff, rather than being particularly isolated from the legislative process as in many states, is involved in the process as a direct agent. This is also true to some extent of the auditor in Maryland.

A more restrained, and as yet unproven, approach to achieving action is exemplified in Illinois where a special purpose agency uses a "decision memo." This goes to the supervisory committee after sufficient time has elapsed to judge reactions to the report, so they know the political context. The costs and consequences of implementation are outlined for each recommendation.

A highly restrained, yet common approach for many auditors, as well as some special purpose agencies, is to rely entirely on an executive agency response to the findings. The trend, however, is toward more active involvement by the legislature.

Subsequent Follow-Up Monitoring and Compliance Review. Special staff have been assigned this responsibility in several states. They may be located: in the same staff which conducted the study (New York, Illinois special purpose, many audit agencies)—this allows a person familiar with the study to follow-up, but is considered to present problems of role conflict, that is, enforcement impedes future objectivity; under the committee which supervises the program review staff, but not part of the staff—New Jersey utilizes such a "compliance officer" role, which seems to be demonstrating advantages in greater objectivity, in a more professional disposition to persuasion and cajolery, and in performing the important function of providing feedback to the review staff on the realism of recommendations; under some other committee like a Government Operations Committee (California, Florida) which may be especially assigned to oversee implementation—this has the advantage of completely separating the role of program review from that of utilization, compliance, and enforcement; in fiscal bureaus or under appropriations committees, as in Michigan, where the two appropriations committees have jointly established the formal position of "Legislative Audit Coordinator" to institutionalize follow-up of audit and evaluation reports through the appropriations and standing committees.

Legislative Intent and Program Objectives. Elusive and controversial as legislative intent and program objectives can be, legislatures which are using the new tools of program review find it helpful, and in many cases feasible, to specify these in advance. Where this is possible, it renders the program under study immensely more amenable to treatment by the new tools of program review. Several devices are worthy of special attention: extension of the modes through which legislative intent is communicated to committee transcripts, reports, and staff analyses—a particularly powerful tool in this area is the joint memorandum of intent issued with the appropriations bills by more and more legislatures (South Dakota, California, Florida, New York); requiring executive agencies to submit a proposed set of objectives and indicators, and an evaluation plan for approval by the standing committee of jurisdiction prior to program implementation (Wisconsin); requiring the submission of an "evaluation note," analogous to the "fiscal note," for every bill which establishes or modifies a program—the note would specify program objectives, indicators, and standards (under wide discussion); providing for review of executive administrative rules and regulations by committees and by the legislature if necessary (Alaska, Arkansas, Connecticut, Idaho, Iowa, Kansas, Kentucky, Florida, Michigan, Minnesota, Montana, Nebraska, New York, Oregon, South Dakota, and Wisconsin).

The legislative appropriations process is a key to utilization of program review in legislative decisions. Legislatures recognize program review as a natural part of the process. Michigan has taken the most distinctive step to structure the use of time, focusing directly on program review in the months prior to submission of the governor's budget. This is being done concurrently with implementation of an executive budget system which places high priority on program review.

Program-Oriented Executive Information Systems. There is a strong connection between states which are strengthening program review and those which are moving ahead with program-based executive systems. Several states illustrate the strong role a legislature can have in initiating steps to meet its needs and in supporting adequate executive systems. The Hawaii, California, Wisconsin, and South Dakota legislatures have been exemplary.

Executive information systems supportive of program review include budgeting, accounting, and management information systems. Legislatures, including those mentioned above, are getting involved in joint design of these systems as a reliable basic source of information on all programs available in a short time frame without the special efforts of an in-depth study.

Legislatures are requiring "variance reports" of projected versus actual program results as a basis for "program status monitoring." (Hawaii, Texas)

Self-Evaluation. No information system design can foresee special issues and problems which will arise. Consequently, the executive as well as the legislature needs a capability to conduct selective in-depth program review. Innovations here include: stipulation of specific requirements for program review in legislation establishing each program (Congress); dedication of a proportion (1–3 percent) of an agency budget to program review (California); support of "systematic experiments" and pilot programs rather than jumping into a statewide program; legislative monitoring of the quality of executive program reviews and utilization of their findings.

Most American legislatures take the view that executive systems are necessary both as a management aid to the executive and as an oversight aid to the legislature and that a legislative role in monitoring executive systems and conducting its own in-depth studies is equally necessary.

Environmental Characteristics Associated with Program Review Efforts

The relationships between state legislative approaches to program review and various environmental characteristics identify some significant patterns which can suggest conditions hospitable to or even required for the alternative approaches discussed above. In this section selected "independent" environmental variables are analyzed for their effect on "dependent" legislative approach variables. This constitutes an initial effort to answer the question: "Why does a given state pursue a particular approach to legislative program review?" An important and related question is: "To what extent are political leaders constrained by various conditions in their selection of an approach to legislative program review?"

For several reasons the analysis presented here should be considered only a beginning. While it identifies some patterns with significant implications, in many areas no clear-cut patterns emerge. Further, the variables for which data are available are not necessarily the ones which answer all the important questions which need to be asked. In some cases readily available indicators are not adequate. These limitations will be made evident in the discussion which follows.

Methodology. The variables selected as a means of exploring the relationship between environmental characteristics and legislative program review patterns can be divided into two categories, dependent and independent variables. The three dependent variables reflect the legislature's approach to program review: whether or not a concerted program review effort has been identified; the type of organization selected to perform this mission; and the nature of the product.[10] All of these variables have been discussed in the previous section.

The independent variables reflect state environmental characteristics along four major dimensions: the broad nature (simple or complex), resources (budget), and style (professionalization) of legislative organization; *executive* power (strength of governor) and knowledge base (supporting information systems); cross-cutting characteristics of *state government* as a whole for conflict resolution (partisanship) and substantive action (program innovation); and indicators of *state development* (population, per capita income, total state and local expenditures).

These four dimensions of the environment may be conceived as progressively less direct in their linkage to legislative program review, as shown in figure 2. But as other studies have shown, variables with apparently more distant linkages may nevertheless have very substantial impact.[11]

The raw data on which the analysis is based are presented in table 2. The analyzed data are presented in table 3. The sources and nature of each environmental indicator presented in the tables and used in the analysis are discussed below.

The first dimension includes three independent variables. The first is the nature of legislative organization which is seen

Figure 2

Proximate Linkage of Environmental Variables to Legislative Program Review

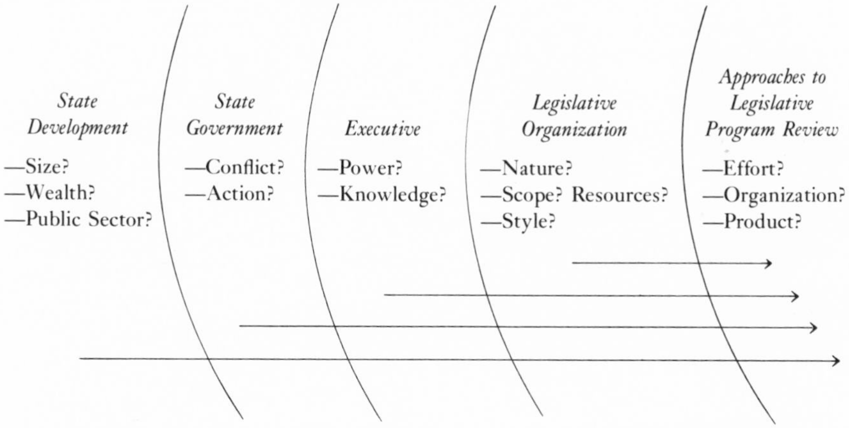

dichotomously as either "simple" or "complex," depending upon the number of staff units, the functions they perform, their size and decentralization.[12] This variable is a direct measure of the extent to which specialization of function and division of labor among all organizational units within the legislature affects organizational arrangements for program review. The second variable is the legislative budget which is taken as an indicator of the total resources under direct formal control of the legislature for performing legislative functions. Major components in this variable are legislator salaries, operating expenses, and staff. This variable may be viewed as an independent measure of the scale of resources available for functions such as program review.[13] The third variable is the "Legislative Professionalism Index" a composite indicator of where a legislative body stands on a scale of organizational development.[14] A legislature that scores high on professionalism pays high salaries to legislators, makes high expenditures for staff assistance, processes a larger-than-average number of bills, and has lengthy sessions. These variables are among the many measures advocated by the legislative reform movement of the 1960s.[15]

The second independent dimension regarding the power and knowledge base of the executive branch has two variables. The

Table 2

Data: Approach to Program Review and State Characteristics

States	No PR	All W. PR	L. Aud./No PR	L. Aud./W. PR	All Non Aud. PR	Special	Fiscal	Committee	Research	Hybrid	Multiple	Simple Leg.	Complex Leg.	Limited PR	Intensive PR	Govn. Power	Innovation	Partisanship	Legislative Professionalism	Prog. Acctg.	Prog. Approp.	Pg. Ef. Meas.	Ex. B. Eval.	No Ef. Anal.	Op. Meas.	Dec. Basis	Leg. Budget	Total Budget	Population	Per Capita Income
Alabama	x											x				14	.406	45	.104					x			1.9	1.5	3.5	3087
Alaska		x	x				x					x		x		16	x	x	−.188	x	x		x				2.8	0.6	0.3	4875
Arizona	x		x									x				9	.384	31	−.100		x	x			x		2.7	0.9	2.0	3913
Arkansas	x		x									x				13	.394	44	−.765	x	x	x		x	x		0.8	0.7	2.0	3078
California		x		x	x		x	x	x		x		x	x		18	.604	17	2.294			x	x				31.6	11.1	20.5	4640
Colorado		x		x									x	x		14	.538	4	−.173							x	2.2	1.1	2.4	4153
Connecticut		x	x		x	x							x	x		16	.568	6	.226	x							2.5	1.6	3.1	4995
Delaware	x											x				13	.376	1	.317								0.8	0.4	0.6	4673
Florida		x	x		x			x					x	x		8	.397	40	.279	x	x	x			x		15.1	2.7	7.3	3930
Georgia		x		x								x		x		13	.381	47	.248		x		x	x	x		5.0	2.0	4.8	3599
Hawaii		x		x								x			x	19	x	x	1.010	x	x	x	x		x		4.1	0.8	0.8	4738
Idaho		x		x								x		x		13	.394	12	−1.545		x		x	x			1.4	0.3	0.8	3409
Illinois		x		x	x	x					x		x		x	19	.521	5	1.043				x				11.7	5.1	11.3	4775
Indiana		x			x				x			x		x		12	.464	11	−.150		x		x	x			3.2	1.9	5.3	4027
Iowa	x											x				11	.413	14	−.382	x	x		x	x			3.1	1.3	2.9	3877
Kansas		x		x									x	x		10	.426	36	−.260	x	x		x			x	2.1	0.9	2.3	4192
Kentucky		x		x					x			x		x		14	.419	24	−.218	x	x		x		x		3.1	1.6	3.3	3306
Louisiana		x	x		x		x						x	x		13	.459	43	.273	x			x				3.8	2.0	3.8	3252
Maine		x		x								x		x		11	.455	35	−.114	x	x			x			0.8	0.5	1.0	3375

Maryland		x		x	x		x			x			x	x		16	.482	13	.219	x	x		x		x		5.1	2.1	4.1	4522
Massachusetts		x			x	x							x	x		10	.629	9	2.185				x	x			12.5	2.9	5.8	4562
Michigan		x		x	x		x				x		x		x	18	.578	10	1.538	x	x	x	x		x		13.3	4.5	9.1	4430
Minnesota	x		x										x			15	.525	16	.203	x							4.4	2.3	3.9	4032
Mississippi		x			x	x						x		x		8	.298	48	−.122					x			2.2	1.1	2.3	2788
Missouri	x											x				16	.377	26	.202	x	x	x	x		x	x	3.7	1.7	4.8	3940
Montana		x		x								x		x		15	.378	23	−1.827	x	x						1.0	0.4	0.7	3629
Nebraska	x											x				15	.425	30	−.107	x	x		x				1.3	0.6	1.5	4030
Nevada	x		x									x				14	.323	25	−.697		x			x			1.0	0.3	0.5	4822
New Hampshire	x		x									x				9	.482	32	−1.357					x			0.8	0.3	0.8	3796
New Jersey		x	x		x					x			x		x	18	.585	8	1.455	x	x	x	x		x		4.8	3.0	7.4	4811
New Mexico	x											x				8	.375	22	−1.006				x				1.1	0.6	1.1	3298
New York		x			x	x	x				x		x		x	19	.656	15	2.145	x	x		x		x		25.8	12.4	18.4	5000
North Carolina		x			x		x					x		x		8	.430	42	−.096	x	x	x	x		x		1.4	2.2	5.2	3424
North Dakota		x			x				x			x		x		13	.444	29	−1.364					x	x		0.5	0.3	0.6	3538
Ohio	x											x				16	.528	7	.599	x		x	x	x			5.6	3.5	10.8	4175
Oklahoma	x		x									x				13	.368	34	−.101		x			x		x	3.3	1.3	2.6	3515
Oregon	x												x			14	.544	21	.396		x	x	x				1.9	1.1	2.2	3959
Pennsylvania		x			x		x						x	x		17	.560	3	1.715	x		x				x	15.9	5.7	12.0	4147
Rhode Island	x		x									x				11	.503	33	−.065	x	x				x		0.9	0.5	1.0	4126
South Carolina	x											x				6	.347	46	.325	x				x			2.4	1.1	2.7	3142
South Dakota		x		x								x		x		10	.363	28	−.821		x	x			x		0.6	0.3	0.7	3441
Tennessee		x		x									x	x		15	.389	37	−1.190	x	x						2.2	1.4	4.0	3300
Texas		x	x		x		x					x			x	7	.362	38	.795	x		x	x				7.6	4.1	11.7	3726
Utah	x											x				17	.447	20	−1.366	x	x	x			x	x	0.8	0.6	1.1	3442
Vermont	x											x				9	.414	41	−1.203	x	x	x	x			x	1.0	0.3	0.5	3638
Virginia		x	x		x	x						x			x	15	.451	39	−.613					x			2.7	1.9	4.8	3899
Washington		x			x	x							x	x		18	.510	19	.142	x							4.8	1.9	3.4	4132
West Virginia	x		x									x				8	.386	27	−.366								2.9	1.0	1.8	3275
Wisconsin		x		x	x		x				x		x		x	11	.532	18	.837	x	x		x		x	x	5.7	2.4	4.5	3912
Wyoming	x		x									x				14	.346	2	−2.355		x	x					0.2	0.2	0.3	3929
Totals	20	30	16	15	19	7	10	2	4	2	5	32	18	22	8					29	30	17	25	16	17	8	238	99	208	

first is the "Combined Index of the Formal Power of Governors," which is the sum of four ratings on budget power, appointive power, tenure potential, and veto power.[16] In utilizing this index the author does not assume that legislative and executive powers are in a zero-sum relationship with one another. Rather, there are important areas of mutual interdependence. In some states the desire for an effective government may result in support for both a strong executive and a strong legislature. Consequently, a corresponding measure of formal legislative powers, clearly differentiated from the "Professionalism Index," needs to be developed, but it has not been possible to do so in preparation of this paper.

The second variable relates to the knowledge base of the executive. This is presented under the heading of "Supporting Information Systems" in table 3 and includes several variables. These identify states with program-based accounting systems in operation, where legislative appropriations are made on a program basis, where the budget document shows program effectiveness measures, where primary budget office functions include evaluation of program performance, where the budget office conducts no analysis of program effectiveness, where most operating agencies conduct analysis of program effectiveness, and where executive decisions are reported to be based on analysis of program effectiveness to a substantial extent.[17]

The third independent dimension regarding characteristics of state government includes two variables; the role of partisanship in conflict resolution and the decision-making processes,[18] and the nature of resulting state decisions as indicated by relative innovation[19] and leadership in new programs. The "political rationality" of partisanship may either conflict with the rationality of program review or may find it a useful adjunct. States which introduce new programs may or may not be equally willing to review them.

Finally, the fourth independent dimension regarding state development includes three variables; the population, per capita income, and total state and local expenditures.[20] Population is a useful indicator of state size. Population per square mile, or density, is not used here but could provide an additional indicator of forces requiring a governmental (collective) response. Per

Table 3

Analysis: Approach to Program Review and State Characteristics

	Legislature		State			Composite		
Approach	Organiz. Complex	Expend. (millions)	Expend. (billions)	Population (millions)	Per Cap $	Innovation	Partisan	Profession
No PR	1/20(.05)	2.0	0.9	2.35	3,829	.413	26	−0.416
All W. PR	17/30(.57)	6.6	2.7	5.4	3,732	.476	23	+0.270
Limited PR	12/22(.55)	5.5	2.1	4.4	3,486	.460	25	−0.044
Intensive PR	5/8 (.63)	9.5	4.3	8.5	4,411	.526	19	+1.026
Leg. Aud./No PR	5/16(.31)	3.5	1.5	3.3	3,998	.435	28	−0.211
Leg. Aud/W. PR	8/15(.53)	6.2	2.4	4.8	4,008	.465	22	+0.090
Special	5/7 (.71)	8.9	3.8	7.0	4,307	.519	20	+0.715
Fiscal	7/10(.70)	11.3	4.7	8.5	4,193	.518	22	+0.953
Committee	2/2 (1.0)	23.4	6.9	13.9	4,285	.500	29	+1.287
Research	1/4 (.25)	9.6	3.7	7.4	3,877	.483	20	+0.439
Hybrid	2/2 (1.0)	5.0	2.6	5.8	4,667	.534	11	+0.837
Multiple	5/5 (1.0)	17.6	7.1	12.9	4,551	.578	13	+1.571
All Non-Aud PR	13/19(.68)	8.7	3.5	7.2	4,091	.498	22	+0.630

Definition of terms for "Approach": "No PR" (states where no concerted program review effort identified); "All W. PR" (all states where a concerted program review effort was identified); "Limited PR" (all states where product was "limited program review"); "Intensive PR" (all states where product was "intensive program review"); "Leg. Aud./No PR" (states where the post auditor reports to the legislature, but where no concerted program review effort identified); "Leg. Aud./W. PR" (states where the post auditor reports to the legislature, and where a concerted program review effort has been identified); "All Non-Aud. PR" (states where a concerted program review effort is being pursued outside of the post audit agency, including states where a post audit agency exists, whether or not that agency conducts a concerted program review effort).

Table 3 (Continued)

Approach	Supporting Information Systems							Governor's Power Index
				Budget Functions				
	Prog. Acctg.	Prog. Approps.	Measures of Effect.	Eval.	No Analysis	Op. Agency Effect. Meas.	Basis of Exec. Decs.	
No PR	10/20	13/20	6/20	8/20	8/20	5/20	4/20	12.3
	(.50)	(.65)	(.30)	(.40)	(.40)	(.25)	(.20)	
All W. PR	19/30	17/30	9/30	17/30	8/30	12/30	5/30	13.8
	(.63)	(.57)	(.30)	(.57)	(.27)	(.40)	(.17)	
Limited PR	13/22	12/22	5/22	10/22	7/22	6/22	3/22	13.1
	(.59)	(.55)	(.23)	(.45)	(.31)	(.27)	(.14)	
Intensive PR	6/8	5/8	4/8	7/8	1/8	5/8	2/8	15.8
	(.75)	(.63)	(.50)	(.88)	(.13)	(.63)	(.25)	
Leg. Aud./No PR	9/16	9/16	6/16	4/16	5/16	5/16	1/16	12.4
	(.56)	(.56)	(.38)	(.25)	(.31)	(.31)	(.06)	
Leg. Aud./W. PR	8/14	11/14	4/14	9/14	3/14	6/14	3/14	15.4
	(.57)	(.79)	(.28)	(.64)	(.21)	(.43)	(.21)	
Special	3/7	1/7	0/7	3/7	3/7	1/7	1/7	15.0
	(.43)	(.14)	(.00)	(.43)	(.43)	(.14)	(.14)	
Fiscal	7/8	3/8	5/8	7/8	0/8	4/8	3/8	14.3
	(.88)	(.38)	(.63)	(.88)	(.00)	(.50)	(.38)	
Committee	1/2	1/2	2/2	1/2	0/2	1/2	0/2	13.0
	(.50)	(.50)	(1.0)	(.50)	(.00)	(.50)	(.00)	

Research	1/4	2/4	1/4	3/4	2/4	2/4	0/4	13.3
	(.25)	(.50)	(.25)	(.75)	(.50)	(.50)	(.00)	
Hybrid	2/2	2/2	1/2	2/2	0/2	2/2	0/2	17.0
	(1.0)	(1.0)	(.50)	(1.0)	(.00)	(1.0)	(.00)	
Multiple	3/5	3/5	1/5	5/5	0/5	3/5	2/5	17.0
	(.60)	(.60)	(.20)	(1.0)	(.00)	(.60)	(.40)	
All Non-Aud PR	11/20	8/20	7/20	13/20	5/20	9/20	3/20	13.2
	(.55)	(.40)	(.35)	(.65)	(.25)	(.45)	(.15)	

Definition of Terms: "Prog. Acctg." (states with program-based accounting systems in operation); "Prog. Approps." (states where legislative appropriations are made on a program basis); "Measures of Effect." (states where budget document shows program effectiveness measures, present and/or future, for most agencies or programs); "Budget Functions, Eval." (states where primary budget office functions include evaluation of program performance); ". . . No Analysis" (states where the budget office conducts no analysis of program effectiveness); "Op. Agency Effect. Meas." (states where most major operating agencies conduct analysis of program effectiveness); "Basis of Exec. Decs." (states where executive decisions are reported to be based on analysis of program effectiveness to a substantial degree).

capita income indicates the level of resources available for coping with collective problems and achieving goals. Total state and local expenditures was selected to indicate the level of public sector resources generated by these closely linked levels of government.

Findings. Analysis of the four sets of environmental dimensions for their impact on approaches to legislative program review suggests that all four sets affect the selection of approaches to legislative program review. Several broad patterns emerge.

States which are conducting concerted review of program effectiveness, regardless of their review product, rank higher on various scales than those which are not doing so.[21]

When differentiated by product, states which are conducting intensive program review rank higher than those which are conducting limited program review. States with legislative audit agencies which are conducting program review rank higher than those with legislative audit agencies which are not conducting program review.

When differentiated by the type of organization used, states which use approaches to program review other than or in addition to the legislative auditor (special purpose; fiscal staff; committee; research or hybrid agency; multiple approaches) rank higher than those which use the legislative auditor only.

The powers of the governor are greater in states which conduct program review than in those which do not; greater in those which do it intensively rather than in a limited way; greater in those in which the legislative auditor conducts program review rather than focussing on other types of audit; and greater in states in which multiple, hybrid, post audit, or special agencies are used than where fiscal, committee, or research agencies are used. This suggests that a strong executive is not a barrier to legislative program review capability. It is consistent with the view that states which seek strong government take measures to strengthen both the legislature and the executive.

The various supporting information systems are associated somewhat more with states which conduct legislative program review and are strongly associated with states where intensive program review is carried on, as well as with fiscal, hybrid, and multiple agency states, but are *not* associated with states where special purpose agencies are located. This suggests that special purpose agencies may reflect a legislative attempt to fill a gap in executive systems or to compensate for limited access to them.

The National Association of State Budget Officers (NASBO) survey [22] suggests that effectiveness measures are an important basis for executive decisions in only a handful (nine) of states, some of which are not usually associated with progress in budgeting; these are also smaller states in which the political process is generally thought to be simpler and less subject to conflicting views on program objectives. This data in particular needs to be interpreted with caution.

Apparently partisanship and objective program review are mutually supportive rather than incompatible inputs to the legislative process.

The patterns suggest that at this time (1975) the status of program review efforts in a state is in some degree a reflection of a complex of factors often loosely associated with our ideas of "development" and "complexity." But development is a continuing activity in the states. From table 4 it is evident that the trend to more sophisticated approaches to program review is a continuing one. States which have established the approach more recently (Mississippi, for example) rank lower on these scales than earlier ones. However, other states, such as Ohio, which rank high, have not yet made their move. Unique factors are likely to operate in every state. The Mississippi legislature is one of the stronger ones vis-a-vis the executive, and program review can be an attractive tool for a strong legislature. On the other hand, the Ohio legislature has delayed proposed action in order to give further consideration to alternative approaches which have been advocated or opposed by various key political leaders.

Overall, the diversity and range of state characteristics within each approach to program review organization and product suggests that many states could progress further to strengthen their efforts, and indeed are likely to do so, within the next five years. While environmental factors of the kind assessed here may tend to constrain the selection of program review approaches in certain broad ways, the variation within classifications suggests that substantial discretion must be exercised.[23]

Table 4

Generations of Legislative Program Review

Agency	1965	1970–1971	1972–1973	1974–1975
Audit	Hawaii Michigan	Idaho	Wisconsin Tennessee Montana South Dakota Colorado	Illinois Kansas Maine
Special Purpose		New York	Connecticut Illinois Washington Massachusetts Mississippi	Virginia North Carolina Pennsylvania
Fiscal		California New York	Michigan Texas North Carolina	Louisiana
Committee	California			Florida
Research			North Dakota Indiana	Kentucky
Hybrid			New Jersey Maryland	

Note: Dates refer to when the agency began review studies or audits with a significant program review component.

Two Key Problems: Legislator-Staff Roles and Communication Styles

The involvement of many legislatures in program review activities raises two significant problems. Both problems can be stated in the form of questions. What is the relationship between the program review staff and the legislators? And what are the required communications systems to insure that the product and reports of the program review staff are transmitted to policy makers for appropriate actions?

Baaklini and Heaphey have noted that American legislatures perceive a political role for staff and provide for keeping that role under control, whereas legislatures of many other countries perceive their staffs as neutral experts without a political role and organize them in bureaucratic fashion.[24] The implication is that, in American legislatures, decisions are political and made by legislators, whereas in many other legislatures, the ostensibly "neutral" staff are making decisions under the guise of their superior expertise.

In some instances the observation regarding foreign legislatures is even applicable to many American legislatures. In many states, for example, legislatures meet so little and legislators spend so little time in mastering the growing governmental programs that many legislators do lack confidence in their political and governmental judgment. As a consequence, they may rely very heavily on staff, particularly where nonpartisan central staff agencies employ key personnel over a period of decades. Hence there are distinct parallels to the bureaucratization of staff in legislatures of several countries.

Legislative program control and program review provide a useful opportunity to focus on this problem in view of the fact that they require a combination of active legislator involvement and unusual staff expertise. American observers generally agree that no matter what professional tools of program review are made available to the legislature, they are of little use without two kinds of active legislator involvement:

(1) involvement in establishing the topics, setting priorities, and providing for the translation of program review findings into "actionable material" for the legislature;

(2) involvement in achieving program control, through enacting legislation, raising questions, obtaining commitments, and persisting to see that these commitments are met.

At the same time many of the staffs which conduct program review are drawn from professions with strong inclinations to "independence," "integrity," and to elitist conceptions of their roles. Among these staffs one can as often hear the sentiment expressed that "the legislators are unqualified," as that "the legislature is always right." It is not uncommon to find in these staffs either a missionary sense that "we are here to rationalize the legislative decision-making style" or a sense that "we have our professional procedures, and our job is done when we have followed them."

To be successful legislative program review must resolve these built-in conflicts engendered by the need for legislator involvement and the presence of professional elitism.

American legislatures, then, face the problem of defining the role of program review staff so as to balance between two objectives:

(1) relevance to the needs of the legislature as a political institution and to the needs of individual legislators as political actors whose viability depends on their survival;

(2) achieving a product which can be accepted as a rational, objective basis for legislative action, even in the cases where there may be opposition from the executive or from the professions.

In awareness of some of these problems, American state legislatures have shown an increased tendency to:

(1) limit the independence of the auditor or director of the program review staff;

(2) establish a special committee to supervise the work of the program review agency, including selection of topics, setting of priorities, setting procedures for conduct of the study, and defining the kind of product desired;

(3) conducting hearings, obtaining other information, and making independent judgments on the course of action to be taken.

American legislatures seem to be agreeing readily that the program review function is nonpartisan and objective and that it requires a staff with a degree of tenure sufficient to guarantee expertise. At the same time, however, there is ample evidence that, with a very few exceptions, American legislatures are ready if necessary to alter their organizational arrangements for program review. For example, in some cases auditors have not been interested in using the newer tools, or legislatures have felt they could not convert fast enough. In these cases a new staff has been organized in a separate legislative agency. This has happened in Connecticut, Texas, Washington, and other states.

On occasion even more drastic action has been taken. American legislative staffs are generally not part of the formal government civil service system. This is also true of their program review staffs, with a few rare exceptions, such as the constitutionally required civil service system for the legislative auditor general of Michigan. Clearly, this means that an unresponsive audit staff can, potentially, be remedied quickly. Without prejudice to the specific case, we note that in 1974 the Kentucky legislature exercised its prerogatives by removing the audit staff, eliminating the statutory position of legislative auditor, and establishing a new organizational approach. This is one illustration of the general fact that American legislatures take seriously their prerogatives to reorganize their agencies and remove their staff, even in this area, program review, where they recognize the greatest need for expertise and continuity.

American legislatures understand "objectivity" as a valuable but limited concept. They do not place great reliance upon "independence" as a source of objectivity. That is, they do not have great faith in the results of program review conducted by professional standards, by independent auditors, and isolated staffs. Rather, objectivity emerges from the give-and-take adversary process, from the interplay of conflicting values and the supporting facts which can be marshalled. This view is increasingly reflected in the composition and working styles of legislative program review staffs. They are interdisciplinary. Valuable findings emerge from the availability and application of diverse analytic tools and perspectives.

In harmony with this view, American legislatures are moving to reduce the areas of decision-making which they feel to be, or can reasonably be argued to be, "beyond their competence." For this reason they are increasingly less satisfied with traditional approaches to program review which avoid assessing matters thought to be the prerogative of the program professionals and concentrate, as a result, on matters of efficiency rather than effectiveness. American legislators increasingly recognize that experts can differ. They view it as their function to identify and resolve such differences rather than to be exclusively directed by experts. When an existing staff group does not meet these needs, American legislators show an increasing readiness to revamp it or replace it with a new one.

The American experience seems to suggest that, to achieve significant legislative program control and review, a core staff must be directly under the control of the legislature. It can be neither identified with the bureaucracy, nor with a "fourth branch." They are learning, however, that simply establishing a staff group as a "legislative agency" is not enough. It has to be socially and procedurally integrated into the legislative institution. Legislatures in parliamentary as well as presidential systems seem to be receptive to developing their own staffs. The small, nonbureaucratic special purpose program review staff might be of special interest to parliaments.

Communication of Program Review Reports. Legislatures have often been viewed as barriers to change and progress. Upon closer examination this impression proves to be largely untenable.[25] For example, the problem of many legislatures is not resistance to progressive legislation, but rather that much of this legislation expresses ideals or goals which are not within the reach of available resources and administrative capabilities.

The American experience suggests that three needs have to be addressed in order to close this gap. Oversight procedures are needed to hold the executive accountable to legislative intent. Some of these were discussed in the section on utilization of program review. Second, the realism of legislative mandates needs to be assessed. This requires using the new tools of program review as a means of change and improvement. Third, there must be a communications process conducive to action on this knowledge. If the legislative program review activities are to contribute to the strengthening of legislatures, they should be communicated to the appropriate decision makers. This communication function is a prime responsibility of the review agencies.

A major criterion by which American program review staff are judged is the extent to which they develop actionable material, that is, the extent to which they give the legislature viable alternatives for independent action. While the emphasis on independent action varies, the government's need to respond to new conditions, and to change its approaches accordingly, seems to be universal. This section will focus on whether, and in what ways, program review staff can be of such assistance to legislatures. Considering the respective roles of legislators and staff, how can their interaction in the legislative decision-making process facilitate such responses? What does or can each contribute?

To be effective, decisions must reflect an extensive grasp of reality, and they must represent a commitment to their implementation. The program review staff can provide the former, and the legislature must enhance the latter. An effective legislative process must link rationality and passion, analysis and emotion. Without the former, things go wrong. Without the latter, things don't happen. This dual necessity relates directly to the American thrust toward program control, overview, and review. New tools are being developed and used to enable legislatures to determine whether legislative objectives are being achieved and whether there are alternative approaches which could be more effective. Program review has the potential for closing the gap between promise (objectives) and performance, which seems to characterize all contemporary governments, irrespective of economic development or conditions.

Why, then, has there been concern that program review itself would reinforce a systematic bias toward the status quo, and not toward innovation, change, or response? As a matter of fact, the outcome depends on how it is done. There may well be a conservative bias if the emphasis is on new rather than established programs and simple program description or strong program critique, rather than identification of alternative approaches which could be more effective. The American experience has not been entirely successful in this area because it tends not to allocate staff attention and resources to the serious identification of alternatives. Consequently, recommendations are often superficial and do not reflect the serious effort which went into program description and review.

We have been discussing problems with the product of program review. Does it tell the legislator *what* he needs to know to be a force for innovation and change? An equally serious problem is the style in which the message is communicated and the resulting impact on action. We see illustrated in the legislative process McLuhan's maxim that "the medium is the message." And we find as many deficiencies in the *medium* as in the *message*.

Legislators are oriented to making decisions based on informal peer-like relationships and visceral reactions to direct communication. Yet in only rare instances has the "art form" for communicating program review entered this mode. This alone is a substantial barrier to achieving the impact potential of the program review tool.

There are three basic ways to handle this situation. The program review staff can be isolated and may communicate in cumbersome written form. As a result, either the legislature fails to see potential for action or acts without enthusiasm, commitment, or understanding. In many of these cases program review may appear to be institutionalized, but at a considerable price in nonrealization of potential. In the second mode the program review staff relies on communication through "intermediary" staff serving leaders or committees. As a result there is some improvement in the immediacy of communication, but the legislator still lacks an opportunity for direct "confidence testing" and for translation of the findings into alternative language. Often, too, the legislator's awareness of the source of the information, and consequently his ability to learn how to use it better, is limited. He is likely to learn of the connection only when he sees some results of his actions. At that point his staff may or may not say "we based that on the program review report." The third way is when the program review staff which conducted the study works directly with a legislator, subcommittee, or task force from the point of topic selection through hearings to writing of a report and extensive discussion of alternatives and recommendations. As a result, the efficiency and effectiveness of communication are multiplied. The legislator learns the potential and limits of the staff who are applying it. He sees his opportunities for action beginning to expand. He has a real opportunity to test whether this kind of information can help him make the program control function a part of his "political identity." At the same time the staff has an opportunity to become sensitive to the concerns of legislators.

American legislatures are beginning to break down the barriers to high-impact communication between legislators and staff. At the same time they are exploring ways to preserve the desired level of staff objectivity and, to some extent, independence. We are convinced that we do, in fact, see here the "governmental laboratories" which a federal system can provide. The range of solutions is, in all likelihood, sufficiently diverse to provide something of interest to most other legislatures.

Conclusion

Implications for Some Broader Problems. Throughout the preceding discussion the implications of developments in legislative program review for larger problems of the legislative institution have been touched upon in four areas: relationships between the legislature and other institutions; power distribution within the legislature, policy functions of the legislature, and representative democratic functions. The general importance of these implications has been identified in Baaklini's introductory chapter, since the new tools and staffing arrangements for legislative program review clearly fall under the heading of "bureaucratic rationalization." Our observations suggest that American state legislatures are adapting the new approaches to meet their needs in such a way as largely to preserve the primacy of political rationality.

As suggested in the opening section, the primary impetus to these developments is the political need to enhance the strength of the legislature vis-a-vis the executive by having available the same tools of rationality hitherto claimed to be a monopoly of the executive. Program review strengthens the legislature by enhancing the quality of information which it can share with any other institution in support of its decisions. While the legislature thereby obtains a greater mastery of bureaucratic rationality, it retains a controlling political perspective to bring it into play.

There are implications for major shifts in power distribution within the legislature. Legislators who are inclined to process more and different information as a basis for decisions may gain power over the decisions affected. New committees and staff agencies are created as power bases. Existing questions about the power of legislators versus staff are lent new urgency, and the priority for introducing new ways for legislators to control and communicate with staff is heightened. There may be a democratizing influence within the legislature in the sense that information previously available to no legislators or only a few is now available to all and to the general public through the dissemination of extensive reports. Clearly such dissemination infringes on any "right *not* to know."

A question of historic dimension has been the relative weight to be given to the legislative functions of advance policy-making and retrospective review. At first glance the strengthening of legislative program review may appear to reduce the relative importance of the legislative policy function. However, as implemented and understood by American state legislatures at this point in time, effective program review is not an alternative function but a complementary one. In "closing the feedback loop" with the policy function, it is likely to strengthen it. In fact, it is generally recognized that a precondition for effective program review is the improvement of such policy functions as goal-setting. At the same time, it is recognized that political conditions may not be conducive to clear goals, hence the need for selectivity in program review. On the other hand, information on the effect of "no goals" may produce a political incentive to goal setting.

The representative democratic functions of the legislature involve a classic democratic tension between meeting the constituencies' articulated demands and their needs as adjudged by the representative. Program review appears, even in its most democratic use of citizen and client surveys, to shift the institution in the direction of reacting to aggregate rather than particularistic information. In the judgment of this observer, however, the commitment to assisting individual constituents is so powerful as to continue relatively undiminished. Program review also appears to shift the focus of attention from election districts to statewide programs. This could alter the nature of representation by diminishing the intensity of local representation by legislators. However with existing technology there is every likelihood that programs can be reviewed on a district as well as a statewide basis.

In conclusion, it seems to this observer that, all things considered, we have here a case where the adoption of a kind of "bureaucratic rationality" by the legislature, but within constraints, can strengthen and legitimize, rather than undermine, its political role.

Author's Note

This chapter summarizes the findings of a national study of state legislative program review conducted during 1974–75 under the auspices of the Comparative Development Studies Center, State University of New York at Albany. Research by a core staff was augmented by consultants with special expertise, by associates located in key states, and by an advisory group which assembled a unique and representative combination of individuals: leading state legislative auditors and evaluators, their congressional counterparts, and academics conducting applied research in the field. Beyond these formal arrangements the legislators and staffs of many states provided invaluable assistance. Four levels of state coverage were involved: five states were studied in depth by expert associates located at the scene; fifteen states were covered by field work; fourteen states were surveyed through a series of meetings and interviews at conferences and by telephone; the remaining sixteen states were studied by written inquiry only, these being ones where initial inquiry did not identify substantial efforts to review programs formally. Study findings are presented more fully by the author of this article in *Legislative Review of Program Effectiveness* (Albany: State University of New York, Institute for Public Policy Alternatives, 1975); *Case Studies in Legislative Program Review* (New Brunswick: Rutgers University, Eagleton Institute, 1976); *Readings in Legislative Program Review: An Annotated Bibliography* (State University of New York at Albany, Comparative Development Studies Center, 1974); "Program Evaluation and Performance Audit by Legislative Bodies: A New Thrust for a Traditional Tool of Government Accountability," *Comment* (Comparative Development Studies Center) 1, 1 (August 1974); and *Legislative Review and Government Programs* (New York: Praeger, 1977).

Notes

1. Abdo I. Baaklini and James J. Heaphey, "Legislatures: Their Origin and the Factors That Contribute to Their Emergence." Comparative Development Studies Center, Graduate School of Public Affairs, State University of New York at Albany. 1974. Presented at the Conference on Legislative Origins, 1–4 April 1974, University of Hawaii, Honolulu.

2. Max Weber, "Politics as a Vocation," in H. H. Gerth and C. Wright Mills (eds.), *Max Weber: Essays in Sociology* (New York: Oxford University Press, 1959).

3. E. L. Normanton, *The Accountability and Audit of Governments* (Manchester, England: Manchester University Press, 1966).

4. Abdo I. Baaklini, "Legislatures in Contemporary Societies: An Overview." Presented at the Second International Conference on Legislative Development, 20–24 January 1975, Albany, New York.

5. Alan Rosenthal, *Legislative Performance in the States* (New York: Free Press, 1974).

6. *State Auditing and Federal-State Relations* (Lexington, Kentucky: Council of State Governments, 1970).

7. The eight states are Connecticut, Louisiana, Michigan, Minnesota, New Jersey, Texas, Washington, and Wyoming. The four states are Connecticut, Florida, Wisconsin, and Colorado.

8. Legislative approaches to intensive program review are reflected in the Hawaii auditor's *Manual of Guides* (updated since 1967) and in the 1974 *Handbook* of the New York Legislative Commission on Expenditure Review as well as the GAO paper "Recommended Principles and Standards for Evaluation of Federal Government Programs" (1976). Among more traditional auditors, the comptroller of the Treasury in Tennessee is documenting new efforts through a series of manuals and memoranda published in 1974. Among fiscal agencies, the Texas Legislative Budget Board has represented its approach in "Recommended Measures for Refinement of Performance and Activity Measures" (1974), and the Maryland legislature's Department of Fiscal Services has prepared an "Outline of an Approach to Program Analysis." The Michigan House Fiscal Agency has prepared a "Proposal for a Continuing Year Budget" (1973) and is currently designing an approach combining program review with zero-based budgeting.

9. Edgar G. Crane, *Legislative Review of Program Effectiveness* (Albany: The Institute for Public Policy Alternatives, State University of New York at Albany, 1975), Chapter IX.

10. This discussion is based on Edgar G. Crane, "Building Legislative Program Review Capability," in *Legislative Review of Program Effectiveness,* Chapter IV.

11. For a review of the literature which has explored the relative impact of such variables on state policy, see Thomas R. Dye, *Understanding Public Policy* (Englewood Cliffs: Prentice-Hall, 1972, 1974).

12. From Edgar G. Crane and John A. Worthley, "Organizational Dimensions of Legislatures," *Midwest Public Administration Review,* 10:1 (March, 1976), 14–30.

13. US Bureau of the Census. *Governmental Finances in 1971–72.*

14. John G. Grumm, "The Effects of Legislative Structure on Legislative Performance," in Richard L. Hofferbert and Ira Sharkansky (eds.), *State and Urban Politics* (Boston: Little, Brown and Company, 1971).

15. For an inventory of other criteria, see Citizens Conference on State Legislatures, *The Sometimes Governments,* 1971, 1973.

16. Developed by Joseph A. Schlesinger, "The Politics of the Executive," in Herbert Jacob and Kenneth N. Vines (eds.), *Politics in the American States* (Boston: Little, Brown and Company, 1965), pp. 217–232.

17. Columns two and four are drawn from "Budgetary Processes in the States," a survey conducted by the Georgia Office of Planning and Budget for the National Association of State Budget Officers, 3 January 1975 (draft). The other columns are drawn from "A Survey of Developments in State Budgeting," National Association of State Budget Officers, Systems, Techniques and Data Committee, April, 1975.

18. The Index of Inter-Party Competitiveness was developed by Richard I. Hoffer-

bert in "Classification of American State Party Systems," in *Journal of Politics*, 26 (August 1964): 550–567. It is a composite index based upon change of party control in presidential, senatorial, and gubernatorial—not legislative—contests from 1932 through 1962. Ranks are from 1 to 50. The state with the greatest party turnover ranks lowest.

19. The Compositive Innovation Score was developed by Jack L. Walker in "The Diffusion of Innovation Among American States," *American Political Science Review* 63 (September 1969): 880–899. It is a measure of a state's quick adoption of innovations developed elsewhere, particularly the adoption of new programs; the most "innovative" states rank highest.

20. US Bureau of the Census, *Governmental Finances, 1971–1972.*

21. "Ranking higher" means that total population, per capita income, proportion of legislatures with more complex organization, state and local expenditures, operating expenditures for the legislature, innovation scores, partisanship, and legislative professionalism scores tend to be higher in magnitude. (No preference is implied.)

22. See note 17.

23. For a thorough exploration of legislative considerations in exercising this discretion, see Edgar G. Crane, *Legislative Review of Program Effectiveness;* and *Legislative Review of Government Programs* (New York: Praeger, 1977).

24. Abdo I. Baaklini and James J. Heaphey, "Legislative Institution Building in Brazil, Costa Rica and Lebanon," *Sage Professional Papers in Administration and Policy Studies* (Beverly Hills, Calif: Sage, 1976).

25. James J. Heaphey and Eduardo Pereira, "Legislatures Impact SocioEconomic Change—The Brazilian Congress Enacts Land Reform," *COMMENT*, V. 2, No. 6, September 1975, (Albany: CDSC at SUNYA Publications).

Legislatures and Information Systems:

Challenges and Responses in the States

JOHN A. WORTHLEY

Among the most significant, consistent, and continuing reform movements in American state legislatures is the application of modern information technology to legislative information needs. This development has already had considerable impact on the policy-making activities of several state legislatures, and the movement appears to be rapidly expanding. The National Conference of State Legislatures, for example, has recently formed an information needs committee, which is focusing on the use of electronic data processing.

The central role of information in the public policy process has long been recognized. But until recently modern technologies were seldom employed by state legislatures to harness, process, and analyze relevant and desired information. During the past eight years, however, several states have taken strides in this direction. To the privation of practitioners as well as scholars very little is known of these developments despite their potentially major impact on the legislative institution and the public policy-making process. Not only are analyses of the developments and their impact lacking, but there have not even been factual descriptions of what has been and is transpiring.

This article is a start at filling that void. It ventures to make an empirical contribution by describing what exists as well as to provide an embryonic theoretical perspective useful to legislative innovators. It thus presents an account of recent developments in legislative information systems and suggests an analytical framework for studying those developments and their impact on both legislature and the political system as a whole. In particular, the discussion analyzes the implications of legislative information systems development for legislative policymaking ability, for executive and government agency roles in the political system, and for institutional development of the legislatures themselves. More broadly, the study hopes to provide a basis for evaluating the impact of the continuing trend toward application of modern technology to legislative information needs. While the discussion is restricted to the American scene, the challenge is not. Legislatures all over the world face the need for information systems. The experience of legislatures in the United States can be useful in addressing that challenge wherever it exists.

Setting: The Challenge

Over the past several years both traditional functions and new roles of American legislatures have crystallized broad information needs and challenges. Two dimensions of the phenomenon are apparent: one concerns internal legislative needs for information; the other relates to external needs, that is, legislative involvement in governmentwide information requirements.

Internally, recent increases and improvements in the activities of American state legislatures, enabling and engendering a more independent and cooperative relationship with the executive branch, have highlighted the importance of gathering and organizing information. Larger staffs, longer sessions, and expanded committee work reflect this development. Dechert,[1] Janda,[2] Chartrand,[3] Robinson,[4] and Weaver [5] have all discussed this subject. Perhaps the most prominent aspect of the situation is that with the growth of the information need there has been a simultaneous explosion in information availability. But mere availability of data does not assure its delivery or useability. Indeed, many legislative officials complain that they receive both too much and too little information. There can be so much data that it is overwhelming and thus not useable. It becomes a burden to absorb, evaluate, and classify even portions of the accumulated data. As a consequence, legislators often receive too little information, that is, not enough of the right kind of information, at the right time, in the right form. There is a great void in the area of information management, of turning reams of data into useable information. As Weaver puts it: "The problem is not that Congress gets too little information but that too little of the great mass it gets is relevant and readily, rapidly available." [6] All of this has produced a focus on development of computer-based information systems for handling the situation.

Legislatures need information on bills, budgets, and policy issues. Because of the ever increasing number of current bills introduced in legislatures, information on bill status is a challenging demand. Because so many past statutes pertain to current legislative efforts, statutory retrieval is also a major information challenge. The complexity and bulk of current public budgets present an enormous information problem for legislative budgetary processes, and the burgeoning legislative role in public policy and program formulation and evaluation entails a mammoth information requisite.[7]

In the external dimension, the legislature's traditional functions necessitate legislative judgment on executive agency requests for information systems resources. The progressive application of computer technology to executive information needs, involving major financial commitments, has made this legislative role both technically complex and all the more consequential. The challenges pertain chiefly to coordination of government information resources and protection of confidentiality rights. The numerous agencies of government each require data (frequently the same or similar data) and, consequently, information systems to perform their functions. Considerable problems of cost, inefficiency, and redundancy arise without some sort of interagency coordination.[8] While the executive can, and sometimes has,[9] provided a coordinating mechanism, the legislative function usually compels some kind of legislative involvement. Confidentiality of personal data held by executive agencies is more and more a problematic issue confronting legislatures. Federal laws mandating freedom of information as well as protection of privacy are forcing many state legislatures to meet this issue head on.[10] Finally, legislative appropriations and oversight functions necessitate further policy decisions on information systems existing and requested in government.

While these two dimensions of the information challenge have been periodically surveyed,[11] they have seldom been recognized as two interrelated aspects of the same issue. Yet, surely, solutions to the internal needs will be elusive if the two dimensions are not linked. Budget and program/policy information is normally located in executive agency data files. Thus the way the information systems of those agencies are structured affects, in no small way, the legislature's access to the information it needs. In like vein, the external problems of coordination and data confidentiality are typically so difficult that their solution must depend on a well-functioning legislative system. Just as a legislature finds it frustrating, if not impossible, to gain information from a disorganized executive information system, so too it is difficult to coordinate and make policy from agency information if the legislature has an underdeveloped or inoperative internal information system. The two dimensions are, in brief, intertwined and interdependent.

The first significant recognition of this interrelationship occurred in December 1974 at a conference cosponsored by the National Legislative Conference and the State University of New York at Albany. While previous conferences and writing on legislative information needs focused on the internal dimension alone, this conference considered both the internal and external challenges. The approach was based on an appreciation of the practical inseparability of the two dimensions.

In sum, the information challenge facing legislatures consists of two dimensions which can be conceptually distinguished and separately approached, but which are fundamentally related. Legislatures need to provide themselves with information systems. Legislatures need to provide other government institutions with information systems. The account of innovative responses which follows utilizes the conceptual distinction for purposes of clarity, but the analysis of those innovations stresses their interrelationship.

The Response: Innovations

The complex nature of the challenge and the availability of modern information technology have centered legislative response to the information needs problem on the use of electronic data processing (EDP), in particular, the computer. Thus, while there are many significant non-EDP associated innovations in the information needs area, this presentation is limited to EDP connected responses.[12]

The Internal Dimension

Since the early 1960s American state legislatures have seen the computer as a means of expanding and managing the legislative data base and of reducing the time required for members and staff to access and utilize information. Nearly all the states (forty-three) have successfully applied EDP in one or several areas: thirty-six utilize EDP for statutory search and retrieval, twenty-eight for bill status information, twenty-four for bill drafting, and twenty-three at widely varying levels of sophistication for fiscal/budgetary information.[13] Some of these states have been genuinely innovative both in actual use of EDP and, perhaps more importantly, in organizing for the use of EDP.

Innovative Applications. The norm in legislative use of EDP has been to take a rather narrow, cautious approach, limiting applications to procedural needs, such as bill status. But there have been some significant moves toward more substantive applications which provide legislatures with information that is directly useful in the decision-making processes. They are important to point out because they illuminate the potential inherent in computer applications to legislative purposes.

In 1973 the Florida legislature implemented an automated ombudsman system for gathering, classifying, and retrieving data in response to citizen requests for information on all facets of Florida government. The legislature used the system in determining areas where improvements could be made in state government. In systematizing constituent input, the program both helped the legislature serve the citizenry better and provided a means of bringing citizen sentiment to bear on the decision-making process.

Several states, notably California, Maine, New York, Minnesota, and Michigan have used EDP in various fiscal matters concerning education. Probably the most ambitious application was developed in the Michigan legislatures, where the Senate Fiscal Agency has gathered considerable education data on-line with the capability of aggregating by election district. The aggregation capacity has proven to be particularly well received by legislators whose voting on education policy bills can now be informed by more precise information about impact on their home district.

The New York Assembly has improved its budget review process, and strengthened its role vis-a-vis the executive, by developing a capacity to forecast state revenues and monitor the accuracy of estimates. Though this forecasting is of a rather simple, bench-mark type, it would not be feasible were it not computer based.[14] It is a salient example of how even the simple uses of EDP can produce major legislative improvement.

The California legislature was among the first to use EDP for committee research and analysis on federal aid formulas and control. Again a relatively simple application has improved the legislative budget process as well as the assistance the legislature was able to provide local jurisdictions.

A good example of a very specialized EDP application recently occurred in the New York legislature. Countrywide, interstate retaliatory taxation policies have forced states to restrict taxes on out-of-state insurers and to discriminate against in-state insurers. The problem is complex, as was New York's innovative solution. Suffice to say that by applying EDP to analysis of the problem, the New York legislature produced model legislation on the matter and, incidentally, prompted a cooperative arrangement with executive officials in the state.

While other innovative applications of EDP have been tested in American legislatures, those mentioned are representative and also indicative. They show that innovative uses of EDP information systems can provide significant assistance to legislative functions of policy formulation and review but that innovative applications of EDP in American legislatures have been notably sparse despite availability of the technology. A major reason for the later phenomenon, undoubtedly, is the fact that relatively few legislatures have established organizational means of bringing EDP operationally into the legislative process. It is thus pertinent to consider organizational innovations which have been developed.

Innovative Organizational Structures. The conventional experience of American legislatures has been to assimilate an internal EDP capacity rather informally, i.e., by placing the resource under an existing organizational structure. Typically, legislative EDP responsibility has been to the Legislative Council or to the secretary of the Senate or the Legislative Reference Service or a similar unit which, more often than not, possesses neither knowledge nor immediate interest in the uses of EDP for legislative needs. It is therefore not surprising that innovative applications of EDP have been rather few and slow developing. Currently, however, there appears to be considerable interest in a more satisfactory arrnagement for organizing EDP resources within legislatures.[15]

Pennsylvania led the way (1967) in organizing a strong centralized internal EDP unit. Since it has a professional staff of significant size as well as its own computer, the unit is a very independent structural organization. It provides EDP services to both houses and all committees. Called the Legislative Data Processing Center, the unit responds to ad hoc requests from legislators for information and analysis by undertaking activities such as borrowing computer tapes from executive agencies and massaging them to legislative purposes.

Florida has been a pioneer in legislative use of EDP,[16] but it employs a decentralized system. Organizationally, EDP responsibility was early assumed by the Joint Legislative Management Committee, which created two units for applying EDP: a Systems and Data Processing Division and an Informative Division. The former handles coordination and substantive applications, while the latter applies EDP to procedural areas, such as bill status. A third unit, the Management Systems Division of the Office of the Auditor General, a legislative agency, provides EDP linkage to executive data. Recently the legislature acquired its own computer. The net effect has been that Florida has incorporated EDP into its existing decentralized information system. This arrangement has been quite successful and productive, probably because a strong political commitment to use EDP existed from the beginning and, as in Pennsylvania, professional resources were allotted for the purpose.

In 1970 the Mississippi legislature created the State Central Data Processing Authority to provide centralized EDP services to all state agencies, including the legislature.[17] The authority consists of six legislators and a professional staff and is charged with coordinating state government use of EDP as well as with applying EDP to legislative processes. Prior to formation of the Authority, the Mississippi legislature had no EDP applications. Today it is developing a comprehensive computer-based legislative information system.

Texas developed an intricate and highly successful organizational arrangement,[18] in which the EDP coordination unit is part of the Legislative Council but is also under the direction of a legislative committee. The unit has its own professional staff but works closely with the Systems Division of the State Auditor's Office and the Division of Automation of the Highway Department, whose EDP resources the unit utilizes. While this arrangement resembles the Florida one it is more centralized organizationally and more decentralized operationally.

New York is developing an organizational innovation by equipping the Office of the Senate Legislative Leadership with EDP expertise. Procedural applications, such as bill status and budget applications, remain largely decentralized under the secretary of the Senate, the Finance Committee, etc. Policy applications are being centered in the leadership offices by development of staff expertise.

Illinois early (1967) developed a strong and effective mechanism for legislative use of EDP. It created a Legislative Information System Committee consisting of members of both houses and a professional staff. All EDP applications are centralized through the Committee. This organization provides both political linkage and expertise capacity. The system has experienced remarkable success. The Committee has developed a five-year plan for legislative application of EDP and repre-

Table 1

Legislative Information Systems
Internal Organization

State	Centralized	Decentralized	Own Computer	Outside Computer	Control Unit
Pennsylvania	x		x		Professional Director
Florida		x	x		Joint Committee
Mississippi	x			x	Legislative Committee
Texas	x			x	Joint Committee
New York		x		x	Leadership Office
Illinois	x			x	Joint Committee
Kansas	x			x	Legislative Council
Connecticut	x			x	Joint Committee
Oklahoma	x			x	Legislative Council

sents one of the most comprehensive and coordinated legislative systems existing today.

The External Dimension

EDP has been applied in state government since the 1950s. In most cases its use began on an ad hoc, uncoordinated basis which became more and more costly and redundant. Some legislatures acted early to coordinate statewide EDP resources; a few have yet to act; but most have mandated some kind of master planning of EDP resources. Typically, the legislature has passed a general statute requiring one executive agency to act as coordinator. Some legislatures have asserted innovative legislative involvement in this activity.

As early as 1957 the Minnesota legislature took a decisive role in coordinating the state EDP system. At that time it established a unit within the State Department of Administration to centralize EDP resources. A decade later the legislature directed that unit to develop a master plan for government use of EDP. the stated purpose of the plan was "to make available to the legislature and to officials of the Executive Branch comprehensive and accurate information in a form and at a time to be of maximum value in decision making and research." [19] The plan was ratified by the legislature, has been largely implemented, and today Minnesota is the most successful model of a centralized state EDP information system. Besides providing the state with fiscal efficiencies and resources for program effectiveness, the system gives the legislature a ready base for meeting its present and future information needs. Several other state legislatures, notably Arizona, Delaware, and Virginia are pursuing a similar path.

Mississippi developed a different means for successful EDP coordination. In 1970 the legislature established a State Data Processing Authority as a totally legislative agency. The Authority was to develop a master plan, which was successfully implemented two years ahead of schedule, the only example among US states of an EDP master plan not being behind schedule. Today the agency serves all legislative needs, as well as executive needs, and provides a ready capacity for increased legislative use of EDP. Significantly, the Mississippi legislature made no use of EDP until after this agency was established.

In 1970 the New Hampshire legislature established the Department of Centralized Data Processing and gave it a broad and comprehensive mandate to develop and operate a centralized EDP system for the state. The department was placed under the supervision of a commission consisting of legislators, executive officials, and private industry representatives. It, too, serves all legislative and excutive EDP needs. Washington has created a similar unit.[20]

Illinois has created a legislative commission with a comprehensive mandate to coordinate and oversee the state EDP system. As noted above, New Hampshire established a commission, but the Illinois design gives a much stronger mandate to the commission. The commission was largely responsible for creation of a strong central EDP system in the state through the Management Information Division of the Department of Finance. This unit has in turn been a key in development of an internal legislative EDP system.

Florida currently utilizes a coordinated decentralization system and is developing an innovative improvement to it. Several years ago the legislature placed responsibility for coordination of most executive EDP systems within an existing Department of General Services. At the same time the legislature developed its own EDP system and directed the auditor general also to play a coordination role in statewide EDP. Coordination was thus a joint responsibility. Currently the Ways and Means Committee of the Senate is developing a refinement which it calls "functional decentralization." According to the proposal,

Table 2

Legislative Authorized Organization of State Automated Information Systems

State	Centralized	Decentralized	Coordinating Mechanism
Minnesota	x		State Dept. of Administration
Arizona	x		State Dept. of Administration
Delaware	x		State Dept. of Administration
Virginia	x		State Dept. of Administration
Mississippi	x		Legislative Agency
New Hampshire	x		Independent Agency
Washington	x		Independent Agency
Illinois	x		Legislative Commission and Dept. of Finance
Florida		x	Dept. of General Services and Legislative Auditor General
Michigan		x	Governor's Office and Legislative Subcommittee
Texas		x	Legislative Auditor
New York		x	Budget Division
Wisconsin		x	State Dept. of Administration

the legislature would actively participate in the implementation, operation, maintenance, and evaluation of state EDP; the Department of Administration would be delegated responsibility to effect all legislative mandates; and eight functional systems (one of which is the legislative system) would be coordinated and interconnected. The result would be incorporation of the legislative system within the state system, while maintaining most characteristics of independence. Michigan has developed a similar concept.

Texas has an extremely decentralized approach to EDP coordination.[21] Since 1965 a Systems Division has existed within the Office of the State Auditor (who is, in Texas, a legislative agent). This division serves an EDP coordination function in an advisory manner, but its effect is strong because its recommendations to the legislature are influential. Though just as effective, this arrangement is less formalized than the Florida and Mississippi innovations.

Lessons: Experience and Impact

While more in-depth and long-term empirical study is needed before firm generalizations can be constructed the experience thus far with legislatures and information systems supports a number of important observations.

First, legislatures are confronting the information needs challenge in different ways. Though there is a long way yet to go, several legislatures are taking determined first steps, which will provide significant empirical experience for legislative reformers to study. Application of computer technology to internal legislative needs has proven useful. It has saved time, which is so rare a commodity for modern legislatures. It has assisted tremendously in such procedural operations as bill drafting. It has been a significant aid in managing and analyzing substantive information useful in policy-making. Moreover, though application of EDP technology to internal legislative information purposes has been hesitant and relatively unsophisticated when compared with applications in the executive branch, it can be argued that the slow, cautious approach of legislatures has been wise. Executive agencies and private industry have frequently hurried to use computers without first mastering the machine and evaluating its role and ramifications for operational and decision-making processes. As a result, millions of dollars were spent on machines which, in many cases, disrupted rather than assisted agency operations. Legislatures have been among the few institutions to resist the uncontrolled rush to computers.

In the external dimension, too, legislatures have been innovative. More than that, their efforts have been instrumental in improving government information systems. In California it appears that only constant prodding by the legislature turned talk of information systems coordination into action. In Washington the legislative action mentioned above salvaged a foundering executive EDP coordination program. The Texas and Florida experiences further support this observation.

Second, operational recognition that the internal and external dimensions are interdependent is emerging, and the desirability of an approach combining the two is supported by empirical experience. The Tallahassee Conference and the recent work of the National Association of State Information Systems (NASIS) are indications of this. In earlier years legislative information needs and governmentwide needs were seldom clearly connected.

The experience of the states studied indicates a direct relationship between the two dimensions—those states with a relatively well developed internal legislative information system also seem to have a relatively well developed external dimension in which legislative involvement has been instrumental. Indeed, this study discovered no well developed legislative information system in a state which does not have a well developed external dimension. The Texas, Illinois, and Florida legislatures, which are leaders in the development of internal legislative information systems, have also been among the leaders in organizing and coordinating statewide information systems. Similarly, Pennsylvania, Mississippi, Washington, and Minnesota evidence the positive relationship between the two dimensions. And New York and Georgia, both of which have faced difficulties in developing an internal legislative information system, are states whose governmentwide information system is uncoordinated and marked by a lack of legislative involvement. More research on this relationship would be useful in clarifying the dynamics of what appears to be a direct linkage significant to legislative reform.

Third, some internal organizational mechanism formally charged with applying EDP appears to be a key in legislative response to the information challenge. Those legislatures which have been the leaders in applying EDP generally have a designated information systems unit. Pennsylvania's is organized around a professional office, Illinois's under a committee of legislators, that of Texas under the Legislative Council and a committee of legislative agency heads, Florida's under three separate professional units, and Mississippi's is under an independent legislative agency. Though the variations of the arrangement are numerous, the common characteristic is that a definite organizational mechanism exists. Moreover, the experience of all of the legislatures studied indicates that the organizational arrangement employed should be carefully determined by the special characteristics of each legislature. The political climate of the Illinois legislature dictated that, to be successful, a legislative EDP unit should be directly under political control. Thus a committee of legislators was formed. In Pennsylvania, on the other hand, the political concern with information systems was much different, enabling a more independent professional unit to be created. In Florida the extent and organization of staff units necessitated a multiunit organizational mechanism for EDP. And New York, where the legislature has a strong leadership, faced difficulties developing an information system until recently, when development responsibility was placed under the leadership staff.

Fourth, the relatively slow development of legislative information systems may partially be explained by a need for professional information systems staff who combine EDP knowledge with an understanding of and sensitivity to the legislative process and who recognize the computer as merely one tool for facilitating the legislative process. Such staff are rare, but those legislatures with developed information systems have all had such personnel. New York is a good example. Despite the lack of an organizational unit charged with substantive EDP applications, the New York Assembly produced the innovations dealing with revenue forecasting and insurance legislation. The reason this was possible was that New York had staff who were both knowledgeable in EDP and experienced in the legislative process.[22] (Undoubtedly an additional factor was that the innovation developed in the Ways and Means Committee staff, which is the leadership staff of the New York Assembly.)

The message here for legislative reformers is that information systems should help sharpen the policy-makers' judgment rather than presume that information alone dictates a proper decision. Professional information systems staff sometimes forget that information provides only one among several sets of parameters which the legislator must consider,[23] and the fact that they do has caused legislators to distrust and therefore deemphasize information systems.

Fifth, the state legislatures' experience suggests that traditional organizational notions, in particular the centralization/decentralization concept, may be largely moot issues. This study would conclude that in organizing legislative information systems as well as governmentwide information systems, the pertinent point is to organize well (whether it be in a centralized or decentralized mode) and to base the organizational design on the institutional characteristics of the legislature and the state as a whole.[24]

Sixth, clearly the development of computer-based information systems has a significant impact on the legislature's relationship with other government institutions. Without its own source of useable information the legislature has in the past typically relied on and deferred to the executive version, but with an information system of its own the legislature can function from a strengthened position. More rigorous study is needed to clarify the relationship, but the present study indicates that legislatures with developed information systems do indeed function more influentially vis-à-vis the executive and the bureaucracy. In Michigan and New York a notable example of this has been in the area of state aid to education, where a computerized data base has substantially increased the legislature's role in policy-making.

Beyond improving its "competitive" positions vis-à-vis other government institutions, there is evidence that legislative information system capacity improves the legislature's role, i.e., tends to improve cooperative interaction between the legislature, the governor, and the bureaucracy. In New York the legislative information analysis ability prompted a cooperative effort with the executive regarding insurance legislation. In Florida the legislature's establishment of an ombudsman capacity prompted several executive agencies to establish or up-grade their own constituent relations offices. In other words, improvement of legislative information systems may very well help reform the governmental system as a whole.

Seventh, development of legislative information systems has serious implications for power distribution within the legislature. The computer is a well-recognized source of power and therefore a potential threat to existing power structure. Legislators' instinctive appreciation of this may explain the relatively slow development of legislative information systems and the various organizational forms information systems have taken when adopted. Realizing that information systems staff could become quite powerful, that they could, in effect, reduce the area of legislator discretion, legislatures initially reacted against using computers. When they have been introduced, EDP units have been set up to accommodate existing power interests within the legislature. In Florida the information system was distributed to maintain the existing internal power distribution, while in New York the EDP capacity is being placed so as to further strengthen the power base of the leadership. Careful consideration of the practical impact on internal power distribution may thus be a key to successful development of internal legislative information systems.

On a theoretical level, the power of a professional information system staff could pose a threat to the political function of the legislature, i.e., could undermine rather than support the discretion of the elected member. The experience to date, however, indicates that legislatures have been instinctively alert to this danger and have been careful to control the incorporation of EDP capability in the legislature.

Eighth, legislative information systems development has significant implications for the policy-making as well as the representative functions of the legislature. Information and the ability to harness it is surely a critical component of the public policy process and therefore, presumably, the better the legislature's information, the stronger its role in policy-making. This study clearly shows that to be the case: an improved information system facilitates improved policy analysis and a more effective role in policy deliberations with the executive. The cases of Michigan and New York regarding state aid to education policy are representative; in both cases the development of a legislative information system has enabled the legislature to take a determining posture in an area of policy analysis in which previously, for lack of information capability, they generally had to defer to executive branch analyses.

In terms of the representative function of the legislature the Florida ombudsman innovation illuminates the potential impact of information system development.

Ninth, finally, the evolution and "simplification" of computer technology is having a clear impact on legislative responses to the information challenge. Whereas a decade ago computers were very expensive, complex, and understood only by an elite, today computer costs are sinking and the average person is being exposed to them early in life and continuously through it. As a result, government officials are generally more at ease and familiar with EDP uses, and the pool of professional staff prospects who are skilled in both the legislative process and in EDP is on the rise. The result is increasingly efficacious use of EDP in meeting information needs.

Conclusion

The challenge of information needs facing legislatures is formidable. The boggling volume of data available and pertinent, combined with the imposing nature of the technology available has created a major burden requiring innovative action. Indeed, conquest of this challenge may be crucial to meeting other challenges relating to legislative reform and innovation, for information capacity is fundamental. In the words of Francis Rourke: "The efforts of legislatures to regain their lost status focus on the improvement of their data gathering ability, by either improved staffing or the use of computers and other informational hardware." [25] This study has found that American state legislatures have experienced significant innovative responses to the challenge and that these efforts are providing a wealth of empirical data for evaluating the impact of information systems on legislative institutions.

Author's Note

The descriptive data included in this analysis resulted from an in-depth study of information systems in twenty-three states. Official documents were examined and key personnel interviewed during field trips to Virginia, Georgia, Wisconsin, Texas, Illinois, New York, Michigan, Minnesota, Florida, and Tennessee. In addition, officials of the National Association of State Information Systems, as well as of the Information Needs Committee of the National Conference of State Legislatures, provided useful data. The author obtained information on states not personally visited through letters and phone calls to information systems officials.

Notes

1. Charles R. Dechert, "Availability of Information for Congressional Operations" in Alfred de Grazia (ed.) *Congress: The First Branch of Government.* (Washington: American Enterprise Institute, 1966).

2. Kenneth Janda, "Information Systems for Congress," in de Grazia, *Congress.*

3. Robert L. Chartrand et al., *Information Support, Program Budgeting, and the Congress.* (New York: Spartan, 1968).

4. James A. Robinson, "Decision Making in Congress" in de Grazia, *Congress.*

5. Warren Weaver, *Both Your Houses.* (New York: Praeger, 1972).

6. *Ibid.*, p. 165.

7. These needs, at the congressional level, were recently clarified and documented by the Legislative Reorganization Act Implementation Planning Task Team, "Preliminary Analysis of Congressional Information Needs," Washington, 19 October 1973.

8. See National Association of State Information Systems (NASIS), *Information Systems Technology in State Government, 1973 Report.* (Lexington: Council of State Governments, 1974).

9. See John A. Worthley and Lenore L. Heaphey, "EDP Systems Coordination: The States Experience," *Comment* 2, 4 (May 1975): 1–8.

10. See John A. Worthley, "Legislators Confront Privacy Invasion," *Comment* 2, 3 (March 1975): 1–4.

11. See NASIS, *Information Systems Technology*, for a survey of the external dimension and James E. Elkins, "A Survey of the Use of Electronic Data Processing by State

Legislatures," The University of Georgia, 1974, for a compilation of developments in the internal dimension.

12. Some internal innovations are described in Elkins, "Use of Electronic Data Processing"; in Congressional Research Service, *Modern Information Technology in the State Legislatures* (Washington: Government Printing Office, 1972); and in Congressional Research Service, *The Congress and Information Technology* (Washington: GPO, 1972), Chapter 7. The Elkins survey is very cursory and the Congressional Research Service efforts are both out of date. There is no survey of external innovations. The information presented below is based on extensive research in the states.

13. These figures are reported in Elkins, "Use of Electronic Data Processing."

14. The application is described in Robert J. Morgado, "Revenue Forecasting: The Approach of the New York State Assembly Ways and Means Committee," *Comment* V. 2, No. 1, January 1975, (Albany: CDSC at SUNYA Publications).

15. The December 1974 Conference on Legislative Information Needs held in Tallahassee, Florida indicated this developing trend.

16. See *Florida Legislative Information and Processing System: Conceptual Description*, Office of Auditor General, April 1973.

17. See Central Data Processing Authority, *Master Plan for Data Processing Activities*, Jackson, Mississippi, January 1974.

18. See Texas Legislative Council, *Report on the Legislative Information System of Texas*, Austin, Texas, February 1974.

19. *Information Systems in the State of Minnesota* (St. Paul, Minn.: Department of Administration, 1970).

20. See Washington State Data Processing Authority, *Comprehensive Plan*, December 1974.

21. Office of the State Auditor, *Annual Report*, Austin, Texas, 1974.

22. See Morgado, "Revenue Forecasting."

23. See Victor G. Neilson, "Why Evaluation Does Not Improve Program Effectiveness," *Policy Sciences* (Spring 1975): 385–390.

24. Because of the wealth of variations which can be empirically studied, the area of information systems provides a rich field for further research on the centralization/decentralization theme.

25. Francis E. Rourke, "Administrative Secrecy: A Comparative Perspective," *Public Administration Review* 35, 1 (Jan/Feb 1975): 2.

Institutional Development and Legislative Effectiveness:

Rules Changes in the Wisconsin Assembly

RONALD D. HEDLUND and KEITH E. HAMM

Inherent in any analysis of a political decision-making institution, like a state legislature, must be an assessment of the performance of that institution in making choices. Such an assessment, to be valid, should evaluate three relevant components—personnel operating within the system (*e.g.*, their strengths and limitations), the institution's relations with its social environment (*e.g.*, existing levels of support and demand input), and the internal structuring of the institution to facilitate its operations (*e.g.*, the rules and procedures used in decision-making). Further, attention must be directed toward the relative effectiveness of these components in advancing the decision-making capacity. Political scientists have given both direct and indirect attention to all of these factors, but in recent years relatively greater emphasis has been placed upon the first two. Concern with the effects of formalized rules and procedures on the decision-making ability of legislators and legislatures became primarily the domain of legislative support agencies,[1] reform-oriented organizations,[2] and a limited number of academics.[3] Political science interest in such structural features seemed to wane during the "behavioral revolution," yet recent small-group and organizational research indicates that internal institutional constraints cannot be ignored.[4]

The research reported here is based upon a cross-time study

of one legislative body, the Wisconsin Assembly, from 1971–74. The goal is to determine the impact of systematic changes in the formalized rules and procedures for decision-making from 1971–72 to 1973–74. A longitudinal, quasi-experimental design seems appropriate since, as we shall later show, these two sessions greatly resemble one another in many features except for the rules changes under study here. In the following sections we shall discuss our theoretical orientation toward institutional change, discuss the setting for this study, outline our perspective on the role of formalized rules and procedures in legislative decision-making, make an operational series of legislature-level measures of institutional performance in decision-making, and present the results when two differing sets of conditions prevail.

While the primary concern of this research is the effects these rules changes had on the performance of the Wisconsin Assembly, the findings have direct implications for the broader issues raised throughout this volume: How have the new rules and procedures affected the Assembly's relations with other institutions? Have the changes affected the power distribution within the legislature? What do these findings imply regarding the policy functioning of the Assembly? And how do these findings regarding legislative performance relate to the functioning of a representative legislature? Although we make no claim that this single study of Wisconsin necessarily applies to other settings, our conclusions do suggest adopting a new outlook regarding the effects of institutional change on an institution's capability for decision-making.

Institutional Change and State Legislatures: The Theoretic Base

To observe that American state legislatures, like their national, regional, and local counterparts throughout the world, are subject to change and development is to state the obvious. Recent widespread increases in state legislative salaries and support services and reapportionment of legislative districts are only the most visible demonstrations of this point. Legislative institutions are constantly evolving in response to a number of general and specific external and internal factors. Some of these changes may be so subtle as to elude the casual observer, while others are so dramatic and far-reaching that they restructure the legislature entirely. Inhibiting the political scientist's study of legislative change has been the absence of a comprehensive theory of institutional development. Yet political scientists have affirmed the importance of change in considering legislative institutions.

> Predicting the consequences of changes in political institutions, particularly in regard to the performance of these institutions, should certainly be one of the major purposes of political science. . . . Purposeful as well as accidental structural changes will continue to be made, and it behooves us to understand something about the linkages between institutional characteristics and the behavior of the political system.[5]

Specification of a theoretical orientation is prerequisite to any systematic study of institutional change. After reviewing the literature, two alternative solutions were considered for use in this study. The first option involved adopting a "reformist orientation." Such a framework views the consideration of legislative change as a problem concerned with devising a more adequate "mechanism" for converting legislative inputs into public policy. Typical of this approach is the recent Citizen's Conference on State Legislatures report analyzing and comparing the performance of the fifty state legislatures on five dimensions—functionality, accountability, informedness, independence, and representativeness.[6] Using multiple indicators of each dimension, the study ranks every state according to the specific indicators and makes suggestions for change intended to "improve" legislative performance. Guiding these recommendations is an implicit framework for assessing legislative performance, summarized by seventy-three specific criteria. Although these criteria are logically derived and make intuitive sense, they are not an interrelated set of propositions and generalizations which could be labeled an explanatory theory. Thus, while an impressive and unique set of empirical data were collected for every state legislature and logical recommendations for change were made upon the basis of findings, the reformist approach used therein and elsewhere is basically "atheoretic," value laden, and presumptive regarding change and its consequences. A reformist orientation was therefore deemed unlikely to offer the desiderata sought for our study of institutional change in the Wisconsin Assembly.

The second alternative involved using political and social science notions of system change and its antithesis, stability. Recent work by social psychologists like Katz, Kahn, and Allen and political scientists like Deutsch, Easton, Huntington, and Almond and Powell serve as sources for the notions of system change which may be elaborated into a comprehensive theory appropriate for assessing institutional development in state legislatures.[7] Throughout all of this literature is the presumption that social systems undergo change. In discussing the systems approach to political science, Easton noted:

> It is clear, therefore, that if a systems conceptualization suggests little else, it does present a dynamic model of a political system. . . . A political system is a goal-setting, self-transforming and creatively adaptive system. It consists of human beings who are capable of anticipating, evaluating, and acting constructively to prevent disturbances in the system's environment. In the light of their goals, they may seek to correct any disturbances that might be expected to occasion stress.[8]

Similarly, Deutsch included notions of change in his communications model of politics.

> Every autonomous decision system . . . eventually is likely to rearrange its own inner structure, and these changes may be either viable or pathological . . . depending on whether they increase or decrease the probability of the future successful functioning of the system. . . .[9]

This apparent inevitability of change in a social system raises questions about the conditions fostering such change, the essence of such change, and the outcomes of such change. Understanding these facets becomes an important requisite for building an adequate theory of institutional changes and development.

Prior theories of social change have tended to view system change as the consequence of disturbances, crisis, and stress in the system and/or in its environment, which are directed toward the system. As such conditions arise, the system is given an impetus for change and development. In discussing such change, Deutsch argued for using the "feedback" concept. In this context feedback from prior performance may provide the system with

> . . . a major internal imbalance or disequilibrium that functions as its drive, in the sense that the system tends to move toward a state in which this internal disequilibrium will be reduced, or more loosely expressed, in which its internal "tension" will be lowered. Moreover, this inner disequilibrium must be of a particular kind, such that it can be reduced by bringing the whole system into some particular situation or relation vis-à-vis the outside world. This situation of the system to the outside world we may call a *goal situation*, or briefly, a *goal:* once the system has reached such a goal its inner disequilibrium will be lower.[10]

Therefore, if a social system encounters negative feedback from its prior performance, the system may seek some type of accommodation—change—so that it can reduce disequilibrium. Failure to reduce such disequilibrium creates the potential for system disintegration and disappearance. As applied to legislative institutions, this approach to change would argue that so long as the persons, structures, and processes associated with the legislature perform tolerably well in keeping its level of internal disturbance low, a state of "homeostasis" exists. However, when a legislature is no longer capable of controlling disturbance caused by feedback, a state of stress or crisis will result. This state will remain until the legislative institution adapts so that it can develop a new relationship with its environment, or until the crisis forces the system to disappear. Thus, it is in the best interests of everyone associated with a system for accommodation to take place when sufficient stress appears.

In order to convey this notion of system accommodation over time, we have taken two models suggested by Grumm—one a variant of the familiar Eastonian political systems model and the other a variant of the Wold-Jureen economic supply-price-demand model—and combined and modified them for use with a legislative system.[11] This model—Figure 1—depicts the environment, input, processor, and output components of a legislative system and their interrelationships over five points in time. The environment provides two types of input for the legislature—stressful inputs in the form of demands and negative support and sustaining inputs in the form of resources and positive support. These inputs enter the processor—the legislature which is composed of persons, structures, and processes—which acts upon them converting inputs into outputs—public policies which provide rewards and deprivations. This conversion process requires progression from one time frame to the next. Outputs are in turn transmitted through feedback to the environment and the processor from the second to the third time frame and serve to formulate, in part, the nature of the environmental inputs and the character of the processor at the third point in time. Partial continuity exists in the various components of the model across time. For example, the horizontal arrows indicate the continuity across time of environmental conditions, processor—personnel, structure, and process—and output base. Although this is a simplified model for legislative change, it combines a number of elements taken from a systems approach with several dynamic features of system change. All of the basic elements of a systems approach remain—environment, inputs, processor, outputs, and feedback—including the hypothesized interrelationships among them. In addition, dynamic elements are specifically included to call attention to change in the environment, change in the relationship between the environment and the system, change in the internal disturbances within the system, and change in system performance. This is the dynamic model we postulate for institutional change and it is this model which suggests the hypotheses we test here.

The Wisconsin Assembly, 1971–1974

The setting for this study was the lower house of the Wisconsin legislature during the 1971–1974 period. A number of discrete studies of the Wisconsin legislature have concluded that the Senate and Assembly are professionalized and institutionalized in comparison with other states. For example, Chaffey compares Wisconsin with Montana on several legislative

Figure 1

Cross-Time Model of Legislative System Change

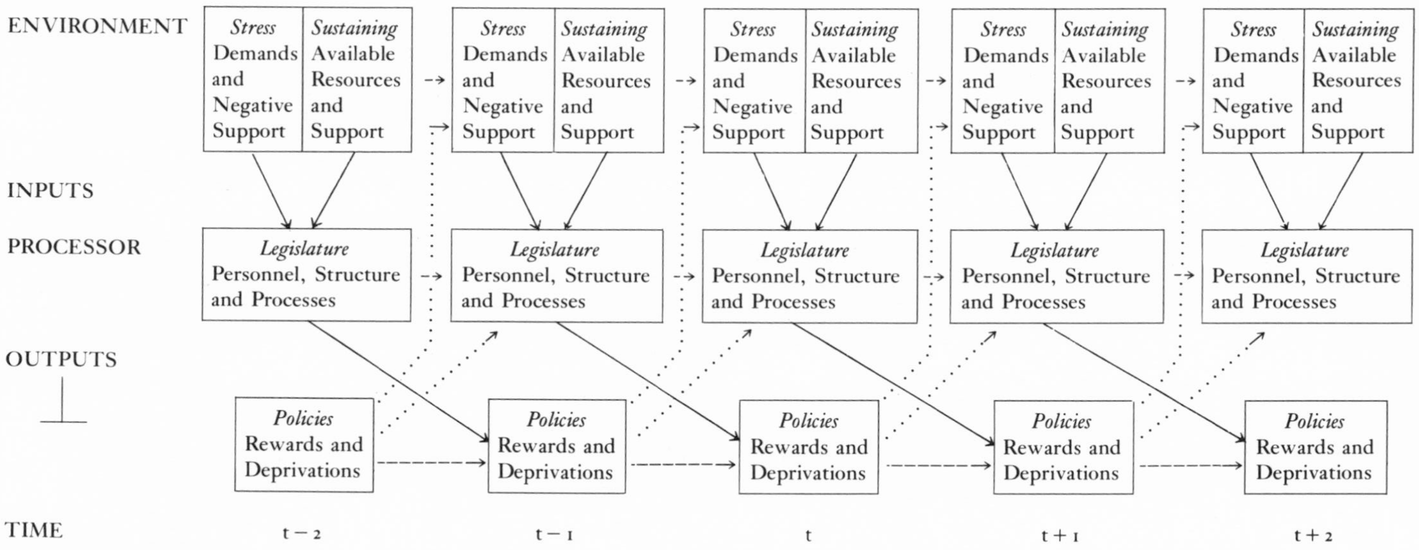

Key: Solid lines indicate direct flow
Broken lines indicate continuity effects
Dotted lines indicate feedback

operations which serve as indicators of institutionalization and uses Wisconsin as the example of an institutionalized, professional legislature.[12] The Citizen's Conference on State Legislatures study of the fifty states ranks Wisconsin fifth overall on their five dimensions. Wisconsin ranks near the top in four of these categories—seventh in functionality, third in informedness, fourth in independence, and tenth in representativeness—and low in only one: twenty-first in accountability.[13] Rosenthal, in his study of state legislative committees, reports on self-evaluations by seven state legislatures including Wisconsin. Wisconsin has the highest ranking for constituent service and policy and program formulation among the states studied and the second highest ranking on policy and program control.[14] All of these independent evaluations lead us to conclude that Wisconsin is, in comparison with other state legislatures, highly professionalized and institutionalized.

However, the professionalization and institutionalization of a legislature should not be perceived as insulating forces creating a system completely immune from environmental disturbances. For example, an increase in the number of stress inputs may be of such a magnitude that the existing information handling capability of the legislature is not sufficiently organized to respond in an adequate manner.[15] Such an imbalance between system and environment may force the system to alter its internal arrangement to cope adequately with the increasing stress.

The Wisconsin Assembly after 1961 is an example of an institution experiencing a dramatic increase in demand inputs, as measured by the number of bills introduced. Figure 2 demonstrates the changing level of demand inputs for the twenty-year period beginning in 1953. The most noteworthy change is in the unprecedented increase in the demands made during the 1971–72 session. An increase at this rate may have seriously affected the information handling capacity of this decision-making body. Thus, the Assembly offers an appropriate setting to assess the nature of institutional change in response to demands using a quasi-experimental, longitudinal research design. A series of systematic rules changes made after the 1971–72 session, and discussed in the next section, serve as the "natural setting treatment" for assessing the effects of institutional change

Figure 2

Percentage Increase in the Number of Bills
Introduced into the Wisconsin Assembly
(1951 Base)

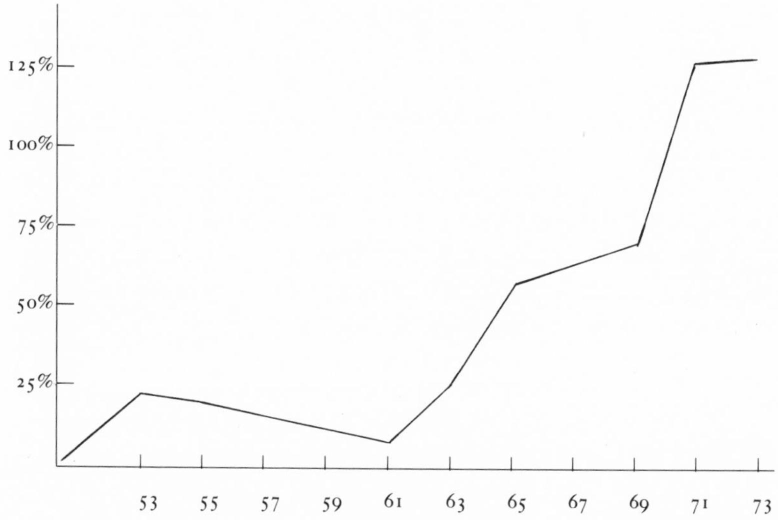

on the capacity of this decision-making body to cope with an increase in demand inputs. Our special interest is in the positive and negative effects these rules changes had on legislative performance.

Given that our research design is quasi-experimental and that a number of factors are likely to affect legislative performance in addition to the experimental treatment under study, our concern must be with the potential effects of these other nontreatment causal variables. (Since we were not capable of controlling the effects of these other variables, our concern was that their impact be either constant or random over the period studied.) As displayed in Table 1, the Assembly operated under a set of fairly stable conditions across the two sessions under consideration. System resources, the actual resources which a state has at its disposal, do not vary across sessions. Demand input from agencies or interest groups, as measured by executive, party controlling the Wisconsin Senate, and interest groups registered, is included, since the demands cannot be directly inferred from system resources; rather they must be communicated by individuals in the society. In this case, the variables show only slight or no variation between sessions. The internal decisional system must also be taken into account if one is to test accurately the effects of the rules changes. Legislative professionalism, as measured by the turnover in membership and the number of terms served,[16] is constant over the 1971–1972 and 1973–1974 sessions. Partisan balance, the extent to which one party dominates the Assembly, is also roughly equal for the two sessions. Variation does exist in leadership positions, but these differences are partially obviated by the somewhat predictable and automatic pattern of leadership succession, *i.e.*, Representative Anderson and Representative Shabaz became speaker and minority floor leader respectively after having served apprenticeships in other leadership positions. In addition, personal characteristics of the legislators, *i.e.*, educational level, occupational status, and age, are also roughly of the same magnitude. The informal norms of the Assembly are assumed to be the same given the continuity in membership from session to session. No appreciable difference was noted in the staff services available to representatives across these sessions. Thus, other potential causal factors appear constant over the 1971–1974 period.

Formal Rules and the Wisconsin Assembly

One of the requisites usually cited for the existence and maintenance of social organizations is regulation of behavior via formal rules. In political decision-making bodies like state legislatures, satisfying this requisite is critical; and few, if any, legislatures exist without formalized rules and procedures. Recent textbooks on the legislative process have noted the pervasiveness of formal rules. The comments of Jewell and Patterson are typical.

> Formal rules and procedures are among the most important functional requisites of a legislative body. Together with the informal rules of the game . . . they constitute the primary means of normative regulation for legislators. It is difficult to imagine a legis-

> lature or any other organization existing and functioning for long without clearly defined rules.[17]

From a functional point of view, then, formal rules and procedures appear to play a critical role in the maintenance of a legislative system.

Formal rules serve this purpose because of the variety of vital functions they perform for the organization. Keefe and Ogul categorize these functions on both a specific and a general level.

> Rules serve a multiplicity of purposes. They establish the order of business and provide for priorities and regularity in its consideration; they dilute opportunities for arbitrary and capricious treatment of the minority; they offer customary and traditional ways for settling disputes and for coming to decisions; and, in their perpetuation from year to year and decade to decade, they impart continuity to the life of the chamber. Their essence is *systematization*, their major contribution *orderliness.*[18]

In summary, formal rules perform these regulating functions by establishing a regular order of business, assuring an orderly manner for processing demands, protecting segments of the system and the polity from unfair treatment, expediting settlement of disputes through routinized procedures, and providing continuity for the structure in which legislative decisions are made.

Although formal rules and procedures are generally conceived to be part of the structural context in which decisions are made, they also have another effect. Legislative case studies have demonstrated numerous instances in which the nature of the formal rules affected the outcomes of decisions and even the nature of the proposed solutions. Two congressional observers, Bibby and Davidson, noted this interrelationship in their study of depressed-areas legislation.

> . . . "the rules" have influence over legislative outcomes. They are resources, and mastery of them is a form of power in Congress. . . . the rules are nevertheless not independent of the power struggle that lies behind them. There is very little that the houses cannot do under the rules, so long as the action is backed up by the votes and inclination. Yet votes and inclination are not easily obtained, and the rules persistently challenge the propo-

Table 1

Control Variables for Each Legislative Session in the Wisconsin Assembly

Control Variables	Session 1971–72	Session 1973–74
System Resources:		
Percent in SMSA[1]	58.9	58.9
Percent Employed Manufacturing[1]	24.8	25.2
Demand Input from Agencies or Interest Groups:		
Governor	Governor Lucey Democrat	Governor Lucey Democrat
Senate	20 Republicans 13 Democrats	18 Republicans 15 Democrats
Interest Groups[2]	394	395
Lobbyists[2]	531	485
Internal Decisional System:		
First Term Members	29%	29%
Number Previous Terms (For 1945–67 Average = 2.25)[3]	2.23 average	2.23 average
Partisan Balance	66 Democrats 34 Republicans	62 Democrats 37 Republicans
Leadership		
Speaker[4]	Rep. Huber	Rep. Anderson
Majority Floor Leader[4]	Rep. Anderson	Rep. Earl

nents of legislation to demonstrate that they have both resources at their command.[19]

Formal rules not only are an important element in the context of legislative decision-making, but they also have a direct as well as an indirect impact on the decisions that are made.

Like most other legislatures, the Wisconsin Assembly is governed by a series of rules regulating the conduct of individuals and groups within this legislative system. Predictably, rules are included to cover the role of elected officers, the process by which legislation is presented and considered, the duties of committees in the deliberative process, and the details of legislative debate and decision-making. During the 1960s few major

Table 1 continued

Minority Floor Leader	Rep. Froehlich	Rep. Shabaz
Assistant Minority Floor Leader	Rep. Shabaz	Rep. Thompson
Educational Level[5]		
Not Beyond High School	20%	18%
College Degree	49%	52%
Higher Degree	30%	31%
Occupational Status[5]		
Attorney	20%	19%
Farmer	15%	12%
Retired	3%	4%
Other	62%	64%
Age Average[5]	44 Years	42.5 Years
Salary[5]	$8900	$9900
Informal Norms	Assumed Constant Over Period	
Staff Services	Slight Increase Over Period	

[1] Figures provided by the Bureau of Research Statistics, Wisconsin Department of Industry and Human Relations.

[2] Figures supplied by the Division of Elections and Records, Office of the Secretary of State.

[3] David Ray, "Membership Stability in Three State Legislatures: 1883–1969," *American Political Science Review* 68 (March 1974): 110.

[4] On 18 December 1971 Representative Huber resigned from office to accept an executive appointment. He was succeeded as speaker by Representative Anderson. Representative Earl became the majority floor leader.

[5] Figures provided by the Wisconsin Legislative Reference Bureau.

changes were made in these rules.[20] At the beginning of the 1971–1972 session, two moderately important changes were brought about because of a tremendous increase in the level of demand for policy decisions with its resulting potential for system stress and because of a change in the Wisconsin constitution calling for annual sessions of the legislature. The first of these changes involved a modification in the scheduling of work throughout the two-year session. Four successive floor sessions were to be scheduled by resolution at the beginning of each session, three to occur during the first year of the biennium and one to occur during the second. The intent was to provide committees, especially the important Joint Finance Committee, time to meet during the early part of the session so that the flow of legislation to the floor could be regularized and made more constant. The second alteration was an informal consequence of the change in scheduling. It involved no formal rule change but was important because it informally modified the procedures by which bills were scheduled. Under the new arrangement, the majority floor leader became a critical checkpoint for determining when bills were scheduled in the Assembly. Although the four periods within the session facilitated a sustained work schedule throughout the two-year period, many important pieces of legislation did not come to a vote; the familiar end-of-the-session "log jam" reappeared; and many legislators, reporters and citizens felt frustrated because the legislature was not able to vote on certain legislation. In light of the constantly increasing level of demand input and the apparent inability of the Assembly and Senate to respond to the resulting system stress, the stage was set for a series of additional changes in the system which were intended to improve the information-handling capacity.

The rules changes proposed by the Democratic leadership at the outset of the 1973–1974 session, and eventually enacted, met with considerable skepticism from virtually all Republicans and from some Democrats. Much of the reluctance was generated because of the perceived "sweeping" impact of the three major changes being proposed. The first change gave to what previously had been a "housekeeping" committee—the Rules Committee—the power to make any measure a special order of business that would take precedence over all other measures after a request from any member. Ordering debate and amendment limits during floor consideration and designating floor managers to oversee the debate process were also provisions of this first change. The floor deliberations aspects of this proposal were similar to the powers held by the Rules Committee in the U.S. House. The second rules change implemented a discharge petition for removing measures from committees. If a committee held a proposal for twenty-one days and failed to report it out, a petition signed by at least fifty of the ninety-nine members could withdraw that measure and place it on a calendar. This procedure supplemented a provision permitting withdrawal of a bill from a committee by a majority vote. The third major change placed automatic limitations on debate if the Assembly was one or more days behind its scheduled calendar. Under this provision, debate on any question was limited to twenty minutes with five minutes being the maximum time for any speaker. The arguments offered in support of the rules changes centered around abstract notions of improving legislative responsiveness and reasonableness by ending the mass confusion associated with the last days of a session. The majority floor leader defended these as responsible steps which could bring about greater effectiveness and help insure consideration of important legislation. The opposition, however, stressed the effects these rules changes could have upon the individual legislator. The debate limitation was called a "gag rule." One of the more senior Republicans with twenty years service noted that this change represented a departure from the prior practice of unrestricted debate. He stated:

> This legislative body has been noted nationally for its fairness and the way it operates. . . . There has been a long tradition of listening to what anybody has to say.[21]

Further arguments against the Rules Committee's new role centered around a belief that this change could further centralize power in the leadership's hands. Thus the competing arguments seemed to be greater legislative efficiency in performing its decision-making function versus the centralization of power in the leadership with an associated diminuation of individual prerogatives.

In order to secure passage of these changes, the Democratic leadership turned the normally brief and perfunctory first day of the session into a two-day battle. They pressured Democrats, using strategies like withholding announcements of Democratic committee assignments and chairmanships until after adoption of the new rules and continuing debate into the late evening hours. These tactics, plus the persuasion based on general frustrations from the previous session, were successful. On the final adoption vote, fifty-seven Democrats and four Repub-

Table 2

Perceived Reasons for the Introduction of New Rules by the 1973–74 Session of the Wisconsin Assembly According to Party (percentages by column)

	Party	
Perceived Reason	Democratic	Republican
Efficiency	57	49
Efficiency and Effectiveness	26	3
Effectiveness	8	3
Political Leadership	2	35
Political Leadership and Efficiency	7	10
Total Percentage	100	100
N	53	29

licans voted for adoption and twenty-eight Republicans and four Democrats voted against; five Republicans and one Democrat did not vote.

During brief interviews with eighty-eight of the ninety-nine representatives shortly after the adoption of these new rules and procedures, a majority of both Democrats and Republicans thought these changes were proposed for reasons of efficiency and effectiveness; only a few more than one-third of the Republicans perceived that the desire for increased power for the leadership was an important factor (see Table 2).

Legislative Performance: Operational Measures and Hypotheses

The problem for study in this report concerns the Wisconsin Assembly's capacity to perform its decision-making function under two sets of conditions which correspond to the 1971–1972 session and the 1973–1974 session. As we have shown, these sessions differ primarily with regard to one major characteristic—the nature of the formal rules and procedures governing decision-making. Other potential differences likely to affect the decision-making capacity are either assumed to be constant over the two sessions—*e.g.*, the factors listed in Table

1—or are assumed to be random in their effects across the two periods studied. Thus our major independent variable is legislative session.

The greatest potential difficulty with regard to making the concepts used in this study operational arises from the phenomenon to be explained—legislative performance. Prior studies of system operations have usually encountered great difficulty when formulating measures of system performance and have frequently avoided specifying any measures.[22] Recent studies of social and political systems have tended to equate measures of performance with effectiveness. Katz and Kahn defined effectiveness

> . . . as the extent to which all forms of energic return to the organization are maximized. This is determined by a combination of the efficiency of the organization as a system and its success in obtaining, on advantageous terms, the inputs it requires.[23]

Congruent with this definition is Price's equation of effectiveness with a system's achievement of its goals.[24] In both definitions, effectiveness involves more than the internal operations of a system. Inherent is how the system relates to its external environment in terms of inputs and outputs. In this report our concern is with the legislature's effectiveness in performing its decision-making functions.

Effectiveness in this context is generally conceded to be a multidimensional concept. Thus, we began making effectiveness an operational factor by specifying four major dimensions taken from Price—productivity, expeditiousness, efficiency, and adaptiveness. Each dimension was, in turn, specified, using multiple indicators which could be observed directly (see Figure 3). Productivity conveys the notion of the system's ability to transform demand inputs into decisions. An increase in the information-handling capability, which the streamlined and centralized 1973–1974 formal rules should produce, should affect the system's productivity positively.

> H_1: Productivity, as indicated by the eight operational measures, should be higher for the 1973–1974 session of the Wisconsin Assembly than for 1971–1972.

Figure 3

Operational Measures and Dimensions of Concept
"Effectiveness in Performing Decision-Making Functions"

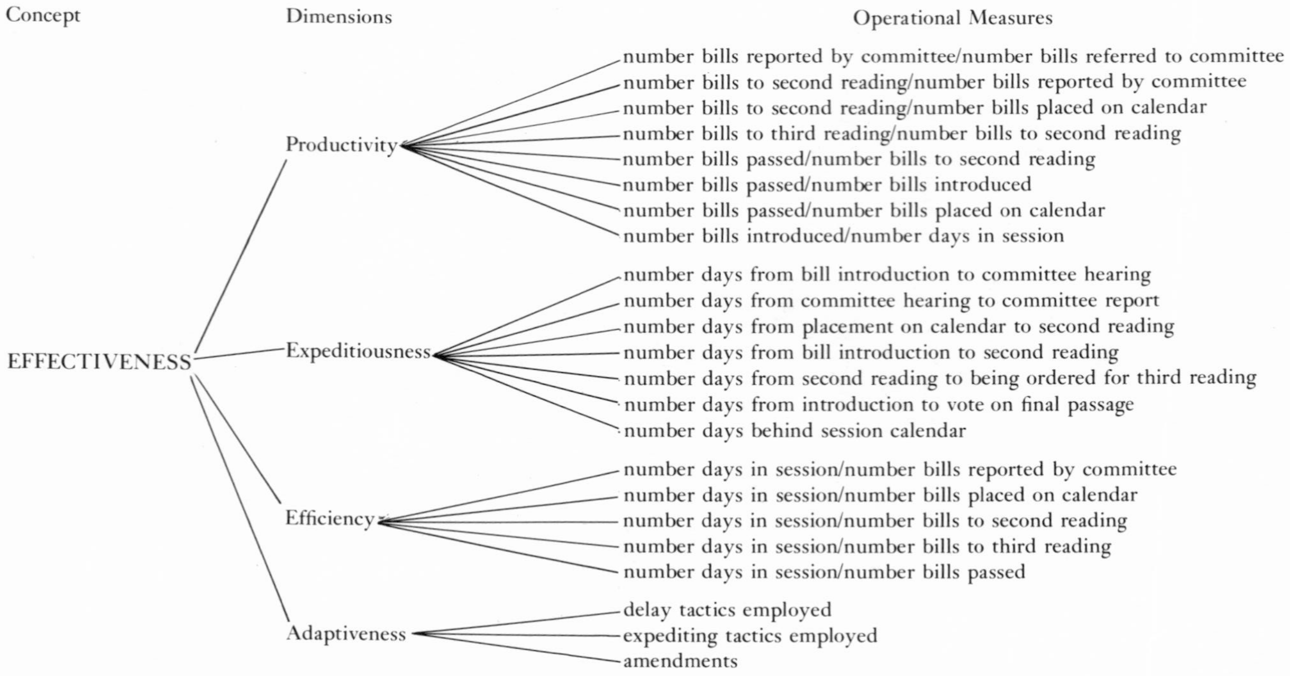

Expeditiousness may be equated with the speed with which the system converts the various demands into decisions. Thus an increase in the information-handling capability of the legislative system should result in an increase in the speed with which decisions are made.

> H_2: Expeditiousness, as indicated by the seven operational measures, should be higher for the 1973–1974 session of the Wisconsin Assembly than for the 1971–1972 session.

Efficiency normally refers to the "ratio between input and output, effort and results, expenditures and income, cost and resulting pleasure." [25] However, in discussing the legislative system, the concept of efficiency cannot be treated adequately in terms of input and output. Rather, we are concerned with the cost of producing decisions in the legislature, regardless of whether the decision is, in fact, a policy output. In this case, as the information-handling capability of the system increases, the system should experience a concomitant increase in efficiency.

> H_3: Efficiency, as indicated by the five operational measures, should be higher for the 1973–1974 session of the Wisconsin Assembly than for 1971–1972.

Adaptiveness conveys the idea of the system's ability to reorient itself in the face of a crisis or disturbance. Thus as the information handling capability the system increases we should also expect to see an increase in adaptiveness.

> H_4: Adaptiveness, as indicated by the three operational measures, should be higher for the 1973–1974 session of the Wisconsin Assembly than for 1971–1972.

The selection of quantitative operational measures in Figure 3 reflects our concern with providing meaningful, valid, reliable, and objective indicators of effectiveness in legislative performance. The use of a more qualitative, judgmental method for collecting comparative data would have raised serious questions about measurement. For example, asking "neutral" observers of or active participants in the Wisconsin Assembly to compare these two sessions on productivity, expeditiousness, efficiency, and adaptiveness was not pursued because of the built-in bias such judgments were likely to reflect and the problem of establishing a norm for comparison. On the other hand, the official records of the Assembly reflect accurately any differences between these two sessions on the four dimensions selected and provide for a more objective and quantifiable assessment of system performance.

Collecting these data, however, was exceedingly tedious and time-consuming. All bills introduced into the Assembly or sent from the Senate to the Assembly were evaluated with seventy-nine different kinds of information, which were coded into machine-readable form. These data were used for the analysis undertaken in the next section. The specific operational measures used here were taken from the original list of seventy-nine. In determining what information regarding each bill was germane for indicating the productivity, expeditiousness, efficiency, and adaptiveness dimensions, we were guided by in-depth discussions with legislators and legislative observers as well as our own evaluations regarding the operations of the Wisconsin Assembly. Certain important "check points" in the legislative process, features of legislative deliberations and mitigating factors in evaluating legislative performance of the Wisconsin Assembly were continually mentioned. These became the key variables around which our operational measures were developed. In explicating the variables selected, we will demonstrate how these variables fit into and are important elements of the legislative process as it operates in the Wisconsin Assembly.

Upon introduction of a legislative proposal or receipt of a proposal from the Senate, the vast majority of all legislation—92 percent in 1971–72 and 95 percent in 1973–74—is referred to one of the substantive Assembly committees. Those bills not sent to committee are immediately placed on the calendar. Each committee holds hearings on most bills and, after considering possible amendments, reports its deliberations and recommendations to the Assembly. (A favorable committee recommendation is an important element in securing final passage.) If a bill is not sent to another committee, it is placed on the calendar where it awaits a second reading. During this second reading, representatives amend and "perfect" the bill, preparing it for final consideration. At the time of second reading, a bill may be referred to a second committee (this normally occurs when a bill is sent to the Joint Finance Committee for a fiscal review), tabled, indefinitely postponed (killed), or sent to third reading. If a bill is not going to be passed, it is usually killed at this time. Third reading is the stage for final decision on a bill. When a bill is ordered to third reading, it is also ordered to be engrossed, so that all amendments and technical changes will have been made prior to the final vote, after third reading. Approval of a bill clears its way for being messaged to the Senate, although reconsideration of the vote and delay in messaging a bill may take place. Throughout this process, a number of tactics can be used to delay or speed up a bill's progress. Among the former are raising points of order, asking that the bill be tabled, delaying sending the bill to the Senate, reconsidering the vote for final disposition, and rereferring a bill to committee. Expediting tactics include withdrawing a bill from a committee, making a bill a special order of business, and suspending the rules so that it can be read a third time without the usual delay.

In order to evaluate properly some of these variables, a standardizing factor was introduced. Since our concern in these operational measures was with performance and since we were comparing across two legislative sessions which differed in terms of time and work load, we chose two appropriate factors for standardizing purposes—the relevant number of session days and the number of bills. In all instances, these factors or appropriate variations of them, were used as denominators in calculating our quantitative measures, thus standardizing our operational measures across the two legislative sessions.

Legislative Performance 1971–72 and 1973–74: The Findings

Using information indicating the number of bills reaching certain key points in the legislative process, the number of days necessary for legislation to reach these points, and the relative popularity of certain tactics in considering legislation, the operational measures listed in Figure 3 were calculated for the treatment (new rules, 1973–74) and nontreatment (old rules,

1971–72) sessions of the Wisconsin Assembly. Once these measures were calculated, appropriate comparisons were undertaken. When possible, a statistical test of difference was applied to the comparisons, but in a number of instances, no appropriate test was available. The following sections provide cross-treatment comparisons of the measures on the four effectiveness dimensions and present their implications.

Legislative Productivity

Since legislative productivity is defined here as the system's ability to convert demand inputs into outputs, the appropriate measures should relate to the amount of legislation undergoing such conversion. The most straightforward measure probably would be the output (the number of bills passed) standardized for the number of demands made (the number of bills introduced). However, other similar measures might be used to indicate system productivity, subsystem productivity and process productivity. Thus this study includes the number of bills passed standardized for the number of bills introduced, as well as the subsystem productivity measure consisting of the number of bills reported by committee standardized for the number of bills referred to committee and the process productivity measure of the number of bills reaching second reading standardized for the number of bills placed on the calendar. The analysis will involve comparing pairs of ratios—one of the pairs calculated for each session. Since these data have an unknown mean, and an unknown distribution, no statistical test could be used to analyze the significance of differences in the ratios. Further, the absence of a standard value for these ratios established from prior experience demands that our analysis of these data be restricted only to a direct comparison of two ratios. In order to provide a simplified indication of the trends in these data, a positive or negative sign has been added to indicate if the comparison of 1971–72 to 1973–74 is consistent with our expectation that productivity should be higher under the treatment conditions. (A positive sign indicates higher productivity for 1973–74 on that measure; a negative sign indicates lower productivity.)

Table 3

Comparative Analysis of Legislative Productivity Measures for the 1971–72 and the 1973–74 Sessions of the Wisconsin Assembly (ratios of measures)

Productivity Measures[1]	Nontreatment 1971–72 Session	Treatment 1973–74 Session	Direction of Trend[2]
Bills Reported by Committee / Bills Referred to Committee	$\frac{934}{1848} = .505$	$\frac{740}{1762} = .419$	–
Bills to Second Reading (Committee)[3] / Bills Reported by Committee	$\frac{592}{934} = .633$	$\frac{587}{740} = .793$	+
Bills to Second Reading (Total)[4] / Bills Placed on Calendar	$\frac{703}{1154} = .609$	$\frac{662}{859} = .771$	+
Bills to Third Reading / Bills to Second Reading	$\frac{507}{703} = .721$	$\frac{489}{662} = .739$	+
Bills Passed / Bills to Second Reading	$\frac{478}{703} = .680$	$\frac{481}{662} = .727$	+
Bills Passed / Bills Introduced	$\frac{478}{1997} = .239$	$\frac{481}{1868} = .257$	+
Bills Passed / Bills Placed on Calendar	$\frac{478}{1154} = .414$	$\frac{481}{859} = .560$	+
Bills Introduced / Days in Session	$\frac{1997}{138} = 14.47$	$\frac{1868}{113} = 16.53$	+

[1] Some of the data cited in this table are at variance with the official record cited in the *Bulletin of Proceedings for the Wisconsin Assembly: 1971–72 Session*. Our coding followed the official *Assembly Journal* and agrees with the *Senate Bulletin*. Conversations with the Wisconsin reviser of statutes and a check of official bills in the secretary of state's office confirm the data reported here.

[2] A positive sign indicates movement consistent with our hypothesis, *i.e.*, greater productivity in 1973–74.

[3] This is the number reported out of the first committee which received a second reading.

[4] This number includes those bills to second reading after committee deliberations as well as those bills which by-passed the committee system.

For seven of the eight measures in Table 3, the treatment session was more productive than the nontreatment. Only for the ratio of bills reported by committees to bills referred was the 1971–72 session more productive. This indicates that with regard to the movement of bills to second reading and final passage and with regard to the overall consideration of legislation, the treatment conditions were more conducive to higher productivity than were the nontreatment ones.

This one exception was confirmed independently by the leadership of each party. In their judgment, committees during the treatment session became more selective regarding their action on legislation. They thought fewer bills came from committees during 1973–74 and that there was more committee deliberation and study on the bills within each committee. Whether this trend toward greater committee selectivity in reporting legislation is an appropriate indicator of low legislative productivity is debatable. On the whole these quantitative measures seem to indicate that the rules changes in 1973–74 Wisconsin Assembly did increase the Assembly's information-handling capacity and did improve its productivity.

Legislative Expeditiousness

In the definition above, expeditiousness is viewed in terms of the amount of time a system requires for completing certain tasks. Traditionally, legislators and legislative observers have reacted against evaluating legislative performance in terms of how quickly the legislature acts; they have preferred using some measure of the quality of output. Although we are sympathetic and basically supportive of this position, the present research used indicators of required time as only one of four measures of Assembly effectiveness. Further, we believe that one result of the new rules should be to expedite the Assembly's legislating.

The primary factor we considered in this dimension was time. Time was measured by session days. The choice of session days as our indicator resulted from our evaluation of possible alternate time units; minutes and hours as well as weeks and months were all excluded because these units were either too small or too large and because calendars and legislative business usually calculates time in terms of days. We concluded that session days was the most meaningful. In calculating days, however, perfunctory meeting days, such as most Fridays and special sessions, were excluded to assure comparability and meaningfulness of time units. Tabulations were kept regarding the number of hours in session per day to serve as an independent check for comparability. A comparable number of hours per day per session was noted. The results convinced us that our use of session days was the most valid and reliable measure of the time dimension for these two sessions of the Wisconsin Assembly.

Across time measures indicate that the treatment session—1973–74—met in formal session fewer days than did the nontreatment one, 113 for the former and 138 for the latter. This net reduction of 25 days—18 percent—suggests that the new rules may have expedited legislative decision-making. Another similar but more qualitative measure concerns the traditional end-of-session "log-jam" surrounding legislative deliberations. Prior sessions of the Assembly had sometimes been noted for their colorful and marathon endings. This was not true for 1973–74: the Assembly adjourned at an early evening hour, after an admittedly hectic day, while the Senate, operating with a set of rules which permitted the use of delay tactics, continued until five A.M. the following morning. But while this overall measure is supportive of our second hypothesis, attention to more specific comparisons is necessary.

In order to assess the Assembly's expeditiousness, seven important time spans in the consideration of legislation were selected for detailed treatment. All bills reaching a certain point in the legislative process were examined in terms of the number of session days required to reach that point. Since we could generate a mean and distribution by using all bills, a t-test could be applied to these data. Comparisons across the two sessions—Table 4—show that on only two measures were the sessions basically the same—days between committee hearing and committee report and days between second reading and being ordered for a third reading. On each of the other four, the differences are statistically significant using a t-test and are in the predicted direction—*i.e.*, more expenditious treatment was given legislation in the 1973–74 session than in 1971–72. The major exception is in the number of days required to hold hearings and evaluate testimony, to consider amendments, and to pre-

Table 4

Comparative Analysis of Legislative Expeditiousness Measures for the 1971–72 and the 1973–74 Sessions of the Wisconsin Assembly (means and t = tests)

Expeditiousness Measures (by bills)	Nontreatment 1971–72 Session	Treatment 1973–74 Session
Mean Days, Introduction to Committee Hearing	14.8	13.0
N (Bills)	1051	1074
t = test	3.15, $p<.002$	
Mean Days, Committee Hearing to Committee Report	14.5	14.1
N (Bills)	727	608
t = test	.529, Not Significant	
Mean Days, Placed on Calendar to Second Reading	15.6	11.9
N (Bills)	680	633
t = test	7.13, $p<.0001$	
Mean Days, Introduction to Second Reading[1]	34.6	30.7
N (Bills)	703	662
t = test	3.42, $p<.001$	
Mean Days, Second Reading to Being Ordered for a Third Reading[2]	3.1	3.3
N (Bills)	567	509
t = test	.40, Not Significant	
Mean Days, Introduction to Vote on Final Passage[3]	36.1	31.1
N (Bills)	497	483
t = test	3.34, $p<.001$	

pare the committee report. (The other insignificant difference is between two points in the legislative process.) The new rules did not have any significant impact on these aspects of the legislative process; however, the findings that fewer days were required in 1973–74 from placement on the calendar to second reading, introduction to second reading to final disposition suggests that the treatment positively affected the expeditiousness of the 1973–74 Assembly. The shorter time period in 1973–74 from introduction to committee hearing can *not* be traced directly to the provisions of the new rules used in this session. Hence this greater expeditiousness probably reflects either the indirect effects of the new rules or direct committee

Table 4 continued

Number Days Behind Session Calendar[4]		
25% of Session Days	6	8
35% of Session Days	9	11
50% of Session Days	16	8
60% of Session Days	22	7
65% of Session Days	2	11
73% of Session Days	13	13

[1] Some bills which got to the second reading were withdrawn from committees and made a special order of business. This accounts for the larger number of cases in this category than in the Placed on Calendar to Second Reading category.

[2] A significant number of bills (83 percent 1971–72 and 79 percent 1973–74) were ordered to third reading on the same day as the second reading. This short delay usually occurs with noncontroversial legislation.

[3] The vote on final passage is a largely pro forma vote which confirms prior decisions to pass legislation made after second reading. The critical votes thus occur during second reading on motions to indefinitely postpone, rerefer to committee, refer to second committee, *etc.*

[4] The dates corresponding to these session days are as follows:

Percentage	1971–72 (N = 138)	1973–74 (N = 113)
25	April 27	April 4
35	May 26	May 3
50	July 15	June 20
60	September 14	July 19
65	September 28	October 4
73	October 19	October 24

subsystem responsiveness to perceived stress arising from practices in previous sessions.

One apparent inconsistency in this table needs to be explained. If one adds the average number of days to second reading using the first three time periods—introduction to hearing, hearing to report, and report to second reading—the total exceeds the time span indicated through the overall measure by approximately ten days in each session. Bills sent to the Assembly from the Senate and certain other bills are *not* referred to any committee and thus move directly to second reading. A fairly large number of bills—between 100 and 150—have a short delay for this time span and are *not* included in the calculations using committees. These, together with the suspension of the rules to withdraw bills from committees, also account for the larger number of bills in the overall measure compared with those going to second reading through committees.

Another quantitative indicator of expeditiousness found in Table 4 concerns the number of days the Assembly was behind the session calendar. In Wisconsin each calendar is an agenda drawn up at periodic intervals, usually daily, indicating where bills are located in the legislative process. An examination of the completion dates of calendars would thus indicate how far behind the legislature was. (The periods selected in Table 4 were used to assure comparability given the differing number of session days in 1971–72 and 1973–74 and to take cognizance of the fact that approximately the last quarter of each session was working from a diffeent type of calendar.) This comparison indicates that each session was about equally behind during the first and last thirds of the session, but that the 1971–72 session fell further behind during the middle third. (The reason for this difference is, in part, the extended deliberations on the budget bill during the middle third of 1971–72.) This comparison reinforces the other indicators in Table 4 that the Wisconsin Assembly appears to be significantly more expeditious in its decision-making function under the treatment conditions than under nontreatment conditions.

Further evidence regarding an expeditious handling of legislation can be seen if one examines in detail how members in each session dealt with legislation which survived the critical second reading and amending stage. (Bills normally are killed or "passed" at this stage of the legislative process in the Wisconsin Assembly, although a third reading and final vote is also required.) In 1971–72 a wide variety of parliamentary tactics was used to move bills around so that important legislation could come up for floor consideration. At times this scene became confusing and chaotic with few rank-and-file members realizing what was happening. Bills ordered to a third reading were sent to a second committee, numerous minor bills were laid on the table in one long legislative day in order to clear the calendar, and some bills that had been tabled were subsequently taken off the table and passed. (Table 6 will demonstrate further the differential use of these parliamentary tactics.) On the other hand, the 1973–74 session was much more consistent and orderly in moving legislation. Bills which were not to pass were "sidetracked" during second reading so that ordering a bill to third reading became more indicative of favorable action. Greater expeditiousness and orderliness in the legislative process thus seems evident in the 1973–74 session of the Assembly, when one considers the process used for moving bills from one legislative decision point to another.

Legislative Efficiency

Efficiency and effectiveness are two concepts that are frequently confused, especially when used to evaluate system performance. In this chapter we have followed the lead of social psychologists and organizational theorists who use effectiveness as the more general concept to refer to the interaction of a system with its environment. Efficiency, on the other hand, is a more limited concept referring to an organization's internal activity which is undertaken to maximize that organization's performance. Many social scientists have avoided using the efficiency concept when studying organizations because of cost-benefit connotations inherent in most measurements suggested for the concept. For the same reason many political scientists have avoided the term, especially those who have studied legislative systems.

As measured here, efficiency in legislative performance *is* indicated in terms of one cost inherent in legislative operations—time. Although this is one type of cost incurred by the legislature, our analysis is not intended to be a strict cost-benefit analysis, nor is it intended to be a strict input divided by output measure; rather we use efficiency to indicate the amount of time required for the legislature to perform one series of operations on one type of output—policy.

Table 5 includes five measures of system efficiency. Each of these expresses the average amount of time—measured in session days—required for bills to reach given points in the legislative process. In their present form, these measures have not been weighted or adjusted to indicate the amount of time expended on nonpolicy output-oriented tasks or the amount of time given to the legislation which did not reach that point in

Table 5

Comparative Analysis of Legislative Efficiency Measures for the 1971–72 and the 1973–74 Sessions of the Wisconsin Assembly (ratios of measures)

Efficiency Measures	Nontreatment 1971–72 Session	Treatment 1973–74 Session	Direction of Trend[1]
Number Days in Session / Number Bills Reported by Committee	$\frac{138}{934}=.148$	$\frac{113}{740}=.152$	–
Number Days in Session / Number Bills Placed on Calendar	$\frac{138}{1154}=.119$	$\frac{113}{859}=.132$	–
Number Days in Session / Number Bills To Second Reading	$\frac{138}{703}=.196$	$\frac{113}{662}=.170$	+
Number Days in Session / Number Bills To Third Reading	$\frac{138}{507}=.272$	$\frac{113}{489}=.231$	+
Number Days in Session / Number Bills Passed	$\frac{138}{478}=.289$	$\frac{113}{481}=.235$	+

[1] A positive sign (+) indicates movement consistent with our hypothesis, *i.e.*, greater efficiency in 1973–74.

the legislative process; however, we believe that for our purposes of assessing the comparative efficiency of these two sessions of the Wisconsin Assembly, these five measures are adequate. For two of these five measures—committee reports and placement on the calendar—the 1971–72 session was more efficient. In large part this difference reflects the larger number of bills sent from committees during this nontreatment session. The other three measures, however, show a greater efficiency for 1973–74. Included in these measures are indications of the average amount of time required for bills to get to second reading, to get to third reading, and to get to the point of passage. Thus measures of efficiency which focus on the later stages of the Assembly process tend to show greater efficiency for the 1973–74 session, while measures of the early stages suggest that 1971–72 was more efficient. These conclusions seem to agree with our earlier findings that the nontreatment session facilitated the flow of more legislation from committees.

While the absolute differences in the values of these measures appear small, each session day represents the combined work-expenditure of many people, not only the efforts of the approximately one hundred representatives, but also the extensive staff services and support agencies. Any improvement in efficiency of the legislative process is likely to be translated into time available for other legislative tasks, like constituent interaction and case work. Unfortunately, our data do not allow us to assess the impact of changes in relative time efficiency on other legislative tasks.

Legislative Adaptiveness

Our theoretic orientation to system change shows that a response on the part of a legislature takes place through time frames which follow the initial stress-producing situation. A similar notion can be applied within the system. In this context, a legislature itself may experience internal stress as it seeks to change and to respond to the more general stress resulting from its relationships with its environment. This internal stress on a system may require change which we will label adaptiveness. The concept adaptiveness can take on both productive and counterproductive features. That is, some portion of the system may respond to the stress of system change by seeking to reorient the system internally so that it will resemble as closely as possible the former state, while other elements may seek to reorient the system to further advance change within the system in response to external stress. In terms of the present research problem, we expect elements within the legislative system to respond differentially to the changes being made to improve the effectiveness of legislative performance. A certain group will probably seek to compromise the changes made so as to restore legislative performance to its earlier state. (These persons are probably satisfied with the former state of affairs and see no reason for change.) On the other hand, the advocates of change may find other groups who seek to take the changes to some more advanced state which will be characterized by even more drastic alterations.

In this study legislative adaptiveness to system changes in-

Table 6

Comparative Analysis of Legislative Adaptiveness Measures for the 1971–72 and the 1973–74 Sessions of the Wisconsin Assembly (percentages and means)

Adaptiveness Measures (By Bills)	Nontreatment 1971–72 Session	Treatment 1973–74 Session
Delay Tactics for Bills Read a Second Time		
Percent Bills Having Points of Order Raised	6.5	10
Direction:	More bills had points of order raised in 1973–74	
Mean Number Points of Order Raised	.10	.14
Direction:	More points of order raised in 1973–74	
Percent Bills with Motion to Lay Bill on Table	44	17
Direction:	More bills reaching second reading had motions to table in 1971–72	
Percent Bills with Successful Motions to Lay Bill on Table	40	12
Direction:	Greater success in tabling bills during second reading in 1971–72	
Expediting Tactics		
Percent Successful Motions to Withdraw Bills from Committee	76	71

cludes three possible responses—delay tactics, which will probably compromise system change; expediting tactics, which will probably advance system change; and amending tactics, which may either advance or retard system change. Our concern is with general patterns of adaptiveness and not with how tactics are used in specific instances. Thus we have chosen to measure these adaptive responses in terms of their general use for all appropriate bills and their relative popularity across sessions.

Table 6 summarizes comparisons for nine adaptiveness measures and indicates the direction of the patterns across these two sessions for four indicators of delay tactics, three indicators of expediting tactics, and two indicators of amending tactics. Points of order were used considerably more often in 1973–74, while motions to table bills were considerably more popular in

Table 6 continued

Direction:	Greater success withdrawing bills from committees in 1971–72	
Percent Successful Motions to Make Bill Special Order of Business	71	79
Direction:	Greater success making bills special order of business in 1973–74	
Percent Successful Motions to Suspend Rules to Read Bill Third Time	94	91
Direction:	Greater success suspending rules to read bill a third time in 1971–72	
Amendments		
Mean Number of Amendments Offered per "Amendable" Bill[1]	4.3	5.5
Direction:	More amendments were offered per "amendable" bill in 1973–74	
Mean Number of Amendments Adopted per "Amendable" Bill	1.8	3.0
Direction:	More amendments were adopted per "amendable" bill in 1973–74	

[1] An "amendable" bill is one where at least one amendment was offered. In 1971–72, 42 percent of the bills getting to the amendment—second-reading—stage had at least one amendment offered, while in 1973–74 a comparable figure was 37 percent.

1971–72. Greater use of tabling in 1971–72 reflected in part the necessity for disposing of the greater number of bills getting out of committees, which created a severe backlog of legislation. On the other hand, in 1971–72 certain expediting tactics, those requiring large-scale support, were generally *more* successful than in the 1973–74 session. More specifically, the rules changes allowing bills to be withdrawn from committee through petition in 1973–74 did not appear to result in greater success for removing bills from committees than was the case during the nontreatment session. Only in terms of making bills a special order of business did the 1973–74 session have greater success. One of the important considerations regarding this aspect of expediting tactics is the role of the Rules Committee in making bills a special order of business. Although this mechanism was available in 1973–74, only thirteen bills were made a special order of business by the Rules Committee. This indicates that the specific changes made in the Assembly's rules and procedures could have an impact on institutional effectiveness without being used continuously.

Regarding the use of amending tactics, more amendments were offered and adopted in 1973–74; however, more 1971–72 bills had amendments offered than was the case for 1973–74 bills. Three factors probably contributed to this change in the amendment process: amendments may have been used more widely in 1971–72 to secure support within the majority party, 1973–74 legislation was more in need of "perfecting" amendments, and the amendment process became a more viable means for delaying legislation in 1973–74.

Two conclusions regarding adaptiveness to change by the Wisconsin Assembly seem in order. First, changes undertaken by the 1973–74 Assembly through the adoption of new rules were not always implemented as envisioned. The Rules Committee was rarely used as a device to get legislation made a special order of business and less success was experienced in removing legislation from committees with the addition of a discharge petition than under the previous provisions for voting legislation out. Second, legislative systems do appear to adapt. Not all of this adaptation is supportive of change and not all adaptation runs counter to that change; however, the mixture from 1973–74 suggests that in spite of adaptive behavior that might compromise the effects of the rules changes, on the whole these adaptive behaviors do not appear to have diminished greatly the impact of the rules changes on legislative effectiveness.

Conclusions and Implications

The purpose of this research has been threefold: to examine system response to perceived stress in the form of demand inputs; to provide operational definitions for one aspect of institutional performance, "effectiveness"; and to analyze the effects of institutional change on the effectiveness of system performance under longitudinal, quasi-experimental conditions. The 1971–72 and 1973–74 sessions of the Wisconsin Assembly served as the nontreatment and treatment conditions. Findings indicate that the internal rearrangement, via changes in the rules and procedures, was successful in terms of increasing the productivity, expeditiousness, efficiency, and adaptiveness of the system for the time period under consideration. However, each of the rules changes should not be given equal weight. Usage of the discharge petition to remove bills from committee was initiated with majority support in only seven instances during the 1973–74 session. In addition, the Rules Committee utilized its expanded powers to make bills a special order of business in only thirteen cases; however, those occasions involved very important legislation, like the 1974 University of Wisconsin merger. The greater productivity attributable, in general, to these changes in rules and procedures probably stems in large measure from the effects of limiting debate.

In addition to our specific findings, we see theoretical significance in our work. While we have not attempted to test a theory in a rigorous manner, our observations may serve as a guide for future research. Decisional systems such as state legislatures appear capable of responding to an imbalance within their environment created through an increased flow of demands. Response of the system, through alteration of its rules and procedures, appears to produce some of the desired results of increasing the information-handling capability of the system. A system need not enter a period of prolonged impairment of its performance from stress in order for that system to take some action to improve the effectiveness of its performance.

Our concern has centered on the effects of rules changes on legislative performance. We are convinced that this concern for performance was the primary goal for adopting these new rules and procedures; however, the changes and concomitant alterations in legislative performance probably had some additional unintended consequences. One such consequence relates to the legislature's potential for interaction with other political and social institutions. Although we have no specific data from our study pertaining to the Wisconsin Assembly's relations with other institutions, we would expect that a more efficient and effective legislature would be better able to act in its decision-making, thus freeing it from dependence upon other institutions like pressure groups and administrative agencies. Furthermore, greater efficiency implies that the legislature is capable of processing demands in a shorter period of time. This increase in the level of performance should result in the legislature being able to compete more effectively with other governmental institutions.

In the Wisconsin setting, the Assembly's interaction with two other political institutions does appear to have been affected by the rules changes. As a result of the rules changes, the Democratic control of the Assembly, and a sympathetic leadership the Assembly became a vital component in the Democratic governor's legislative program. The governor appeared at times to exert control over the Assembly, making use of the new rules and procedures so that his own legislative program would become law with as few changes as possible. Since the Senate was controlled by the Republicans during both of these sessions, the governor considered it important to have the Democratically controlled Assembly make a firm and united stand. The new rules and procedures facilitated this, and as a result, the governor's program appears to have been less subject to compromise than had been true in the 1971–72 session.

As it affected the relations with the Senate, the rules changes may have fostered more partisan feeling and position-taking than seemed to exist in other years. Senate-Assembly differences have always been evident, but they seemed to be more partisan in 1973–74. Although legislators may not have perceived this, a strong partisan position on legislation emerging from the Assembly undoubtedly affected that chamber's relations with the Senate. The absence of data precludes any precise delineation of whether these relations were more positive or negative as a result of the rules changes and the heightened partisanship. Perhaps the most instructive insight regarding the effects of the new rules and procedures is that the 1975 session of the Wisconsin Senate adopted its own new rules and procedures which in some ways resembled those adopted in 1973–74 by the Assembly.

A second additional consequence of the rules changes can be seen in the redistribution of power within the Assembly. More power was placed in the hands of the leadership, while debate and floor participation by individual members was more limited and subject to leadership control. As members of the Rules Committee, the leadership could more effectively influence what legislation reached the floor as well as the activities of members, especially on the floor and in debate. Individual members surveyed at the end of the 1974 session indicated a perception that the leadership had gained an advantage with the new rules and procedures.[26] Unlimited debate became very difficult in 1973–74, as did other frequently used delay tactics. Any minority, but especially the minority party, found it increasingly difficult to extract compromises in return for their cooperation. On the other hand, interviews with legislators showed that few members perceived the leadership to be using their new-found power in an arbitrary manner. Exceptions to the strict limits on debate were freely concurred in and the majority was generally careful about not arbitrarily imposing itself upon the minority.

A third area of univestigated consequence involves public policy. While this paper has mapped out the results which accrued from changes in rules and procedures for legislative performance, it has not provided information on the substantive quality of the legislation the Assembly passed or the distribution of rewards and deprivations which were conferred on the various interest sectors in Wisconsin. However, assemblymen who were interviewed at the end of the 1973–74 session offered some subjective evaluations on these two points. First, while a majority of those interviewed concurred in our assessment of the effects on efficiency and expeditiousness of the legislature, only 18 percent of those interviewed would state that the rules had affected the quality of legislation positively; the greatest response, over 60 percent, was that the changes had no noticeable effect. These responses suggest to us that the changes, for all their effects on performance, may have been merely tangentially related to the quality of the enacted legislation. However, this finding should be tempered by the knowledge that these same respondents were willing, in most cases, to indicate that a beneficiary emerged in the actual distribution of rewards and deprivations to the various interest sectors in the state. In summary, the changes in rules and procedures affected certain segments of the population in a positive fashion, without necessarily helping to upgrade the quality of legislation which the Assembly adopted.

Finally, we may evaluate the changes as they affect representative government. Perhaps the most appropriate method for accomplishing this evaluation involves the utilization of a balance sheet system. The effects may be charted in terms of positive and negative components with an overall evaluation possible at the conclusion of this operation. Initially, from a positive perspective, we could argue that the changes in the rules provide the majority with the means for making decisions. It would appear that the minority in the 1973–74 Assembly, no matter how vocal, rarely prevailed in those instances in which the majority (with the consent of the leadership) was committed. This general statement would not have been as applicable in past sessions of the Assembly, although superficial observations indicate that throughout the past few sessions, centralization of power was occurring with a concomitant use of superior resources by the Democrats to enforce party discipline both within the caucus and on the Assembly floor. Thus, there may be a trend toward reduction in the discretion of the representative in implementing his constituents' demands. At the same time, however, it is difficult to gauge the extent to which this restriction in decision-making is taking place. Nevertheless, indications from the maneuverings involving the 1975 state budget, including the utilization of the Rules Committee's powers, suggest that the emphasis on party discipline, while apparently producing schisms within the Democratic party, is intensifying. Yet, we must also keep in mind that the interpretations of these restrictions on the individual representative have occurred concurrently with accepting requests for additional time to extend remarks. This change in the rules appears mainly to have eliminated the uninhibited verbosity which prevailed in previous sessions. In summary, it is difficult to evaluate the effects of the changes on representative government. We note that both positive and negative consequences may be associated with the change, but perhaps a better perspective will be available when we are able to take a long-term look at the consequences.

Given that legislative systems appear to be confronted with an ever increasing spiral of demands, the finding that systems can adjust by an internal rearrangement of their structures and processes and can improve the effectiveness of their performance confirms the postulated effects of internal arrangements upon system functioning. This observation, however, raises supplementary questions. Can an internal rearrangement of structure and process be sufficient to meet any type of system stress? What mitigating factors will affect system response? Is system change constant and in the same direction? The future task involves conducting a rigorous test of the theoretical relevance of these findings and building an adequate theory of institutional change. Comparative as well as theoretically based research must be used for such theory testing and theory building.

Authors Note

A number of people have made significant contributions to the completion of this research project. Financial support came from the University of Wisconsin—Milwaukee Graduate School through a faculty research grant and computer time and from the Milwaukee Urban Observatory. Also important has been ongoing research support by the Political Research Laboratory and the Social Science Research Facility (especially Paul Keuler and Jerome Schuh). A number of graduate and undergraduate students have greatly assisted in the collection of these data; most notable have been Patricia Siewert, Judy Titel, Irving Gottschalk, Robert Stein, and Russell Allen. In addition, the insights and comments of Cornelius P. Cotter, Meredith W. Watts, and Wilder W. Crane on an earlier version of this paper directed us toward greater precision and accuracy. A special acknowledgement goes to our wives. We alone, however, assume responsibility for the data, analysis, and conclusions contained herein.

Notes

1. Typical of such reports have been the Pennsylvania General Assembly's Commission for Legislative Modernization, *Toward Tomorrow's Legislature* (Harrisburg, Pennsylvania: 1969); Kentucky Committee on the State Legislature, *The First Year: A Summary*

Report on the State Legislature Covering the First Year of its Operations, September 1967–1968 (Louisville, Kentucky: 1968).

2. Recent assessment of legislative operations by reform-oriented organizations include the Citizens' Conference on State Legislatures, *State Legislatures: An Evaluation of their Effectiveness* (New York: Praeger Publishers, 1971); Charles Tantillo, *Strengthening the Rhode Island Legislature: An Eagleton Study and Report* (New Brunswick, New Jersey: Rutgers University, 1968).

3. Some recent studies of legislative performance conducted by political scientists include Alan Rosenthal, *Legislative Performance in the States* (New York: The Free Press, 1974); Thomas A. Flinn, "An Evaluation of Legislative Performance: The State Legislature in Ohio," in John J. Gorgan and James G. Code (eds.), *Political Behavior and Public Issues in Ohio* (Kent State, Ohio: Kent State University Press, 1972), p. 153; John S. Saloma, III, *Congress and the New Politics* (Boston: Little, Brown, 1969).

4. For example, Daniel Katz and Robert L. Kahn, *The Social Psychology of Organizations* (New York: John Wiley and Sons, Inc., 1966).

5. John G. Grumm, "Structural Determinants of Legislative Output" in Allan Kornberg and Lloyd D. Musolf (eds.), *Legislatures in Developmental Perspective* (Durham, N.C.: Duke University Press, 1970), p. 429.

6. John Burns, *The Sometimes Governments* (New York: Bantam Books, 1971), Chapters V–IX discuss the nature of these five dimensions. Chapter XI presents the ideal model advocated for state legislatures, makes recommendations for each state legislature, and ranks the legislatures on the five dimensions.

7. Katz and Kahn, *Social Psychology of Organizations;* Francis R. Allen, *Socio-Cultural Dynamics: An Introduction to Social Change* (New York: The MacMillan Company, 1971); Karl W. Deutsch, *The Nerves of Government* (New York: John Wiley and Sons, Inc., 1965); Samuel P. Huntington, "Congressional Responses to the Twentieth Century" in David B. Truman, *The Congress and America's Future*, 2nd Edition (Englewood Cliffs, New Jersey: Prentice-Hall, Inc., 1973), pp. 6–38; Gabriel Almond and G. Bingham Powell, Jr., *Comparative Politics: A Developmental Approach* (Little Brown and Company, 1966).

8. David Easton, *A Framework for Political Analysis* (Englewood Cliffs, N.J.: Prentice-Hall, Inc., 1965).

9. Deutsch, *Nerves of Government*, p. 221.

10. *Ibid.*, p. 184.

11. John G. Grumm, "The Legislative System as an Economic Model" in Allan Kornberg, *Legislatures in Comparative Perspective* (New York: David McKay Company, Inc., 1973), p. 236–242.

12. Douglas C. Chaffey, "The Institutionalization of State Legislatures: A Comparative Study," *The Western Political Quarterly* 23 (March 1970): 180–196.

13. Citizens Conference on State Legislatures, *State Legislatures*, p. 40.

14. Rosenthal, *Legislative Performance in the States*, p. 12.

15. Roger Hanson claims that the critical feature of the legislative environment is its information-handling capability; in fact, he argues that all other features affecting the decision-making capability depend upon this one capability. See "A Critique of the Citizen's Conference on State Legislatures *Study of State Legislatures: An Evaluation of their Effectiveness*," a mimeograph report for the Research Division of the Institute of Government of the University of Georgia.

16. Chaffey utilizes this concept in his article, "The Institutionalization of State Legislatures: A Comparative Study."

17. Malcolm C. Jewell and Samuel C. Patterson, *The Legislative Process in the United States*, 2nd Edition (New York: Random House, 1972), p. 278.

18. William J. Keefe and Morris S. Ogul, *The American Legislative Process: Congress and the States*, 3rd Edition (Englewood, New Jersey: Prentice-Hall, Inc., 1973), p. 245.

19. John Bibby and Roger Davidson, *On Capitol Hill: Studies in the Legislative Process*, Second Edition (Hinsdale, Ill.: Dryden Press, Inc., 1972).

20. During the early 1960s the rules and procedures in both houses of the Wisconsin legislature were the subject of a study by Paul Mason. As a direct result certain minor changes were made in both the Senate and Assembly. The only other major change was periodic experimentation with an informal consent calendar.

21. Byron Wackett, as quoted by Eugene C. Harrington, "Assembly Wrangles on Rules," *The Milwaukee Journal*, 2 January 1973.

22. For example, Bertram M. Gross, "The State of the Nation: Social Systems Accounting," in Raymond A. Bauer, *Social Indicators* (Cambridge, Mass.: The M. I. T. Press, 1966); and John S. Saloma, III, *Congress and the New Politics*.

23. Katz and Kahn, *Social Psychology of Organizations*, p. 165.

24. James L. Price, *Organizational Effectiveness: An Inventory of Propositions* (Homewood, Ill.: Irwin Press, 1968).

25. *International Encyclopedia of Social Sciences*, 5:437.

26. Ronald D. Hedlund and Keith E. Hamm, "Conflict and Perceived Group Benefits From Legislative Rules Changes," a paper delivered at the 1975 Annual Meeting of the American Political Science Association, San Francisco, California, 2–5 September 1975.

Administrative Impact of New Legislation

RICHARD NUNEZ and JOSEPH WHORTON

A major portion of new legislation enacted each year has a significant and direct impact on the bureaucracy. Such legislation may include statutory mandates for specific administrative performance, authorization for new programmatic action, or amendment of existing programs with an eye toward reform. Oftentimes the legislation relates to general goals or objectives and is vague in terms of the specifics of administrative implementation. As a consequence, interpretation and implementation are left to the bureaucracy. Administrative interpretation of the law, in the form of regulations and guidelines, can result in programs that operate in ways which differ from legislative intent, cost more than anticipated, and, in some cases, fail to achieve their stated purpose. When a program fails, blame is often placed on the law and the legislature is criticized for failing to consider ". . . grubby details of planning, organizing, staffing and developing the administrative systems to translate laws into working programs." [1] Behind such criticism is the belief that legislation can and should more clearly define the parameters of administrative discretion, as a means of protecting the integrity of the legislation, and include, as a part of the legislative process, detailed and specific information regarding the administrative impact of the proposed legislation. Administrative impact, in this sense, refers not only to program costs, but also to such matters as which agency will administer the new program and the manner by which it will be implemented.

This chapter argues that both of these objectives can be met if the legislature uses an administrative impact statement which would contain information regarding the administrative feasibility of any proposed legislation requiring administrative action.

One theme which runs throughout this volume is the attempt of legislators to improve their performance. A large part of this effort involves an interface with the executive branch concerning such matters as budget, program review, and program audit. The chapters by Crane, Beckman, Worthley, and Kayali detail attempts by legislators to improve the quality of information concerning administrative performance. The post audit activity Crane found in many state legislatures, is evaluative and is geared toward improving administrative performance and insuring that the intent of legislative enactments are being met. Likewise, the House Committee on Appropriations, as "overseer" of the administration, closely scrutinizes the content and need for administrative budget requests. The introduction by the US Congress of statutory reporting requirements is still another example of a technique legislators use to monitor the progress of administrative implementation of law. The legislatures of Brazil, Denmark, and India have also institutionalized devices whereby they can increase control over administrative performance and, where necessary, question specific administrative acts.

While these actions do help close the traditional gap between the legislative and the executive function, they are for the most part ex post facto review. In cases where the impact of legislative proposals are assessed, (i.e., the work of the Congressional Research Service), the specifics of administrative implementation are, more often than not, left to the executive. The use of an administrative impact statement would add another vital dimension to this analysis and in many instances it would formalize a process already being undertaken.

The demand for more specific legislation, containing detailed provisions aimed at limiting administrative discretion, is a constant theme in much of our legal literature. For legal scholars, the concept of the rule of law is threatened by the enactment of statutes that are vaguely worded and do not have specific provisions. In their view, such broad delegation of powers to the administrator means that the legislature has shunned its duty and that the wrong people are making the laws.[2] Benjamin Cordozo, in his classic phrase, "This is delegation running riot," [3] captured the feeling of horror with which the legal profession and many reformers read vaguely worded statutes.

Yet vague and ambiguous statutes continue to be enacted. Why? To provide an explanation, we need to investigate two interrelated phenomenon; the nature of legislative decision-making and the linkage between legislative decision-making and the bureaucratic process.

The Nature of Legislative Decision-Making

A new proposal, phrased in a written bill, has, by the final legislative stages, been viewed and reviewed, analyzed and criticized, supported and opposed from many angles. Despite the diversity of legislative proposals, questions about a new bill can be grouped into four main categories: 1) questions of political feasibility, 2) questions of legal feasibility, 3) questions of financial feasibility, and 4) questions of administrative feasibility.

In the real world of decision-making, these questions overlap and interrelate with each other. This interaction is represented in figure 1. Viewed as a whole, the legislature and, consequently, legislation is placed in the area of political questions. In this arena the members' right of debate is the mechanism for raising political questions, and members' votes are the vehicle for handling them. While questions of legality, financing, and administration have a specificity of content that can be separated from the political when placed in the legislative process, they invariably become subjected to the dynamics of the political arena.

Legal questions concerning new administrative proposals are routinely brought to the legislature's attention. Since all legislatures operate under a fixed set of procedural rules and within limited areas of power usually stated in a written constitution, doubts may arise whether proposed legislation violates the procedural rules or exceeds the limits of legislative power. In some legislatures, it is sufficient for a single member to raise doubt of legality during his debate or for the question to be raised by a

Figure 1

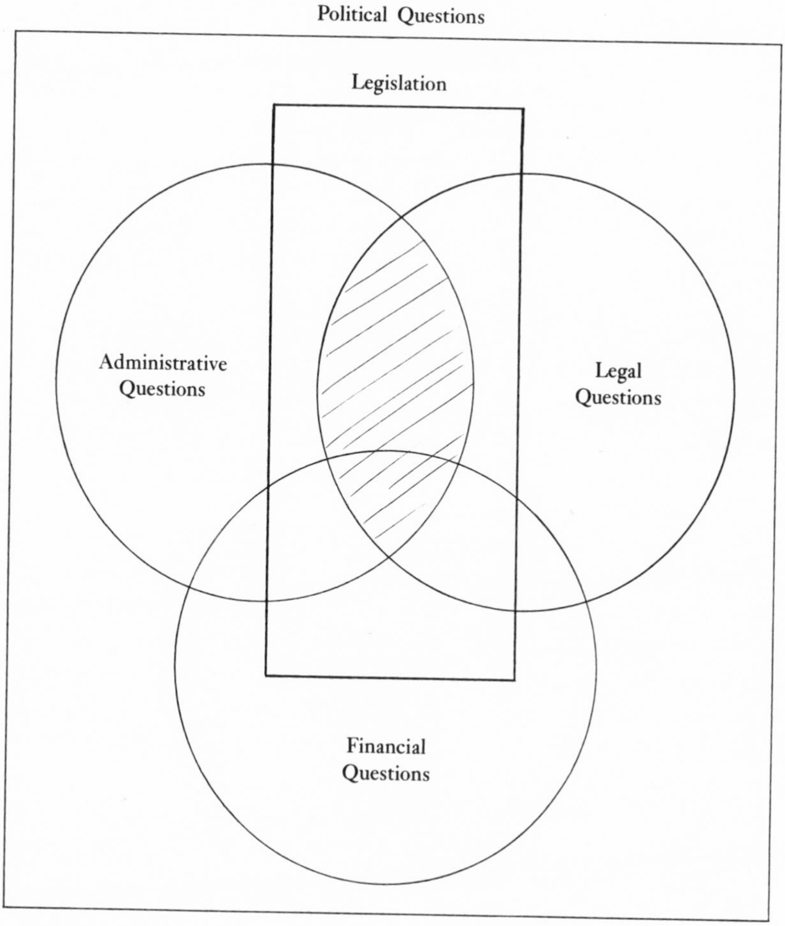

vote of the members to initiate a formal legal review process. Even in those legislatures described as rubber-stamp legislatures, there often exists one, two, or perhaps three institutional mechanisms for testing and approving a bill's legality. For example, standing committees on the laws and constitution and a special legislative legal officer, similar to an attorney general, all serve as the legislature's institutional units for raising and answering questions surrounding a bill's legality. It is of no significance whether the final opinions on a bill's legality issued by these special units are purely advisory or are binding; it is sufficient that the question of legality, as a separate issue, has been raised during the legislative decision-making process.

As with the political and legal questions, legislatures are institutionally equipped to raise and handle financial questions about a new administrative proposal. As part of established legislative procedures, bills with fiscal impact are reviewed by standing finance committees, by the office of the legislative leadership, by special legislative auditors, etc. Rarely would a bill carrying sizable financial impact slip through without considerable analysis. Viewed historically, the early improvements in legislative staffing were aimed at increasing the legislature's ability to handle financial questions.

The fourth question, administrative feasibility, is not usually addressed in some systematic and institutional way as are questions dealing with the political, legal, and financial impact. Where administrative impact is considered at all, it is usually general in nature, dealing with broad program goals, or occurs after the fact in the form of program review, post audit, or legislative inquiry. Why then, are administrative questions ignored? Or, to paraphrase the reformers, why are "the grubby details" omitted from the debate and the statute?

The most direct answer is that a bill's administrative feasibility may not be the most important aspect from the legislator's viewpoint. The prime focus on each bill is its political acceptability to the members. All other considerations, whether legal, financial, or administrative, are of secondary importance. Therefore legislative leaders must make whatever changes are necessary to win a bill the widest desired consensus on the floor.

What changes are most often made as a bill moves through the legislative process? As a small sample, an analysis of the New York State legislature over a three-year period reveals that, of bills which were amended and survived the political process (i.e., became law), over 95 percent of the amendments deleted specific material and/or substituted vague words or phrases.[4] In essence, for an overwhelming percentage of the bills subsequently enacted into law the legislative process was a process of rendering the bills more and more vague, until the necessary political consensus was achieved. We may assume that the sponsors of a bill would prevent amendments or would not give up specific language in their bill, if they had the necessary votes to pass it in its original form. Thus amending is a vote-gathering process. To win votes, specificity is sacrificed. Critics are correct in charging that the legislature avoids grubby details of administration, but they are wrong in placing blame. Vagueness may not be a legislative defect or oversight; it is a deliberate political maneuver that reformers fail to appreciate or understand. Pragmatically, vagueness increases political acceptance.

Vagueness in the statute also permits the legislature to address itself to social problems that demand attention, even though the present state of technical knowledge does not offer a known solution (e.g., drug addition and fuel shortage). In these instances the legislature adopts public policy in the truest sense of the word, leaving it to the bureaucracy to develop solutions via policy implementation. For example, much of the early New Deal legislation, vaguely worded, was aimed at restoring public confidence in the ability of government to end the depression. The lack of specifics regarding methods of implementation and administration was due in part to the need to buy time so that new solutions could be developed. Consequently the bureaucracy enjoyed wide latitude in interpreting and administering the new legislation.

Critics often assume that the legislature's failure to enact administrative details is an indication that it has defaulted on its commitment to the administrative program. In fact, the legislature may not be committed to any specific administrative program, but is only committed to specific interests that are demanding law as an answer to their needs and problems. The wishes of the interest groups are primary and the administrative aspects of the program are secondary.

In some cases the legislature does not ignore the grubby details. Although the administrative aspects of a bill may not appear in the formal language of a bill, the legislature often weighs the pro and con arguments of administration. Budget hearings and staff testimony before congressional committees are the primary sources of information regarding administrative feasibility. Characteristically this information is not made a formal part of the law, principally because legislators want to avoid infringing on the executive's prerogative to make technical administrative decisions. There is, however, an understanding between the administration and legislature as to how the new law will be administered. Subsequently, when legislators vote on a bill creating a new agency or program, this implied commitment of how the bill will be administered is an integral part of the bill.[5]

Legislative Decision-Making and the Bureaucratic Process

There is a large body of administrative theory which holds that there should be a clear distinction between legislating and administering. Under this rubric administration is the execution of laws passed by the legislature. To properly fulfill their role, administrators argue that they need flexibility and great latitude. For the legislature to narrowly define the administrative content of a new piece of legislation would not only usurp the administrator's prerogative, it would also reduce the practice of administration to a drone-like state.

This attitude on the part of administrators is not just motivated by self interest. Administrators recognize that the environment in which they work is essentially one of uncertainty. Programs, no matter how well conceived or planned, cannot cover every contingency. The administrator, therefore, needs the flexibility to alter programming to the situation. In the same vein, much legislation is experimental, addressing subject matter on which there is no prior administrative experience. In this instance it may be necessary to try a number of different administrative procedures before the right formula is found. If the legislative process is one of political compromise and consensus, then bureaucratic decision-making peocess is one of "satisficing." In order to "satisfice," the administrator cannot be bound too narrowly by the law he is charged with executing. Finally, the administrator argues that if he is to have the responsibility for program administration then he must also have the authority to act.

In practice the lines between the executive and the legislature continually cross and it is not always possible to make clear distinctions between the two. In 1967 the Senate Subcommittee on Separation of Powers made very clear that the US Constitution makes no statement of differences between legislative and administrative powers.[6] There is, in fact, a constant interaction between the two branches, an occurrence which is not too surprising, considering the fact that they serve the same clientele. The interaction takes several forms. As has been stated, the bulk of legislation passed by Congress does not originate there but in an administrative agency concerned with the legislation. Legislators, through the device of congressional inquiry, are in frequent contact with the administration on behalf of their constituents. This quasi-ombudsman process provides legislators a constant feedback regarding administrative competence and performance. Likewise feedback from political groups whose interests the agency serves alerts the legislature whenever the program is badly administered or administered differently from the commitments made during the legislative process.[7]

In addition to continuous feedback from outside groups, there are several units within legislatures that exercise the function of legislative oversight, which usually encompasses a review and analysis of the administrative operations of a program. For example, the Federal General Accounting Office and the newly created Congressional Budget Office [8] analyze the administrative aspects of programs and report their findings to Congress. Several state legislatures have established committees to review agency rules and regulations which may be approved or nullified by legislative action. Numerous writers have pointed out the ways in which the legislature may exert its influence upon the bureaucracy to modify or revoke an administrative process or policy.[9]

What we have, then, is a delicate balance between the needs of administrators for flexibility and the latitude to administer and the needs of legislators to enact law which is specific enough to insure that the intent of legislation will be met. One possible method for achieving this end is the administrative impact statement.

Administrative Impact Statements

As a bill moves through the legislative process, it gathers additional pieces of evidence. To the bill are attached the tally of committee votes, official legal opinions, and estimated financial costs. In addition a bill creating a new program could carry a statement indicating that questions about the program's administrative feasibility were considered and analyzed.

Written administrative impact statements would remove the assumption, often repeated and often erroneous, that administrative aspects of new programs were not considered by the legislature during its decision-making. The requirement that the administrative impact statement be written would place responsibility for it squarely upon the desk of a known unit within the legislature itself. Drafted by such a specially created unit, an administrative impact statement would be attached to every program bill as it moved through the legislative process, thereby giving a clearer picture of the administrative, as well as the legal and financial, aspects that were known at the time of legislative decision-making.

Contents of Administrative Impact Statements

How much and what kinds of information would administrative impact statements contain? Clearly how detailed they would be would depend upon many factors, such as the program's novelty, the sums of money to be appropriated, the competence of the research staff, but the primary deciding factor would be the legislature's desire to know the administrative details—maybe not the grubby details, but, at a level of specificity or generality that is politically acceptable for a particular bill. The legislature may wish to know the following. Are scientific and technical tools available to handle the social problem? Does there exist an adequate pool of competent personnel to administer and work within the proposed program? Simply, can this program, as drafted in this bill, be successfully administered?

For program bills that are not politically controversial, or are broadly supported, the administrative impact statement might contain additional information on more detailed questions, whether simply or elaborately explained.

Undoubtedly even the most thoroughly documented facts or supported conclusions in an administrative impact statement might provoke contrary facts and opposing conclusions, just as the new environmental impact statements have, in themselves, become centers of controversy. This is not new; official legal opinions and financial estimates are often contradicted by opposition ones. Controversy does not destroy the value of the impact statement. Nevertheless, with or without controversy, the purpose of the administrative impact statements would be to routinely place before the legislature questions and information concerning the administrative aspects of bills being considered, thereby making the bill's administrative feasibility part of the legislative decision-making. The legislature would be able to incorporate questions of administration into the larger political context, as it now incorporates legal and financial questions (see figure 1).

It must be emphasized that such administrative impact statements would be staff-prepared documents that moved with bills through the legislative process. The impact statement would not have legal status in itself and would not add specificity to the bill. Being informational and advisory, it could be ignored, if overriding political factors required a contrary decision, in the same manner that legislative leaders often ignore legal and financial opinions when political considerations demand.

Administrative Feasibility Unit

The proposal for administrative impact statements leads to a related proposal—the creation of a special legislative unit, an administrative feasibility unit, with responsibility for drafting the impact statements.

Staffed with experts in public administration who are also knowledgeable about the specific administrative environment in which the legislature is operating, the proposed administrative feasibility unit would be closely tied into the formal legislative process, so that every program bill would be studied routinely in its administrative as well as its legal and financial aspects.

To have an influence on the decision-making process, the feasibility unit would be located near the political leaders in the legislature. Whether the unit were a separate office or integrated into the leader's office, whether the staff were permanent civil service or politically appointed, whether the unit served as an advocate of administrative effectiveness or merely in an advisory capacity could all be decided by the political and social values of the society in which the legislature was located. This proposal is solely that the administrative feasibility unit be created and that administrative impact statements be an accepted integral part of the legislative decision-making process.

The proposal, while adding to the information base necessary to legislate, would not infringe on the special needs of administrators, nor would it close out legislative options for program review and evaluation. The proposal, in fact, contributes to some very basic administrative principles. It is similar in nature to the planning-programming-budgeting-and-management-by-objectives models. It would clearly set program goals and test feasibility before implementation. The impact statement can be seen not only as an aid to better legislation but also as an aid to better administration. The administrator would have a better understanding of his charge and would also have reasonable assurance that the program he is asked to administer is, in fact, workable. In addition, interest groups and individuals affected by proposed legislation would have a better understanding of how they might be affected. Considerable duplication, conflict, and ambiguity among various administrative agencies could be eliminated by specifying how particular programs are going to be administered.

Finally, the proposal can be viewed as an extension of rational decision-making. Herb Simon holds that structure determines outcomes by determining the factual and value premise of decisions.[10] The political process of legislative decision-making provides the values. Legislatures already provide a portion of the factual content through their legal and financial feasibility studies; the impact statement would add the final factual need, administrative feasibility.

Conclusion

The question of administrative feasibility is only one of several questions the legislature weighs and balances within the larger framework of a bill's political feasibility. Looking for administrative details within the legal language of a bill and finding them missing, reformers and critics accuse the legislature of failure, of dereliction of duty. But this is a misdirected attack, starting from the incorrect assumption about the role of legislatures. Legislatures seek consensus in responding to society's demands and needs, as these are expressed by political groups. The driving force behind the legislative process is the search for consensus among the significant political groups and in this search, if administrative details must be sacrified, so be it; that is the genius of the legislature's compromising mechanism.

The proposed administrative impact statement would introduce the question of administrative feasibility into legislative decision-making, in the same manner that the legal and financial questions are introduced, as separate issues which do not disrupt the larger on-going political decision-making and consensus-seeking process.

Notes

1. Harold Seidman, *Politics, Position and Power* (New York: Oxford Press, 1970), p. 6.

2. For early classical statements of this position, see John Dickinson, *Administrative Justice and the Supremacy of Law in the United States*, (New York: Russell and Russell, Inc., 1927, reprinted 1959).

3. *A. L. A. Schecter Poultry Corporation, et al., v. United States*, 295 U.S. 495; 55 sup. ct. 837; 79 1. ed. 1570 (1935). Concurring opinion by Mr. Justice Cordozo.

4. The analysis of laws included the years 1973, 1974, and 1975 covering the terms of three governors (Rockefeller, Wilson, and Carey) and a change of political party control of the governorship and the legislature. Details of the analysis will be published in a separate study.

5. See Eric Redman, *The Dance of Legislation* (New York: Simon and Schuster, 1973) for a vivid description of the role that the bureaucracy plays and the administrator's commitments made to the Legislators prior to passage of a new program bill.

6. US Senate Subcommittee on Separation of Powers. *Separation of powers, Hearings* 90th Congress, first session,(Washington, DC: Government Printing Office, 1967).

7. For an illuminating discussion of this process, see Aaron Wildavsky, *The Politics of the Budgetary Process* 2nd Edition. (Boston: Little, Brown and Co., 1974), Chapter 3.

8. Public Law 93–344, 12 July 1974.

9. See, for example, Joseph P. Harris, *Congressional Control of Administration*, (Garden City, NY: Doubleday and Company, 1965), and Frank Newman and Harrys Keaton, "Congress and the Faithful Execution of Laws—Should Legislators Supervise Administrators?" 41 *California Law Review* 565 (1953).

10. Herbert A. Simon, *Administrative Behavior*, 2nd Edition. (New York: The Free Press, 1957) Chapter 3.

Part 3

Legislative Reforms and Innovations in Selected Countries

Legislative Reforms in the Brazilian Chamber of Deputies 1964–1975

ABDO I. BAAKLINI

Introduction

The year 1964 in Brazil marks the end of an era and the beginning of a new one. President Juan Goulart, backed by a freely elected legislature and enjoying popular support, was overthrown, and a civilian-military coalition took over through the use of power and coercion. The new "revolutionary" political order, dominated by the military, suspended constitutional life, adjourned the legislature, and for a while ruled by executive decrees. In an effort to rally civilian support behind it, the new regime resurrected the themes of order and progress as its official political ideology. Order and progress were to be achieved through curtailment of political conflicts, restriction of the electoral and legislative processes, disbandment of existing political parties, and institutionalization of a strong executive composed of members of the newly forged military-technocratic alliance. A bicameral legislature was allowed to continue in existence only after it had been stripped of its essential powers. After tolerating a multiparty system until 1969, the executive decreed that elections would be contested by candidates from two new government-created political parties, a progovernment party called ARENA (Aliança Renovadora Nacional) and a loyal opposition party called MDB (Movimento Democrático Brasileiro).[1] Political science literature on Brazil since 1964 has concentrated on how the executive has succeeded in preventing any meaningful democratic life, substituting instead an authoritarian, oppressive military regime.[2] While the literature has succeeded in highlighting one important aspect of political life under the authoritarian military regime, it has neglected an equally important aspect, the resistance to the military repression. In one of his insightful observations, Dahrendorf said:

> The structures of power in which the political process takes place offer an explanation not only of how change originates and what direction it takes, but also of why it is necessary. *Power always implies non-power and, therefore, resistance. The dialectic of power and resistance is the motive force of history. From the interest of those in power at a given time, we can infer the interests of the powerless, and with them the direction of change.*[3] [italics mine]

Resistance to power may take various forms and approaches. It can range from open guerrilla warfare to minor actions by bureaucrats, judges, and legislators. It can reject the system and try to destroy it from outside, or it can operate within the system. This chapter will examine one facet of this resistance by examining the persistent efforts of the Brazilian Chamber of Deputies in the area of legislative reform. While the present discussion will be limited to legislative reforms in the Chamber of Deputies, it is necessary to point out at the outset that similar reforms did take place in the Senate. In fact, the contents of resolutions 20 and 30 of 1971, which spelled out the procedural and structural changes in the Chamber, are also embodied in similar resolutions applicable to the Senate.[4] Confining our discussions to the Chamber has been dictated by reasons of space and to avoid duplication.

Why Legislative Reform?

Political scientists, especially non-Brazilian ones, have the luxury of undertaking their research and arriving at their conclusions, condemning or praising the political setup, without having to suffer the consequences of their appraisals. They are normally concerned with what exists, and sometimes in evaluating what exists against some of their theoretical and value assumptions. Politicians and groups in Brazil, on the other hand, cannot afford such a luxury. They are directly affected by what exists, they bear the consequences of what they say and what they do, and finally they are interested in what should be from within the constraints of what is possible. Legislators as politicians have to live in a political system while working to change it. It is this process of accommodation and resistance, as manifested in the efforts of the Brazilian Chamber of Deputies, that we seek to capture, and we suggest that this process of accommodation and resistance has gradually been strengthening the legislature as a political institution in the country.

As with almost all political acts, the legislative reforms in Brazil included several actors with conflicting and overlapping visions of what the reforms were intended to achieve. We can distinguish three distinct actors: the executive, the legislators, and the legislative staff. Each viewed the legislative reforms from its own perspective as a means of enhancing its goals. Sometimes the means to the realization of different goals were the same; sometimes they were different. Nonetheless, each saw in the legislative reforms a partial fulfillment of its goals and, therefore, was willing to support it and work for it as an acceptable means for the realization of its vision.[5]

The Executive Vision

In the Brazilian context it is safe to assume that legislative reforms, especially basic structural and procedural reforms, would require executive approval. In fact, many of the basic changes introduced reflected the vision and needs of the executive. These included reforms regarding political party leadership in the legislature, the leadership of the legislature, the committee system, and the procedures the legislature was to follow in dealing with proposed bills. In its commitment to order and progress, the executive thought to eliminate from the legislative process structures and procedures that could lead to conflict and procrastination. In conformity with the thrust of the literature on development, the executive in Brazil was committed to a strong "nonpolitical" technocratic central authority whose goal is the preservation of political order as a precondition of accelerated economic progress. This vision translated into the legislative process meant the substitution of rationality and efficiency for politics and partisanship. If the legislative process was to help executive action, it should reflect the logic and procedures of the planning board, not the politicians. Legislative reforms should therefore strengthen the institution's ability to deal with comprehensive socioeconomic planning, to avoid unnecessary delays, to overcome localism and regionalism, and above all to avoid personal or partisan considerations as a basis for their actions. If the legislature was to participate in the decision-making process, it would have to avoid the corrupting influence of personal and partisan politics that characterized the regime that the military had replaced. The legislative process should not only be rational and efficient but also swift and supportive of executive actions. Honest legislators, if they "truly" had the "public interest" in mind, rather than their own selfish, partisan, or local interests, could not differ or disagree on what action to follow. Disagreement with or prolonged debate over "comprehensive" executive proposals would undoubtedly be motivated by "corrupt" selfish political factors.

The executive vision undoubtedly reflected the logic of the self-righteous, benevolent dictatorship often advocated in the literature on development as the most congenial political order to speed up the process of socioeconomic development.[6] It rests on the premise that technical-professional decisions are superior to political, value-laden decisions. The fallacies of this logic have been adequately covered elsewhere.[7] It is sufficient to point out that what is advocated as a technical-professional decision oftentimes involves the choice among competing values and interests and is, therefore, as political as any decision can be. Technical-professional decisions in no way preclude political and value choices.

The Legislative Vision

Articulating a legislative vision poses some problems. Contrary to the executive, the legislature speaks with more than one voice and, therefore, it is difficult to discern a one overall vision. In collegial bodies it is more appropriate to speak of clusters of visions which sometimes contradict each other and sometimes complement each other.

The majority of the Brazilian Chamber of Deputies displayed the following clusters of visions regarding legislative reform. One group of legislators subscribed to the executive vision. If Brazil was to avoid political disorder and economic stagnation, they thought a strong, nonpolitical, executive-action-oriented legislature was necessary. This group rallied around the themes of order and progress advocated by the military, and many of the constitutional debates that preceded the legislative reforms advocated a strong executive and a legislature that would manifest the same characteristics and ideology as the executive.[8] The legislative reforms advocated by the executive were, therefore, wholeheartedly supported by this group. After all the military takeover in 1964 had been supported and championed by a significant number of leading civilian politicians and intellectuals, including members of the Congress. A legislative-executive agreement over what constituted the best political order was to be expected.

A second group of legislators, while not in agreement with the executive vision of what constitutes the best political order, decided to go along with many of the proposals the executive advocated. A number of considerations dictated this. By adopting the ideology and logic of the executive, the legislature would insure its survival and would legitimize its role even under a military-dominated regime. Members of this group believed that decisions are pervasively political whether taken by the executive or the legislature and that claims of rationality and efficiency are simply intended to mask the political nature of the decisions reached. If the executive can reach political decisions and mask them as technical-professional decisions, why can't the legislature? The rational-efficiency ideology might be as good an instrument for the legislature and it would enable the legislature to participate in political debates on the same footing as the executive. Members of this group also felt that the legislature needed to establish a new image if it wished to enjoy popular support and respectability. As is the case in many developing and developed countries, the Brazilian legislature had been suffering from a poor image. The military conception that the legislature was corrupt, unrepresentative of the population, undemocratic in its internal structures and procedures, and inherently conservative and inefficient was shared by many civilian intellectuals, such as students, journalists, and professionals. A new image of the legislature was therefore a primary objective of this group of legislators. The legislature should come to be seen as a rational-efficient decision-making institution, whose goals are to promote order and rapid socioeconomic development. The legislature should also be seen to stress its representative nature, its fair, democratic, and efficient structures and procedures. The content as well as the procedures of the legislative reforms should seek to enhance such an image. If intellectuals and the general public thought more highly of the legislature, this group reasoned, the institution would be able to stand up to the executive and in due time transform the dominant role of the executive vis-a-vis the legislature. In brief, this group wished to use legislative reforms as a means to gain support and legitimacy within the executive branch and among the population so that the legislative institution could survive and in due course change the authoritarian military nature of the political regime in Brazil.

A third group of legislators sought reforms that fell within the executive's zone of indifference. They stressed technical and organizational reforms, such as the creation of a computer center, an information center, a legislative internship program, a press section to facilitate the work of the journalists, and finally the establishment and upgrading of central professional staff units. All of these proposals were thought to be technical and therefore politically acceptable to the executive. Indeed the executive may have encouraged reforms along these lines under the assumption that a legislature served by a rational-efficient legislative bureaucracy was more likely to support executive action. If legislators broadened their factual information base, perhaps they might overcome their provincial particularistic orientation and act in the national interest. As far as the legislature was concerned, the establishment and broadening of an independent factual information base might enable the legislature to participate in decisions and debates and would permit it to challenge the factual premises of executive-sponsored proposals.

The legislative reforms, as we shall see, embodied much that these three groups envisioned. However a fourth group of legislators resisted the reforms as being inspired by the executive and therefore as an instrument to weaken the legislature.

The Legislative Staff Vision

Legislative reforms, especially their procedural and organizational dimensions, usually embody to a large extent the vision of the legislative staff. Their direction as well as their implementation depend on the acquiescence of the legislative staff. The Brazilian legislative reforms were no exception.

The Brazilian legislative staff are part of a permanent, career-oriented bureaucracy. Their selection, promotion, transfer, retirement, and salary are governed by central regulations that are uniformly enforced. As with most bureaucracies, the Brazilian legislative bureaucracy adhered to the executive vision of the proper political order. To a permanent, professionally oriented bureaucracy, politics is disruptive and irrational and should therefore be curbed. The legislative process should manifest the ideal attributes of a rational-efficient bureaucracy. The procedural and structural reforms introduced at the staff organizational level manifested this bureaucratic preoccupation. The stress was on a politically neutral, professionally oriented staff to provide the factual premises of legislative decisions. To promote neutralism and professionalism a merit system should be adhered to. Undoubtedly such a system would enhance staff job security and would promote its self-esteem and its power.

The Legislative Reforms in the Chamber of Deputies

Many American legislative-reform-minded groups would be surprised to learn that the Brazilian legislative reform embodies their dream. It is characterized by its comprehensiveness and its nonpolitical, rational, efficiency orientations. It is also characterized by its openness, avoidance of power sinecures, and encouragement of membership participation in various positions of leadership. Perhaps the best way to understand the Brazilian legislative reform is to outline its salient features. We shall do so under five headings: political leadership in the legislature, the committee system, the concern with efficiency, technical innovations, and image-building.

Political Leadership in the Legislature

The political leadership in the Brazilian Chamber of Deputies is divided into two distinct categories, leadership of the whole institution, called MESA or Management Board, and party leadership.

The MESA. Perhaps in no other place is the executive vision of a nonpolitical legislature more pronounced than in the composition, structuring, and jurisdiction of the MESA. To attend to the Chamber's management business, the first constitutional amendment of 1969 continued the practice of electing, by all members of the Chamber, a board composed of a president, two vice-presidents, four secretaries, and four deputy-secretaries. The board's term was fixed at two years and they could not be reelected. While many political considerations both within and outside the legislature (such as party distribution, regional representation, etc.) influences who is elected to the board, it is for all practical purposes the chief executive who determines the president, and consequently the other members, of the board. While the board is supposed to be nonpolitical and nonpartisan, its composition usually reflects the relative strength of the two parties in the Chamber, with the president and the majority of board members belonging to ARENA, thus far the majority party. As a neutral body representing the whole Chamber, the Board is supposed to implement the rules and regulations governing the conduct of legislative business in an impartial and nonpartisan fashion.

The president of the board is the president of the Chamber and its official spokesman. He divides the work among the various board members to insure that the management function of the Chamber is properly attended to. A permanent staff under the direction of a secretary general assist the board. The president, with the help of the general secretary, is responsible for such diverse management functions as printing and distribution of bills, setting up the calendar, preparing the journal, representing the Chamber to the outside groups, and presiding over its meetings. He coordinates and supervises the board's work and insures that its relations with the legislators, committees, legislative staff, and outside institutions are properly managed.

The two vice-presidents assist the president. They preside over the Chamber's meetings upon the president's request and represent him in formal functions outside the Chamber. Quite frequently they head special task forces and study groups authorized by the president and the board.

The first secretary has a very powerful position, for he supervises all the legislative and administrative staff in the Chamber, which number over two thousand employees. He is under constant pressure from legislators and committees to provide them with services and from the staff in matters relating to recruitment, placement, promotion, and the provision of resources so they may be able to discharge their functions.

The second secretary coordinates the Chamber's relations with such outside bodies as the executive, the judiciary, international institutions, and foreign delegations. He acts as a protocol officer and as the Chamber's minister of foreign affairs.

The third secretary coordinates the Chamber's relations with the press. He is also responsible for all publications originating in the Chamber, such as books, bills, journal abstracts, and the calendar of the Chamber.

The fourth secretary manages the fringe benefits of all legislators, staff, and their families. These include medical treatment, family allowances, transportation allowances, assignment of residence quarters, and other services and benefits that the Chamber provides for its members, staff, and their families. Figure 1 illustrates the organization of MESA.

Party Leadership. After the 1969 coup, Brazilian political life was confined to two officially sanctioned parties, the ARENA, acting as the government party, and the MDB, acting as the opposition party. All other parties were officially banned.

The role of the party and its leadership is officially and ex-

Chart 1

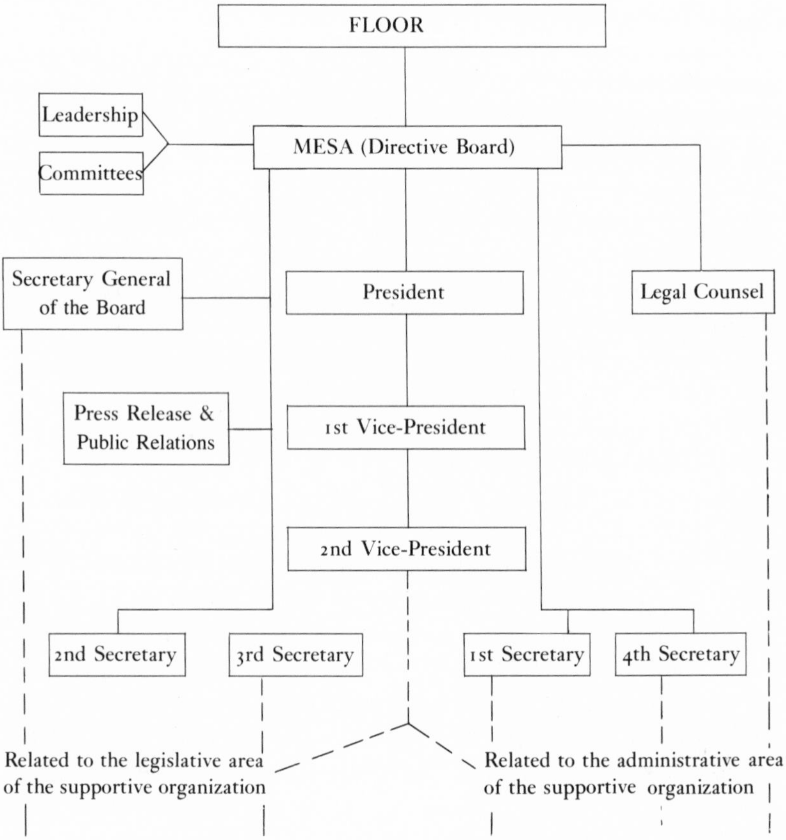

plicitly recognized within the Brazilian Chamber of Deputies.[9] Every four years each party in the Chamber meets to elect its leader, who becomes the official spokesman of his party to the board, the committees, and the floor. To assist him in his work and represent him in the various Chamber activities, each party leader is entitled to select one assistant from his own party for every ten deputies up to a total of five assistants. After that, he is entitled to an assistant for every fifteen deputies.

Assistant party leaders usually hold power in their own right. Since the two parties were created by executive fiat, deputies who belong to the same party do not necessarily share the same ideological and political orientation. Instead each party is composed of cliques, known as "Bancadars," [10] with strong state affiliation. The party leadership in the Chamber is a coalition of the various groups representing the party. The party leader's prerogatives include a separate staff provided by the Chamber, the right to address the floor every session, and the right to communicate his requests and suggestions to the presiding officer at any time during the session. With the help of his assistants he indicates which party members he would like the board to appoint to the various permanent committees. He also sends the board names of party members he would like to have placed in various delegations and official representations. The leader or any of his assistants are entitled to participate in the work of the various committees. While he is not allowed to vote, he is entitled to motion for vote of verification in any committee. On the floor the party leader may petition for a secret voting or may petition that a bill be classified as urgent or priority. In instances where a petition or proposal needs a certain number of signatures to be considered by the committee on the floor, the party leader's signature carries a weight equivalent to the number of deputies belonging to his party. Finally the party leadership participates in a number of policy study groups and has been the source of some interesting policy recommendations.[11]

The Executive branch argues that the depoliticization of legislative leadership (both the party and the whole Chamber of Deputies) through the method of selection and rotation, tends to prevent the abuse of power and the concentration of privilege in the hands of well entrenched politicians.

They also contend that the ability of the institution to act and participate in decision-making in a responsible and constructive manner is increased. The new leadership is selected for its managerial ability and is given tremendous resources to discharge its work. Since it serves for only two years, the leadership can act objectively and forthrightly without fear of losing the support of dominant cliques in the Chamber. A fixed nonrenewable mandate also gives the leadership a time limit in which to complete whatever programs it intends to undertake. Thus it is suggested that actual reform acts and their implementation would not have taken place in such a short time, had it not been for the board's concern to achieve something during its term. Thus during the term of the 1971–72 board, resolutions 20 and 30 were adopted and to a large extent implemented, something that would have taken decades to achieve in legislatures characterized by strong permanent leadership. Furthermore, rotation of the leadership opens the way for new talent, which in turn encourages innovation in and openness of the legislative process.

Critics of the way legislative leaders are selected and how they operate, do not dispute the merit of having a rational-efficient organization to run the Chamber. Nor do they dispute the need to have the leadership elected periodically. In fact they feel that a collegial body such as the legislature stands to gain by such innovations. What they object to is the undue executive influence in selecting the leadership and, more importantly, the way the leadership acts as an arm of the executive for controlling and managing the legislature rather as an adversary defending the legislature against the executive. They argue that periodic rotation of the leadership gives the executive undue power to select individuals who lack a power base in the legislature and, therefore, cannot stand up to executive pressure. Those who have been legislative leaders see the whole issue differently. They see their primary function to be one of mediating conflicts between the executive and the legislature. If the legislature is to be saved from dissolution or suspension (both actions being within the presidential prerogative under Institutional Act Number Five of 1969), then executive-legislative relations must be characterized by compromise, negotiation, and accommodation, and not by conflict and confrontation. This group is opting for time; they look forward to when the appeal of the military and of its call for order and progress has faded and when the legislature, through its new image, has been rehabilitated and its prestige has increased among the people. Finally the legislative staff finds the new arrangement to its liking, because a temporary, inexperienced political leadership finds itself dependent on its professional, permanent staff, and the role of the legislative bureaucracy is augmented. This does not disturb the legislative staff, because it conceives of itself as being competent, dedicated, and motivated to serve the interest of the institution rather than the personal interests of individual legislators.

The Committee System

The rationale for the restructuring of the legislative leadership applied in large part to the selection and functioning of the committees. The concern was to provide the legislature with an open, nonpolitical, and action-oriented committee system. After nomination by the party leadership, the board selects the members for the sixteen standing committees every two years. The two parties have proportional representation in both committee membership and committee chairmanships. Thus although until the last election in 1974, the MDB controlled less than one-third of the seats in the Chamber, it chaired a number of standing committees. Each committee has a chairman and two vice-chairmen. As is true for the board, committees serve for two-year terms only. While members can be reappointed to the same committee, chairmen cannot. It is not uncommon, under this rotational policy, to find a new deputy chairing a committee, since appointment is not based on seniority, nor solely on political power. A member's field of specialization before joining the Chamber, his occupational orientation, and regional considerations influence the party leadership as well as the board in making committee selections. Each deputy, except those on the board, is assigned to one committee as a principal member and to another as an alternate member. No deputy can be a principal member in more than one committee.

In addition to the sixteen standing committees, there are a number of ad hoc committees. These include select,[12] inquiry, external, and joint committees.[13]

Meetings of the committees are open to the public and to other deputies. Deputies who do not belong to a committee may participate in its deliberations short of voting. Committee votes on bills are recorded unless there was a motion for a secret ballot. Committee reports are also printed in the journal. Committees are entitled to hold hearings, subpoena witnesses and documents, and propose legislation. During floor debates, the chairmen and the committee reporter (clerk?) are given priority in addressing the floor when bills originating from their committees are under discussion. The internal rules define how long a committee may take before reporting a bill to the floor. Contrary to the practice of committees in the US Congress, standing committees in the Brazilian Chamber of Deputies must report bills within a specific time. The period allowed varies according to how the bill is introduced. For bills that are classified as urgent, the committee has two days; for those labelled priority, it has five days; and for an ordinary bill, it has ten days. Often these time limitations are extended. As we shall discuss later, the classification of bills and the ways in which they are introduced are innovations intended to speed up the legislative process so as to fit the need of rapid economic growth.

The jurisdiction of standing committees is not confined to the consideration of bills. Article 28 of resolution 30 entitles the committee to explore any policy issue relevant to its subject matter. Thus committees under dynamic chairmen have undertaken functions such as the sponsoring of seminars to educate the public on important national issues. Some committees publish journals in their subject areas, such as *Economica* and *A Revista de Educacao.* Both journals are widely circulated among economists and educators and serve a very important educational and communication functions.

The committee system has been evaluated by the same political actors that judged the legislative leadership. Arguments in its favor are that it is open, efficient, and nonpolitical. Those against it are that it lacks power and rubber stamps proposed executive bills. The committee leaders realize their awkward position vis-a-vis the executive, but feel that by working hard, adopting rational and efficient procedure, and educating the public on major issues, they may be able to reverse the trend in their favor. They are aware that they cannot afford to procrastinate on executive-sponsored bills, for this might lead to adverse public reaction, especially with regard to socioeconomic legislation. Instead their strategy is to equip themselves with the necessary information and to adopt a speedy procedure, which enables them to participate in a meaningful evaluation of proposed legislation within the limited time allotted to them.

There is a general agreement, however, that the committees are now better staffed, have a wider base of information, and are discharging their work efficiently because of a number of procedural innovations that we shall discuss later. They have also managed to establish better rapport with the media and the public. Whether they have become more powerful is still debatable. In the final analysis the power of the committees depends on the power of the mother institution, the full Chamber. But through their policy studies and analysis and through their nonconfrontational approach with the executive, they have managed to strongly influence some bills that the executive adopted.[14]

The Concern with Efficiency

Legislative reforms under this heading were mainly intended to speed up the legislative process, coordinate the various activities within the legislature, and more importantly to insure that the government's economic development programs were swiftly acted upon. Innovations included the establishment of a Joint Budget Committee and rationalization of the legislative process.

The Joint Budget Committee. Advocates of budgetary reforms in the US, especially those who view the budget as an instrument for attaining sound economic and fiscal policies, have often complained that the legislative process is the main obstacle to such a goal. The legislative review of the budget is characterized by confusion, piecemeal work, and lack of coordination. Planning and budgeting are not considered together; revenues and expenditures are rarely coordinated; and authorization and appropriation are the functions of separate committees. To add to the confusion and delay, the budget review in the House is distinct and separate from the budget review in the Senate. The net result, it is argued, is that the legislature never considers the budget in its entirety and, therefore, the budget fails to be a useful instrument for planning and for economic and fiscal policies determination. In Brazil, where the whole ideology of the regime is based on rapid economic growth, the budget takes on disproportionate importance as an instrument of planning, economic, and fiscal policies determination. The need to devise budget review procedures to insure that it can be acted upon promptly becomes understandable.

The constitutional amendment of 1969 called for the establishment of a Joint Budget Committee (JBC) whose sole job is to study the budget, evaluate it, and act upon it. The JBC is composed of forty-five members from the Chamber and fifteen members from the Senate selected annually by the authorities in each house. The committee chairman, although elected annually by the committee members, tends to be alternately a senator and a deputy. While the committee meets as a whole, voting is calculated for each house separately.

The committee starts work in mid-August, when the budget is submitted by the executive. The budget in Brazil is a unified document. It includes all government transactions, such as revenues, expenditures, trust funds, loans, etc. Since the budget is intimately tied to the five-year plan, it also includes all the programs that were completed, those that need to be completed in the present fiscal year, and those that are planned to be completed in successive years. In this sense it gives a total picture of all government activities and programs.

The JBC budget review takes place within procedural and time limitations. Since the programs in the annual budget document are based on previously approved general programs contained in the five-year plan, the JBC cannot unilaterally delete from or add programs to the budget document. This insures the coordination of planning and budgeting. The JBC concentrates, therefore, on the following issues:

—to what extent is the budget document coherent and compatible with prior planning and programs contained in the five-year-plan
—to what extent are increases in routine expenditures reasonable
—to what extent do requested expenditures reflect national goals and priorities

—to what extent is the time schedule attached to the projects reasonable.

Once the budget is reviewed and amended, the committee passes it article by article and reports it to the floor for final enactment. However, to enhance speed and efficiency committee recommendations are final and no further amendments are accepted from the floor except upon the request of one-third of the members in each house. Otherwise the recommendations of the committee are final and are usually accepted on the floor with ease and without amendments.

In accordance with constitutional provisions, the budget needs to be approved within forty-five days from the time it is submitted. This means the JBC must be well prepared before the budget is submitted if it is to undertake any meaningful review. This need has been met by the addition of certain technical and staff capabilities to both houses which we shall discuss later.

Procedural Innovations. Legislatures in contemporary societies undergoing rapid economic change have to act on a myriad of issues ranging from the insignificant to the vital. Sometimes legislative procedures developed when the society was simple and the issues they dealt with were limited and uncomplex. They now need to be brought in line with the complexities of modern issues. In many cases legislatures need to devise a system for establishing priorities applicable to the discharge of their functions. Major bills need to be separated from trivia. Work must be scheduled so as to avoid rush and chaos. A sense of appropriate timing is often needed. The Brazilian legislative reform addressed itself to these issues and devised a rational system of priorities and preferences in handling its work. Bills are categorized in terms of their significance and in terms of their initiators. Each type of bill is given an order of priority in terms of when to be acted upon and the time span within which action is to be completed. Legislative actions may fall into five categories: bills (projetos), amendments (emendas), suggestions (indicacoes), petitions (requirimentos), and recommendations (pareceres). Each type requires a different procedure and time framework. A bill can be initiated by the executive, the legislature, or the judiciary. To become a law, a bill needs to be approved by each house and promulgated by the president.

Priority in considering a bill depends on the source of its introduction and the importance of the bill. A bill can be labeled as urgent, special, priority, or ordinary. The internal rules specify thirteen instances for transmittal under urgent labeling. This right is reserved to the chief executive, the judiciary, the board (MESA), the Chamber (if requested by one-third of the members), and the committee (if approved by two-thirds of its members).[15] Once a bill takes the urgent route, the congress has to act upon it within forty-five days. If it fails to do so and if the bill was introduced by the executive, it can become a law without legislative approval. Labeling a bill urgent is one method the executive commonly uses as a means of determining the legislative agenda. Special bills can only originate in an institution, such as the executive, the judiciary, or the board or a congressional committee.[16] Such bills come after urgent bills and take precedent over ordinary bills. A priority label speeds up a bill already introduced under the ordinary method. Most bills, however, take the ordinary route. Even under the ordinary procedure, committees are under time limitations to report the bill to the floor. If a committee fails to act on a bill within the time limit, the board can recall the bill and refer it to another committee or put it directly on the floor.

Amendments are usually the prerogative of committees. Occasionally, however, amendment takes place on the floor. Bills considered by joint committees (such as the budget bill) or bills reported under the power of delegated legislation (the power given to the executive to issue certain laws) cannot be amended unless requested by one-third of the members in case of the former and one-fifth in the case of the latter.

Suggestions are comments or recommendations introduced by an individual legislator concerning bills under consideration by a committee. Suggestions are referred to committees for action; they are not given an urgent or priority consideration, since they do not require an affirmative or negative action.

Recommendations are usually introduced by committees and refer to bills already introduced. Recommendations are usually sent to the floor in connection with bills or other work done by committee.

Petitions are mechanisms covering a number of areas where information, clarification, or modifications are required. Resolution 30 refers to forty-one instances where resort to petition is sanctioned. Usually the legislature uses it to request information from the executive. Sometimes the legislature petitions the executive for some specific type of action. Petition is a mechanism where the legislature expresses its desires and wishes to the executive without resort to confrontation or embarrassment.

The products of legislative action take a number of forms. Some are bills that pass both houses and are promulgated by the executive. A resolution refers to a measure that requires the approval of either house and usually deals with matters pertaining to internal policies. A legislative decree refers to an enactment by both houses and concerns matters of mutual concern to both the Senate and the Chamber. Finally a presidential law-decree refers to emergency situations where the president enacts a law without prior submittal or approval of the legislature. Presidential law-decrees expire unless submitted and approved by the legislature within sixty days. Table 1 provides the sources and kinds of legislation between 1971 and 1974 of both houses.

The bulk of legislation occurs within the bill category. Of the total 2,404 bills introduced in the four-year period, 348 were introduced by the executive, 4 by the judiciary, and 2,052 by the congress. Of the 2,052 bills introduced by the congress, 84 were introduced by the Senate and 1,968 by the Chamber. Most of the bills were introduced by private members.

If one of the main purposes of legislative reforms in Brazil is to insure that the legislature act positively in a swift and prompt manner on bills proposed by the executive, we should expect that most bills introduced by the executive were approved, while most bills introduced by the legislature were either rejected or not considered at all. Table 2 shows the total number of bills rejected or approved in accordance with the source of their introduction.

A careful reading of table 2 shows that bills introduced by the executive are normally acted upon and not a single bill was

Table 1

Occurrence of Proposals, by Branch of Government
1971–74, 7th Legislature, Chamber of Deputies,
Brazilian National Congress

Proposals Introduced	1971	1972	1973	1974	Total
Suggestions	5	1	3	8	17
Recommendations	58	10	16	6	90
Congressional	—	1	—	—	1
Legislative Decree Bills	54	35	47	37	173
Legislature:[1]	?	?	?	?	?
Deputies[1]	?	?	?	?	?
Committees[1]	?	?	?	?	?
Congressional Decree Bills	58	54	40	70	222
Proposal for Amendment of the Constitution	—	1	—	—	—
Bills	543	553	637	671	2404
From Executive	62	59	93	134	348
From Judiciary	2	—	—	2	4
From Legislature:	479	494	544	535	2052
Senate	8	23	36	17	84
Chamber	471	471	508	518	1968
Deputies[1]	?	?	?	?	?
Committees[1]	?	?	?	?	?
Directive Board[1]	?	?	?	?	?
Congressional	29	13	15	12	69

rejected. In 1973 three bills introduced by the executive were not considered, however, in 1974 two of those bills were approved and the remaining one was still under consideration. It is safe to assume that that particular bill is not important; otherwise, the executive would have introduced it under the urgent method and would have forced the legislature to act upon it within forty-five days.

Bills introduced by the judiciary or by the congress as a whole were all approved during the period under discussion. There were four bills introduced by the judiciary and sixty-nine by the congress.

The record of the two houses in terms of bills approved or rejected seems to be unequal. The Senate managed to have 29 of its 84 bills approved, 45 rejected, and only 10 not acted

Table 1 continued

Complementary Bills	5	7	19	40	71
From Executive	—	—	—	4	4
From Legislature:	5	7	19	36	67
Chamber	5	7	19	35	66
Senate	—	—	—	1	1
Congressional	—	—	—	—	—
Resolution Bills	22	29	52	16	110
Directive Board (Chamber)[1]	?	?	?	?	?
Committees (Chamber)[1]	?	?	?	?	?
Deputies[1]	?	?	?	?	?
Congressional	—	2	—	—	2
Petitions	25	14	25	17	86
of information	25	11	15	15	66
to convoke ministers or secretary of state	—	3	10	2	15
Amendments of Senate[1]	?	?	?	?	?
to Bills	?	?	?	?	?
from Executive	?	?	?	?	?
from Legislature	?	?	?	?	?
Deputies	?	?	?	?	?
Committees	?	?	?	?	?
to Legislative Decree Bills	?	?	?	?	?
Committees	—	—	—	—	—

[1] Data is either not available or does not permit a subdivision in accordance to source of initiation.

upon. The Chamber, on the other hand, had only 144 of its 1,968 bills approved, 521 rejected, and 1,303 not acted upon. In other words, of the 1,314 bills introduced and not acted upon, 1,303 were introduced by the Chamber, 10 by the Senate, and only one by the executive. This leaves no doubt that the legislative agenda is determined by the executive and is structured to deal primarily with legislation introduced by the executive.

A careful review of bills introduced by the Chamber and the action taken upon those bills reveal a very interesting phenomenon. Our data does not distinguish which bills were introduced by the chamber, private deputies, committees, or the board, but it does show that of the 144 bills approved, 129 were introduced by deputies, 5 by committees, and 10 by the board.

Table 2

Total bills by Source of Introduction Number Approved and Rejected Between 1971–74

Source of Introduction	Total Introduced	Total Accepted	Total Rejected
Executive	348	347	—
Judiciary	4	6[1]	—
Legislature	2052	173	566[2]
Senate	84	29	45
Chamber	1968	144	521
Deputies	?	129	520
Committees	?	5	1
Board	?	10	—
Congress (joint legislation)	69	69	—

[1] The two extra bills approved were introduced in the session prior to 1971.

[2] The remaining 1313 bills introduced by the legislature were not acted upon.

Of the 521 rejected, 520 were introduced by the deputies, 1 by a committee, and none by the board. Therefore it is safe to conclude that bills originating in the Chamber have a better chance of being approved if they originate from a committee or from the board rather than from individual deputies. Conversely the likelihood that a bill would be rejected or not acted upon is higher if it is sponsored by an individual deputy rather than by a committee or by the board. These findings, it must be remembered, are in conformity with the intention of the legislative reform, especially as seen by the executive, which is to speed up and facilitate the executive program while keeping conflict and personal politics at a minimum. Priority in the legislative process is given to legislation initiated by institutions whether that institution happened to be the executive, the judiciary, the congress, the board, or the committee.

Legislative action, however, is not limited to bills alone. Table 3 provides a total picture of legislative activities between 1971–84, by showing the various types of activities and the percentage of approval or rejection of each type of legislation. The activities of the legislature in such activities as recommendations, complementary bills, petitions, and amendments seem

Table 3

Legislative Process 7th Legislature, Chamber of Deputies, Brazilian National Congress 1971–74

Kinds of Actions	Total Introduced	Approved %	Rejected %
Suggestions[1]	17	—	—
Recommendations	90	2	—
Congressional	1	—	—
Legislative Decree Bills	173	92	1
Congressional	222	97	—
Proposal for Amendment of the Constitution	1	—	—
Bills	2404	21	23
From Executive	348	99	—
From Judiciary[2]	4	150	—
From Legislature	2052	8	27
Senate	84	34	53
House	1968	7	26
Congressional	69	100	—
Complementary Bills	71	12	5
From Executive[2]	4	125	—
From Legislature	67	5	5
House	66	4	6
Senate	1	100	—
Congressional[3]	?	7	—
Resolution Bills	119	45	1
Petitions General	86	1	3
Petitions for information	66[1]	—	—
Petitions to ask ministers to testify	15	6	20
Amendments of Senate[3]	?	64	10
To Bills	?	63	10
From Executive	?	48	7
From Legislature	?	15	3
Deputies	?	13	—
Committees	?	2	—
Legislative Decree Bills	?	1	—
Committees	?	1	—
Total (Per kind of decision given to the proposal from 1971–74)	3255	33	17

[1] Suggestions and some petitions do not need to be approved or rejected.

[2] The number of approved here is bigger than the number of introduced because there are still some bills being reexamined that are from the previous legislature of 1967–70.

[3] Data on number of bills introduced is not available, thus the number in columns 2 and 3 is the real number rather than the percentage.

to indicate a busy schedule. It also confirms the basic contention of the reformers that the legislature should act as a complementary institution to the executive rather than as an adversary one.

Managerial and Technical Innovations

The reforms discussed in the preceding sections have been primarily political ones that have administrative implications. The reforms discussed here are primarily administrative, with political overtones. These aim at increasing the information base of the legislature. They include measures to increase and improve the legislative staff and to create a joint computer center to serve both houses.

The Strengthening of Legislative Staff. The staff of the Brazilian Chamber has always been characterized by strong centralizing tendencies. It has always been career-oriented, neutral, and selected by merit and competition. Resolution 20 of November 1971, defining the structure and jurisdiction of the staff in the Chamber, strengthened these tendencies.

The Brazilian Chamber of 350 deputies [17] is served by more than 2,000 full-time employees. In a legislature characterized by a nonpolitical leadership, measures were taken to insure that the staff is also nonpolitical. The staff is organized under two general directorates, one headed by a secretary general and the other by a director general. The office of the secretary general works closely with the MESA and is the equivalent to the leadership staff in some US state legislatures. However the secretary general and his staff are permanent career civil servants who serve on the pleasure of the board. If the board decides to remove the secretary general, he and his staff are asked to return to the departments or divisions under the general directorate from which they were drawn. New staff drawn from the central pool of staff then take their place. The general secretary and his staff are responsible for seeing that the various functions performed by the board and discussed in the previous section are implemented; he and his staff are primarily an interface between the political structure and the administrative structure. Chart 2 shows the position of the general secretary vis-à-vis the board and the rest of the legislative staff.

Chart 2

House of Representatives Staff Structure

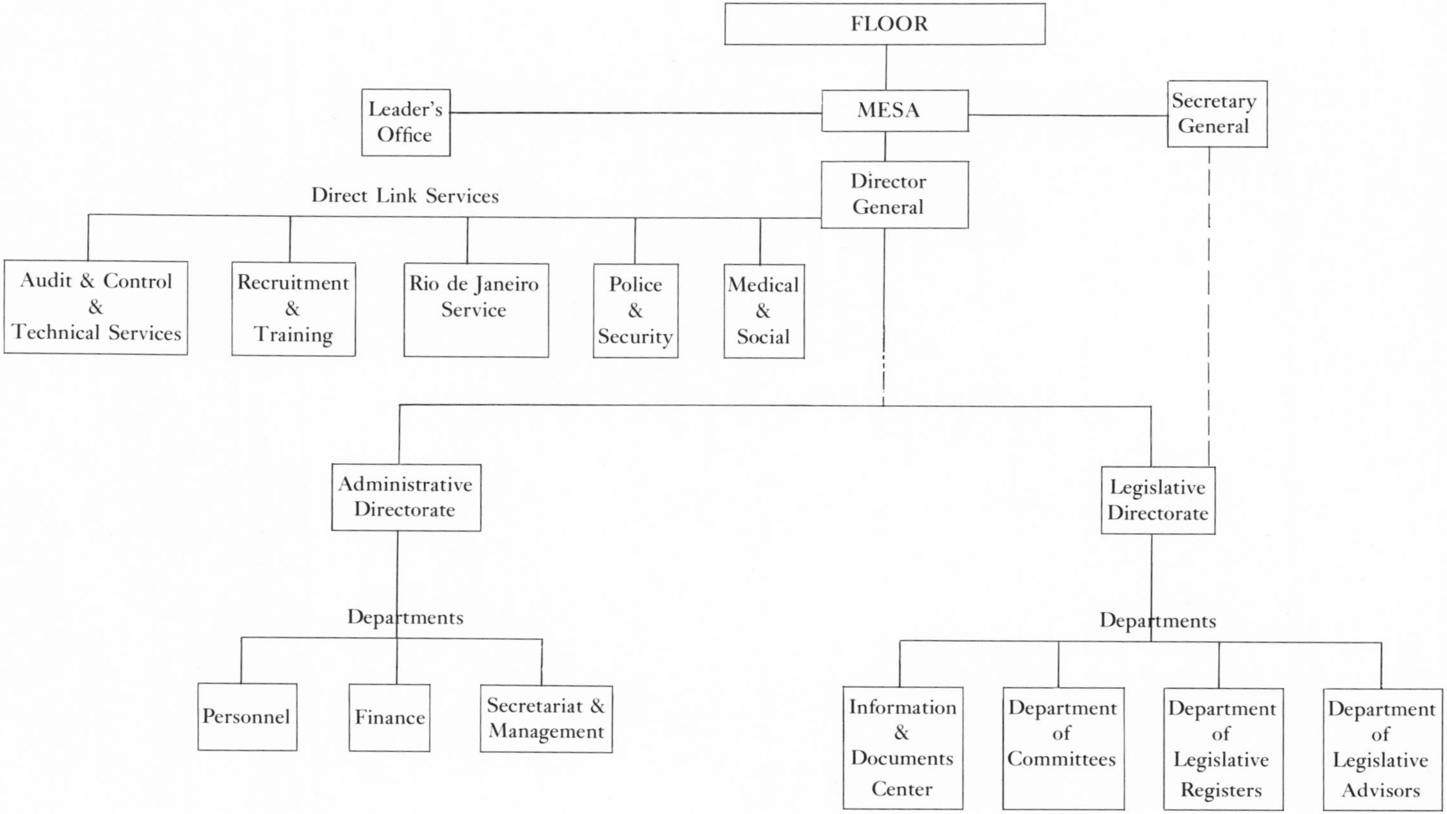

Most of the legislative staff and services fall under the jurisdiction of the director general. His office is the apex of the administrative hierarchy and theoretically any contact between the staff and the political structure of the Chamber has to pass through him. The director general directly controls five services: the office of the Audit and Technical Counsel, a Rio office to manage the Rio de Janeiro operations of the Chamber, a police office to coordinate the work of the Chamber's police, a recruitment and training office to perform personnel functions, and a medical and social office to take care of the medical and social needs of the deputies and the legislative staff.

Two directorates under the director general perform the bulk of the administrative and legislative work. The administrative directorate has charge of all administrative and financial matters in the Chamber. Its three principal functions are represented by its three departments, personnel, finance, and secretarial work and management. The legislative directorate handles the professional and technical legislative function. It is within this directorate that most of the resources of the recent reform were deployed. The legislative directorate consists of four large departments: a center for information and documentation, a department for committees, a legislative register department, and a department of legislative advisors.

The center for information and documentation combines the functions of a legislative reference library and a legislative research service. It supervises an extensive library and generates a lot of information and reports that are used by the legislators or by the legislative staff. Until recently it supervised the legislative advisors section. The department of committees acts as a central unit to serve various legislative committees, a job which includes providing professional, secretarial, and clerical staff to committees, although this staff remains affiliated with the department of committees. The department of legislative register keeps the records of parliamentary debates in both stenographic and taped forms. These records are later edited and published in the parliamentary journal. Sometimes this department helps the department of committees record the minutes of the various legislative committees. The department of legislative advisors is a main innovation of the recent legislative reform. It consists of over forty professional workers whose main function is to provide research regarding pending legislation. This department also provides a pool of talent that the board and the various committees can draw upon for help in the legislative work.

The Computer Center. The computer center is another main innovation of the recent legislative reforms. As a joint Senate-Chamber venture, the computer center is a massive organization in which scores of technicians and legislative specialists work with an IBM 360 computer. It is intended to help the legislators develop an information base independent from the executive. Its purpose is to speed and simplify the legislative process, by eliminating much of the paper work, and to provide a mechanism for legislative research. Thus far the full potential of the computer has not been utilized, for it has been limited to administrative purposes, such as paying the wages of the legislators and their staff, maintaining a computerized medical file on all legislators and staff, and storing library holdings and *major* laws. Recently the computer center started keeping a summary of all legislative debates and other legislative activities. It has yet to be developed as a research instrument but concern over this has led to the appointment of a legislative specialist as the director of the center.

The services of the computer center as well as the various staff units are available to the Chamber and its subdivisions as an institution. This means that the staff serves the institution, not the leaders or members of the majority party. In a survey conducted by the author in 1973, members of the opposition MDB party reported that in most cases they depend on the legislative staff for their information, while deputies who belonged to the ARENA majority party were less dependent on legislative staff for their information.[18]

While the legislature may have been an unwilling partner with regard to some of the provisions of resolution 30, which defined the political structuring of the Chamber, there is no doubt that the provisions of resolution 20, affecting the administrative and technical services, are its creation. In a sense whatever concessions the legislature gave with regard to its prerogatives and procedures, it tried to compensate for by stressing its administrative and technical needs. If the executive's ideology called for a nonpolitical and efficient legislature, the legislature saw that it got the administrative and technical resources needed to perform its functions rationally and speedily. As to the role of a presumably neutral staff, it is no different from the role of a presumedly nonpolitical leadership. Both are used by the legislature to present a nonpolitical face to a military executive that displays intense aversion towards the political.

It is difficult to argue that a legislature with a strong administrative and technical capability is necessarily a strong legislature. In fact, it can be argued that a weak legislature tends to be dominated by a strong and neutral career-oriented legislative bureaucracy. Intensive interviews and talks with a number of leading Brazilian legislators tend to confirm a different conclusion, namely, that the Brazilian legislature, by strengthening its information base and its administrative and technical capabilities, is trying to legitimize its role on the same bases as the executive: rational and scientific bases. This conclusion is apparent in several other activities that the legislature has undertaken in its effort to build a favorable image for itself.

Image Building

Activities and programs have ostensibly been addressed to increasing the efficiency and responsiveness of the legislature. However, the legislature has been careful to capitalize on these activities and programs to build its image among the public. Reforms in this category fall within the executive's zone of indifference, but are strongly supported by the legislature and the legislative staff, since they see in them an instrument for building strong linkages with the public. The first such activity calls for the strengthening of relations between the legislature and the press, which the Chamber does through the efforts of the secretary general and the leadership board, which has one member responsible for providing the press with the information they need. The chamber also gives the press space and communication facilities within the premises of the legislature. This close relationship between the press and the Chamber led them to unite against a common foe. Members of the press and individual legislators have developed various strategies for exchanging information about sensitive subjects that are censored by the executive. Often legislators have risked their security by making a speech on the floor which provides the press with an excuse to report it as part of legislative activities.[19] In other instances journalists act as the legislators' main source of information, especially regarding politically sensitive issues such as political prisoners and violation of human rights by the military authorities. In addition the Brazilian legislature publishes its own daily newspaper covering all the important activities of relevance to the public. Each night the Brazilian radio carries an hour of special programs on the legislature and some of the most important government activities for the day.

Another important device for strengthening the linkage between the legislative and the public is the series of seminars that the various committees of the Chamber sponsor each year. These seminars address themselves to important socioeconomic issues facing Brazil and are usually reported by the press and attended by professionals in the fields under discussion. Sometimes these seminars involve international participants and audiences,[20] and often they are reported in the various publications and journals that originate in the Chamber. As mentioned earlier, each house has a number of professional journals sponsored by the pertinent committees. This publication program is intended to keep the professional public informed and educated on subjects of importance.

The Chamber has also started an internship program, which each month brings about a hundred university students from various parts of Brazil for one month of training at the Chamber in Brazilia. The interns are given the opportunity to observe and participate in the legislative process with the hope that they will develop an awareness of and an empathy for the conflicting demands placed on the legislator. The Chamber's training program involves sending top-level legislative staff to short-term academic programs in the United States and Europe. The purpose of this is to improve the staff's managerial and legislative capabilities by exposing them to other legislative experiences and technologies. These programs also serve to build linkages between the Brazilian legislature and other foreign legislatures and other academic institutes and universities.[21]

It is difficult to assess the full impact of the legislative reforms on the ability of the Brazilian Chamber of Deputies to increase its power as a participant in the policy-making process. Those who support the present regime would suggest that the legislature in Brazil is an equal partner to the executive, particularly with regard to economic and social policies. Opponents would strongly disagree and would point out that the legislature, through its majority, still dances to the tune of the executive. Political scientists and journalists around the world tend to subscribe to the latter position.

It is rather too early to assess the impact of the reforms, however, if the election of 1974 is any indication, there is no doubt that the legislature has become a symbol for resistance to the thrust of the regime's political ideology. Of the twenty-one Senate seats that were vacated, sixteen were captured by the MDB, the opposition party. Over 42 percent of the Chamber seats were also won by the MDB. Political analysts view the 1974 election as a protest vote; they also conceive of the electoral process (especially if elections were allowed to take place in a free atmosphere) and the legislature as the main instrument for change. The new liberalizing policy of which President Geisal speaks and which the press refers to as the policy of "decompression" is another indication of change, as is the curbing of secret military police meddling in the lives of citizens and dissent groups. Recently an opposition Senator delivered a strong speech against police brutality in the alleged murder of a journalist while in prison. Finally the records of the various substantive committees in the Congress and the number of proposals and bills they are producing vividly indicates a more active political role. Even when an individually sponsored bill is rejected or not considered, it is often picked up and presented as an executive-sponsored bill after it has rallied public support. In short, the legislature has become a rallying point for forces opposed to some of the regime's present policies.

Summary

Astute observers of legislatures in developing countries have often celebrated the "resiliency" which these institutions display against the tremendous odds which usually threaten their existence, but these same observers fail to explain how the legislatures manage to survive. Studies on Brazil often dismiss the legislature altogether as insignificant. The Brazilian legislature, however, is no different from other legislatures in many developing countries. Against the tremendous odds it has demonstrated a phoenix-like quality of survival; it has even grown. This chapter has attempted to describe and analyze how this institution managed to survive and how it is trying to function in an adverse environment. To condemn the institution as being "weak" and therefore not worthy of study is to miss the point. By seeming to adopt the same ideology held by the ruling executive, it has carved for itself a place that is becoming increasingly important in the Brazilian political system. It was able to do so by adopting structures and procedures that are ostensibly rational and efficiency-oriented rather than political. It equipped itself with managerial and technical capabilities and it embarked on a public relations and educational program to improve its public image. All of these activities and programs were part of what has been termed legislative reform in Brazil.

Author's Note

Many of the interpretations and conclusions of this chapter are based on the author's personal experience with the on-going legislative reforms in Brazil. During the past four years the author has had the opportunity to work with a large number of legislators and legislative staff who participated in the legislative reforms. The analysis has been, therefore, an attempt to structure and interpret the Brazilian legislative reforms. While many of the legislators and legislative staff members who on many occasions enlightened me with their observations, insights, and opinions may share certain conclusions of this chapter, none of them necessarily subscribe to the whole thesis of this article. In particular I would like to thank Professor Rosinethe Soares for her help as my research associate. Ms. Flavia I. Sequiera was helpful in researching the data for tables 1, 2 and 3. For details on Brazilian legislative reform see: Rosinethe M. Soares & Abdo I. Baaklini, *O Podro No Legislativo*, Camara dos Deputados, Information Center, 1976.

Notes

1. After the revolution the Brazilian Constitution was altered by a number of constitutional amendments and Institutional Acts. Of the three constitutional amendments, the first one of 17 October 1969, is the most important. This amendment placed restrictions on deliberations of proposed legislation, established procedures for joint sessions, especially with regard to presidential messages, and, most importantly, abolished the multiparty system in favour of a two-party system. Of the seventeen Institutional Acts between 1964 and 1969, the most far-reaching in its curtailment of legislative power, is Institutional Act number 5, of 13 December 1968. This act, proclaimed by the president in the name of protecting the revolution against any subversive activities, empowered the chief executive to suspend the membership of any legislator on account of alleged subversive activities. This act has been used to silence opposition and curtail critical debate in the Congress.

2. As an illustration, see Robert Dalland, *Brazilian Planning: Development Politics and Administration* (Chapel Hill, N.C.: The University of North Carolina Press, 1967); Alfred Stepan, *The Military in Politics: Changing Patterns in Brazil* (Princeton, N.J.: Princeton University Press, 1971).

3. Ralph Dahrendorf, *Essays in the Theory of Society* (Stanford, California: Stanford University Press, 1968), p. viii.

4. See Senate Resolution 58/72.

5. The discussion that follows is based on in-depth discussions with a number of legislators and legislative staff. Additional insights as to the goals of legislative reforms were gained through review of the legislative debates on resolutions 20 and 30 and through the reading of the various lectures and seminars that preceded the reforms. In 1965, for example, the University of Brazilia housed a seminar where twelve lectures concerning political reforms were delivered and debated. Another series of lectures regarding political reforms were sponsored by the Chamber of Deputies in 1971 and were later published in a volume titled, *Do Processo Legislativo* (Brazilia: Camara Dus Deputdos, 1972). In 1969 the renowned Brazilian research center, Fundacao Getulio Vargas, submitted a number of reports regarding suggested legislative reforms in Brazil. Most important are the seven reports that were prepared by a task force of deputies under the chairmanship of Deputy Jeraldo Juedes. This task force presented seven reports, the first of which, written by Deputy Marco Maciel, dealt with political parties and their relationship to the legislative process. The second report, by Deputy Tulio Vargas, dealt with floor procedures. The third report, by Deputy Herigue Turner, dealt with the legislative process. The fourth report, by Deputy Fabio Fonseca, dealt with committees. The fifth report, by Deputy Waddemiro Teixeira, dealt with public relations. The sixth report, by Deputy Faria Lima, dealt with legislative advisors. And the seventh report, by Deputy Jose Alves, dealt with legislative administration. All were submitted in 1971 and were the basis for drafting resolutions 20 and 30 of 1972. For a more general work on legislative power, see the book by Senator Ruy Santos, *O Poder Legislativo* (Brazil, 1972).

6. As an illustration of this literature, see Samuel P. Huntington, *Political Order in Changing Societies* (New Haven: Yale University Press, 1968).

7. For the difference between political rationality and other types of rationality, see Paul Diesing, *Reason in Society* (Alabama, Ill.: University of Illinois Press, 1962) and Bernard Crick, *In Defence of Politics* (Baltimore, Maryland: Pelican Books, 1969).

8. See sources listed under note 5.

9. Articles 9–12 of resolution 30, 1971 specifies the structure of party leadership, its method of election, and its prerogatives.

10. "Bancadas" refers to a group of legislators who belong to the same state. Brazil is a federal system composed of twenty-two states. The tendency is for legislators coming from the same state and the same political party to form a group representing state rights and interests. They are usually well organized and assisted by a professional staff with state facilities. They maintain close coordination with state party leadership and other government agencies.

11. Such work includes the recommendations produced by a seminar on National Development under the leadership of MDB Franco Montoro. It also includes the work of a group known by the Brazilian acronym of COCONE. Under the coordination of Senator Virgilio Tavora, this group produced a series of studies on the problems and policies in the northeast. An assistant party leader, Deputy Ruben Medina wrote a book on denationalization based on his experience as a member of an inquiry committee and as a member of the MDB study group.

12. There are five select committees that have taken on the character of permanent committees. They are regional committees that concern themselves with legislation affecting the following regions: drought poligone, Amazon region, Sao Francisco basin, south regional development, and center-west development.

13. The joint committees referred to in article 41 of resolution 30 are not the same joint budgetary committees referred to in the constitution, which we shall deal with later. There are committees of both the Chamber and the Senate that deal with internal congressional matters.

14. The increased involvement of the legislature in policy deliberation and formulations is apparent in the work of the various committees in areas such as tax reform, coffee policy, reforestation, environment and pollution, Amazon free port policy, cattle, advertisement, industries and steel policies. There are ample deliberations over these basic development issues in the records of the various committees that studied these issues.

15. Article 148 of resolution 30.

16. Chapter VI and VII of resolution 30.

17. The number of deputies in the Chamber changes every four years in accordance with the population. In the 1974 election the number of deputies increased to 364.

18. This is based on a questionnaire administered by the author in Brazilia in November of 1973.

19. The press in Brazil operates under strict censorship. One way to avoid censorship is for a legislator to discuss an issue on the floor, thus giving the press an excuse to report it as part of the legislative debate.

20. In January 1975 the Brazilian Chamber of Deputies cosponsored with the Comparative Development Studies Center of the State University of New York at Albany a four-day international seminar on legislatures in contemporary societies which was attended by over fifty international scholars.

21. The program between the Brazilian legislature and the State University of New York at Albany where practical and academic training takes place is the best illustration.

Structural Adjustments of the Danish Parliament in the Twentieth Century

ERIK DAMGAARD

Introduction

To describe how the Danish parliament (*Folketinget*) works, the problems it confronts, and the ways in which it has sought to cope with the political consequences of societal change, it is convenient to depart from the observation that it was instituted in 1849 as a liberal constitutional device to limit the power of the government on the basis of the will of the people as manifested in the choice of representatives. According to the classical model such control would be achieved if the parliament obtained equal power with the executive in legislative and budgetary matters.[1] This is still a basic principle of Danish government, but its concrete implications have changed since the middle of the nineteenth century.

First, after decades of constitutional struggles the cabinet responsibility system was adopted in 1901, which paved the way for more effective parliamentary control over executive actions. Second, two major reforms took place during World War I: introduction of universal suffrage and democratization of the upper-class-dominated first chamber. Third, with the development and ensuing stabilization of the party system in the decades around the turn of the century Danish government essentially became party government with the "four old" parties (Social Democrats, Radical Liberals, Liberals, and Conservatives) as dominating actors until the early 1970s.[2]

Electoral mobilization, party system development, constitutional amendments, and adoption of the cabinet responsibility model of government are all important features of Danish political development. In this chapter, however, I shall regard outcomes in these respects as parameters which condition, but far from fully explain, the contemporary situation of Folketinget. Specifically, I want to analyze legislative politics by applying a demand-response framework. First, I shall show that there has been a long-term trend toward increasing demands on the legislature. Second, I shall focus on some major structural changes and reforms that may be interpreted as adjustments to increasing demands. Third, a number of other reforms pertaining to the functions of Folketinget will be described, and finally, I shall discuss the implications of these findings for the contemporary role and situation of Folketinget. I ought to emphasize at the outset that most of these problems have so far not been subjected to systematic research, hence the analysis should be viewed as a tentative and preliminary enterprise.

Parliament and the Expanded Scope of Government

When the legislature first met in 1850 Denmark was a static, agrarian society. Its population totaled about one and a half million and about half the labor force was employed in agriculture. As the result of economic and social modernization the country changed completely during the next 125 years. The importance of the primary sector was reduced dramatically, while the secondary and tertiary sectors (including government services) assumed increasing importance. In the early 1970s the population was three times that of 1850 and the GNP per capita (in real terms) was six and a half times higher. Only 8 percent of the labor force was employed in agriculture, whereas urban industries employed 68 percent and the public sector no less than 24 percent.[3] The expansion of government activities is of particular importance in this context. As a summary measure of the total government activity one can use the total tax revenue in percent of the gross factor income. That percentage was less than 10 prior to World War 1, but since then it increased steadily, peaking with a jump from 25 in 1960 to 40 in 1970.

OECD figures, calculated on a slightly different basis, show that Denmark was leading the record in 1971 with a total tax revenue of 44 percent of the GNP, while only six years earlier it was a relatively low-taxed country.[4]

Along with this expansion significant changes occurred with respect to the role of Folketinget. A partial view of the increasing pressure upon the legislature is furnished by the number of bills passed over time. In the nineteenth century less than forty bills were passed on the average each year, while the corresponding number was about four times as large in the last decade. Not only did the number of bills increase, but legislation also changed qualitatively. Today it deals with a much wider variety of subject matter. In some areas legislation became incredibly complex while in others important regulatory powers were transfered to the executive. Jean Blondel depicts the qualitative change precisely:

> When theorists began thinking about legislatures, they faced a situation which was wholly different from the one that confronts modern governments. Locke and Montesquieu looked at societies in which state involvement in social and economic matters was minimal if not non-existent. For them, statutes did not mean education or housing acts; they covered problems of private property, individual rights, family law—in short regulation of private relationships between individuals. Slowly the balance tilted, through the nineteenth and twentieth centuries, toward public legislation establishing new agencies and regulating social and economic matters.[5]

The dual development of a growing number of bills and diversification of their contents brought increasing pressure to bear on the legislature and its members. This conclusion would come out even more forcefully if other types of legislative activities were taken into account (number of resolutions, interpellations, questions etc.). But there are still further aspects of the changing situation of Folketinget. At least two other important extensions of the legislator's job must be mentioned. First, the legislature has to some extent become involved with the preparation and administration of legislation in addition to the processing and passing of bills. Second, legislators today participate in meetings of a number of international organizations.

Partly as a consequence of the improved relations between the government and Folketinget brought about by the adoption of parliamentarism in 1901, legislators often were appointed to serve on "legislative" commissions, i.e., commissions usually set up by the government to investigate certain problems with the purpose of proposing new legislation. As of 1974 five such commissions with legislators among the members existed. Parallel to this development legislators also became involved at the executive stage of the legislative process. Several laws have established special advisory bodies to assist or control the minister in administering the measures and regulations called for. In 1974 legislators were serving in at least twenty-five such bodies and a further number of advisory boards and committees included members of Folketinget though they did not formally serve as official representatives of the political party groups.

Before World War I the legislature was hardly involved in foreign policy matters, although some international cooperation took place within the framework of the Interparliamentary Union (IPU). The war and the peace conference in Paris led to a change in this respect however. During the interwar period legislators served as party representatives in the Danish delegations to the League of Nations, and, after World War II, to the UN General Assembly. In the last twenty-five years Denmark has joined a number of other international organizations which have some sort of a parliamentary assembly. As a result, members of Folketinget now participate regularly at meetings of the IPU, the UN, the Assembly of the European Council, the Nordic Council, the North Atlantic Assembly, and the European Parliament. No matter how important these various organizations are considered to be, they demand time from a number of member states' legislators, which in particular is true in the case of the European Parliament.

Thus, for all the reasons mentioned, it is quite obvious that the task of being a member of Folketinget today is totally different from what it was originally supposed to be. Naturally, therefore, one would like to know how the Folketinget readjusted to the changing situation and whether or not the adjustments made have been adequate.

Legislative Responses to Increasing Demands

To maintain itself, any political institution must adjust to environmental changes which significantly affect its functional capacity. At the analytic level one may distinguish between at least three different modes of adjustment to increasing demand or workload pressure. More time may be used, if available, to process an increasing number of legislative items, or alternatively, time used per legislative item may be reduced, if it does not seriously damage the quality of legislative performance. Second, the legislature may reduce the amount of work per member by increasing staff and resources thus leaving more time for members to deal with the important aspects of legislative work. Finally, members may specialize so that different subgroups, formally, or informally, handle specific public policy domains on behalf of the whole legislature.

The logical relationships between the three modes of adjustment are displayed in figure 1. Figure 1 conveys the idea that, if viewed from the point of view of the legislature as a whole, "pure" specialization (e.g., specialized committees) of legislative activities also implies reduction of work and time saving, and that "pure" work reduction also saves time, whereas the reasoning does not hold the other way round. The three key concepts of time, work, and specialization constitute the organizing framework for the following analysis of the adjustments of the Danish Folketinget to the increasing workload of the twentieth century.

Figure 1

Conceptual Relationships Between Modes of Adjustments

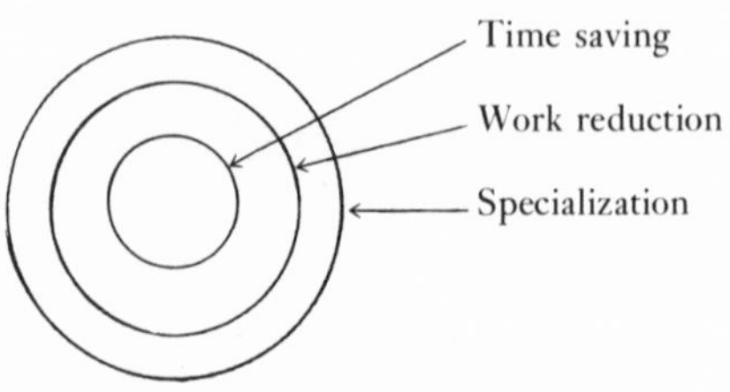

Time Consumption

Data on the use of time since 1850 are only available for floor meetings. Time consumption in this respect may be broken down into three components: number of meetings, hours per meeting, and length of session. The following are some findings of a longitudinal analysis.[6]

First, and perhaps somewhat surprising, the number of meetings is today not larger than in the nineteenth century. During the first half of the twentieth century, however, the frequency of meetings was higher, but then the average duration of meetings was considerably shorter. Therefore it turns out that the total number of hours spent on floor meetings has not increased in this century. On the contrary there seems to be a slight decrease from above 300 hours per year to somewhat less than that in the last two decades.

The length of session is an important variable because it indicates the extent to which members are tied up with legislative work. Originally the average was about six months, but in the latest decades it has been eight months (October-June). We thus find that the increased workload has not been counteracted by more meetings or more time used on the floor, but it has extended the duration of yearly sessions. The logical implication of these findings is that measures have been taken to reduce the amount of time used per legislative item.

In fact, numerous adjustments of that type have occurred. Probably the single most decisive reason for amending rules and changing procedures is the desire to save time if possible. More than twenty adjustments explicitly aiming at time saving can be traced during the period of Folketinget's existence. They deal with such things as avoiding divisions not strictly necessary, limitations of debates, etc. They were made for pragmatic reasons in an incremental fashion and definitely not on the basis of new blueprints for the legislative process or on new theories about how a legislature ought to function in the twentieth century. Adjustments simply occurred when experience had persuaded legislators that things could be done with less time costs by slight changes in their habitual working patterns—for which there sometimes even seemed to be no reason anymore.

Though time-saving adjustments have occurred in a rather large number, they could not prevent the legislator's job from expanding into a full-time position. The era of the classical part-time legislator has definitely phased out. Exactly how much work the legislative job involves is more difficult to pinpoint however. Evidence from 1960 show that the time used on all the activities associated with being a legislator equals that of a normal full-time position anywhere else in society.[7] But, for at least three reasons, even more time is probably demanded from a legislator today.

First, there are no reasons for believing that the structural adjustments described below have effectively counterveiled the increasing workload, which in absolute terms is now higher than ever before. Second, the party system changed quite dramatically at the election of 1973, which increased the number of parties in Folketinget from five to ten, thus producing the most fractionalized parliament in Danish history.[8] One effect of this development is that a small number of members in several parties have to carry the same legislative workload as the larger parties, which means that the average legislator's workload increased substantially. A final observation along this line is that since 1960 less political stability is manifested by frequent general elections. Although the maximum term of Folketinget is four years, the privilege of the government to call elections often results in much shorter effective terms. Since 1960 the average effective term has been only two years and four months, which is less than for any other period since World War I (before World War I the maximum term was three years). Frequent, and often unexpected, elections means stopping the legislative machinery for about two months, conducting exhausting campaigns, and afterward—for those elected—intensified work during the remaining part of the legislative year, perhaps with a new government in office and a very different party composition of the Folketinget.

Anyway, the full-time character of the legislative job is beyond dispute. As a somewhat delayed response to this development one finds acceptance of it in the remuneration of legislators.[9] The original system of per diems according to the length of session was maintained until 1920, although a few upward adjustments of the amount had been made earlier in the twentieth century. As the level of legislative activity during World War I made abundantly clear, the old system had by then outlived itself. The new system, introduced in 1920 and still operative, links the salary of members to that of a civil servant at a certain level in the administrative bureaucracy. It reflects the idea that the legislative job is a full-time one and should be paid as such.

Increasing Resources

Members of Folketinget responded to increasing workload not only by extending the time in session, introducing time-saving changes in legislative procedures, and becoming full-time, salaried legislators, but also to some extent by increasing staff and other supporting resources.

In the nineteenth century Folketinget's staff was very tiny, with only a few university-educated officials. During the first half of the twentieth century a modest increase occurred, but real growth of staff is a more recent phenomenon. The three core offices of the Folketinget are the Bureau, the Secretariat, and the Library and Information Service. In 1954, the total number of academic officials employed was twelve—three in the Bureau, six in the Secretariat, and three in the Library. During the 1960s and early 1970s this staff was gradually enlarged due to a total in 1974 of twenty-one academic staff officials (Bureau: six, Secretariat: twelve, Library: three). As with the time adjustments, the staff increases are on the whole explained by pragmatic considerations: more people were needed to handle a greater amount of work. A possible exception to this is that a decision was made in 1953 to transfer committee secretary service to the Secretariat, where in the past one of the elected committee members usually had been assigned to that function. This decision not only reduced the workload of members, it also defined a new function for the staff to perform.

While the three offices provide services for all members of the legislature, other resources were made available during the 1960s to the *party* groups in Folketinget. Since 1971 it has taken the form of general financial support that can be used at the discretion of each party to improve their legislative efficiency and working conditions. It must be added, though, that the money involved (as of 1972) amounted to only about half a million dollars and that the members of the Danish legislature are generally speaking not very well off in terms of office facilities and personal secretarial support.

In sum, then, some adjustments to changing conditions did take place with respect to the resources that legislators can draw upon their work, especially since the 1960s. Whether these adaptations are adequate or not is a question yet to be discussed.

Specialization and the Committee System

Just as important as time and work aspects of legislative readjustments is the third form of response which takes the form of developing a structure of specialized, permanent committees.

Committees perform several functions for the legislature as a whole. They provide opportunities for detailed scrutiny of proposed legislation, for political compromising among the parties, etc.[10] However, the increasing use of committees and the development of a permanent structure of specialized committees are not fully explained by such general aspects of committee functions. The crucial variable is again the increasing quantity and complexity of legislative work. "Committees are the work houses of legislatures" it has been said.[11] Specialized standing committees allow for simultaneous consideration of a large number of different items. They further constitute an infrastructure for division of work in such a way that issues are handled by those members of the parties who have special knowledge, experience, or interests in the relevant areas.

Folketinget's order of business always permitted use of both ad hoc and permanent committees. In the long-term perspective two trends are conspicuous however. Committees are increasingly used in the law-making process. In the nineteenth century committees dealt with less than half of the bills,[12] while today almost all bills are referred to a committee after first reading.[13] In addition, whereas in the past ad hoc committees were used by far more frequently, the balance has now reversed with permanent, specialized committees as the dominant type. The shift has come gradually, especially since the 1960s, when an increasing number of new specialized committees were set up. The final step was taken in 1972 with a total reorganization of the committee system. It now consists of some twenty permanent committees corresponding roughly to the divisions of the administrative structure of the government. The explicit aim of this reform was to improve efficiency and coordination in legislative work,[14] and this apparently was achieved to some extent.[15]

To sum up, the increasing use of committees and the reform of the committee system—like the adjustments in time and work—have to be regarded as pragmatic responses to problems created by the volume and complexity of modern legislation. Before turning to the current state of affairs with respect to change and reform of the Danish parliament, a few other aspects of legislative readjustments must be mentioned.

New Structures and Functions

So far I have focused on adjustments of existing structures as responses to demands which ultimately arise from the expanded role of government in modern society. By adopting this approach one runs the risk of loosing sight of other reforms or changes that might be important. To make up for this I shall briefly mention a number of reforms which are not directly related to increasing workload but rather to the functions performed by the legislature. Some of the reforms have counterparts in several other countries, but the last one mentioned is a true innovation of considerable theoretical and practical interest.

First of all, the bicameral parliament was replaced in 1953 by the unicameral Folketinget. The upper chamber (Landstinget) was originally designed to favor groups and parties relying on support from upper-level classes. The reform of 1915 changed its composition substantially, and eventually—from the 1930s onward—the party composition of the two chambers did not differ significantly anymore. Since Denmark was, and is, a unitary state, and because there was widespread support for the idea of equal rights and political influence of citizens, the rationale for a bicameral legislature could only be that an upper chamber would contribute mainly by improving the quality of legislative work. However, this line of argument did not obtain much support among politicians. At the end special rights were granted to minority parties in Folketinget (notably the right for one-third of the members to have a referendum on bills passed) and Landstinget was abolished. Though repeal of the upper chamber is an important reform from a legal-constitutional point of view, its political import is that of a dying echo, the last reminder of high constitutional politics of the nineteenth century. The other side of the coin, the new referendum, proved to be an important political reform, however. It functions as a warning to legislative majorities not to rule without paying attention to the views of minority opposition parties on important matters. In 1963 it was proved that a legislative minority could successfully appeal to the electorate, which rejected a set of bills passed by Folketinget.

Control of the government is an essential function of all parliaments though there are a wide variety of structures—within and between parliaments—through which the function is performed. A classical means, short questions to ministers, was adopted by the Danish legislature in 1947. Since then questions have enjoyed an ever increasing popularity with the members. In the mid-fifties the average number of questions asked and answered per year was substantially below one hundred, but then it increased very strongly during the 1960s, reaching a level of about 500 in the last two sessions.

The question procedure is a very simple and handy device for members to call the attention of the government, Folketinget, the mass media, and the public to some matter (and to the member asking!). Question hours have also relieved the formerly very protracted annual budget debate of a myriad of local and other specific questions. Finally, written questions can be asked and answered while Folketinget is not sitting. In 1973/74 about 50 percent of the questions were asked during the summer recess. Thus, there is no doubt that short questions perform functions which older procedures could not as easily take care of.

In 1955 another controlling mechanism was established, viz., the ombudsman institution. The ombudsman is elected by Folketinget, to which he reports about complaints received from citizens and about investigations conducted on his own initiative. This reform aimed at circumscribing the extensive powers given to the executive in the twentieth century with additional safeguards.[16]

Debate on major issues is, like control of the government and administration, a traditional function of parliaments. In 1953 a new possibility was opened for initiating general debates without connection to specific bills or proposed resolutions. The new procedure is the review (*redegørelse*) by a minister of some selected important policy issue area, which may be followed by a general debate not aiming at the making of decisions but perhaps at influencing future legislation. In the last decade there were seven such review-debates on the average per session. This reform is perhaps not of crucial importance, but nonetheless the actual use of this type of report and debate indicates that existing procedures were inadequate for some purposes valued by legislators.

Looking at legislative reforms and innovations from a functional point of view Denmark's entry into the European Community (1973) is of utmost importance. The new problem created by EC-membership was: could Folketinget possibly influence and control decision-making within the European institutional framework given that it has to accept decisions taken by the Council of Ministers at the supranational level? Some loss of power seemed inevitable if the advantages accruing from membership in a large European economic community were to be obtained. To ensure parliamentary control of Danish policy in the EC, the law of accession determined that the government should inform the Folketinget about developments within the Community and, in particular, inform one of the permanent committees (the Market Committee) about proposed Council decisions which would have immediate effects in Denmark or for the implementation of which legislative action was required.

A political crises soon showed, however, that these rules were not sufficient to achieve effective control and hence a more tightly constraining control system was instituted.[17] The basic principle of the control apparatus is that the government must always make sure in advance that its negotiating position in Brussels is not opposed by a majority in the Folketinget. Thus, in effect, the minister receives a mandate from the Folketinget, which he has to stick to while negotiating with European colleagues, unless he asks for, and receives, a new mandate. This control system is unique among the member states of the EC. Comparatively speaking, Denmark has chosen to give higher priority to legislative control than to speed and efficiency in European policy-making. The control system was not developed as a mechanical application of a grand theory of representative democracy but, characteristic of Danish legislative adjustments, upon events which showed that new problems had actually been created by EC-membership. The control system is a pragmatic innovation. It is the Folketinget's response to developments which appeared to threaten its legislative and controlling functions.

Implications of Reforms and the Contemporary Situation of Folketinget

The preceding sections have outlined a number of ways in which the Danish legislature has changed over time. Whether these changes were responses to increased workload or to other factors, they were of a pragmatic and incremental nature.

The questions now relevant are: what does all of this add up to? What is the contemporary situation of the Danish legislature, and which are the problems facing it? Have the adjustments been adequate, and if so, in what sense? In short, one would like to know the implications of these adjustments and the possible problems not solved. But these are tricky questions because there are grave difficulties with defining standards of comparison and evaluation.

To summarize implications of adjustments and to draw conclusions about problems not solved, one needs a model of a modern legislature in a multiparty cabinet responsibility system of government by which the actual parliament can be matched. Here the difficulty arises because there *is no* single generally agreed upon model or theory of what a parliament is or ought to be,[18] except perhaps at such a high level of abstraction that it unfortunately would be of no practical use in this context. This does not mean that no theories exist, but rather that there are *different* and partly incompatible theories about the proper role and functions of parliaments. Consequently, one is forced to work with alternative models in discussing the implications of change and adjustments. As a further complication, the different models are not coherently articulated in theoretical terms, let alone in operational terms. Therefore, the only strategy available is to *construct* alternative models on the basis of scattered and fragmented statements about how the Danish parliament ought to function and how it actually functions. In this section I shall present two such models and then go on to indicate what the adjustments imply for the legislature if evaluated on the basis of both models.

The two models selected may be called the "strong government" and the "strong parliament" model respectively. By and large the models reflect the basic orientations of the majority among the old and established parties on the one hand (strong government) and the minority view among the same parties plus the dominant orientations among the newer parties on the other (strong parliament). Because of that the two models might also be referred to as the establishment model and the reformers' model. Since the reformers' or strong parliament model is the most clearly articulated of the two, and because the strong government model to some extent must be inferred from rejection of essential parts of the reformers' model, it is convenient first to explicate the strong parliament model.[19]

The Strong Parliament Model

The reformers' basic orientations and value judgements can be summarized as follow: the Folketinget ought to be the supreme legislative and budgetary power, it should effectively control the administrative bureaucracy both with respect to policy initiation and to policy implementation, and it ought to be the forum of the nation for political debates. On all three scores the reformers find serious deficiencies in the current situation.

First, Folketinget does not really influence the timing, the topics, or the content of bills proposed. The government, in effect, determines the agenda of Folketinget. Ministers present the bills whenever they happen to be drafted by their civil servants; bills often reflect agreements worked out with interest groups or professions concerned; and bills have no uniform structure insofar as some are very vague and general (e.g., farm subsidy) whereas others are extremely detailed and specific (e.g., education, administration of justice). As a result not even legislators really have a general view of what is going on.

Second, the administration is traditionally held to be the servant of the government, not Folketinget. Hence, Folketinget can only get access to needed information through the ministers in charge of the government departments, which significantly reduces the capacity of nongovernment parties to draft and propose their own bills. However, control of government activities has improved somewhat, since adoption of the new committee system.

Third, Folketinget is not the national forum for important political debates as it used to be. The reason is in part that the procedures for legislative debates have not been sufficiently modernized and in part that television has created a new situation in mass communication. Often very important political discussions take place in TV studios rather than in Folketinget.

In sum, according to the supporters of the strong parliament model, Folketinget is not the actively initiating and effectively controlling political institution it ought to be, nor is it the main stage for national political discussion. The reformers stated their case in Folketinget in 1974 with a series of suggestions about how to redress the deficiencies they perceived.

They proposed setting up a special committee to investigate and report as soon as possible on legislative reforms. Among their suggestions were provisions to ensure

—that Folketinget became involved at a much earlier stage of the legislative process, i.e., before bills were proposed
—that it should receive reports on alternative solutions to problems while the options were still open
—that various new forms of political debate were introduced encompassing not just one government department but much broader societal areas

—that Folketinget's committees ought to review not only proposed legislation but also existing laws to determine whether the aims had been achieved or whether corrections might be needed
—that a new look was taken at the methods of initiating legislation with a view to clarifying the roles of politicians, administrators, interest group representatives, and experts
—that committee hearings were introduced
—that facilities and resources of individual legislators were increased
—that the Folketinget's channels of communication to the public were improved.

As is clearly apparent, the general theme and concern underlying these suggestions is a desire to strengthen the role of Folketinget. This idea was endorsed, more or less emphatically, by the party spokesmen of the Radical Liberals, the Progress Party, the Center Democrats, the Christian People's Party, and the Communists, while it failed to attract support from the government party (at that time the Liberals), the Conservatives, and the Social Democrats (then the largest opposition party, now the government party). The arguments of the three latter parties will serve to construct the status-quo-oriented "strong government" model.

The Strong Government Model

Proponents of the strong government model reacted to the ideas of a strong Folketinget with three types of argument. First, the ideas were considered far too ambitious and unrealistic, at least in the version outlined above. It simply was not a matter suitable for immediate consideration in a committee. They also maintained that important improvements had in fact been made in legislative work, such as the new committee system introduced a few years earlier. Perhaps further improvements ought to be considered but, if so, that would be a natural thing for Folketinget's Committee on Procedures to handle. Last, but not least, the strong government model supporters have argued that some of the reforms suggested might have undesirable effects on the country's political system. Should the civil servants of the government assist Folketinget directly—i.e., not only with the consent of and on behalf of the responsible minister. This is a matter that cannot be discussed solely within the framework of the legislature, because a change in this respect would change the system of government entirely. Legislative and executive functions should not be mixed up but should remain separated so that the minister, and the minister only, is responsible for the activities of the bureaucracy.[20] In addition to that, the government itself was attempting to develop new methods and structures for overall planning and Folketinget ought to do nothing until the government had presented the results of those endeavors.

Support of the strong government model thus means defense of the existing state of affairs as it has developed over time. It does not preclude further adjustments, to be sure, but no reform may be pursued that could eventually alter the present system of government, which is based on government leadership.

Implications of Reforms and Adjustments

By now it is obvious that the answer to the question of whether legislative adjustments and reforms have been adequate or not depends upon the role envisaged for Folketinget in the governmental system. Evaluated on the basis of the strong government model, the adjustments have by and large been adequate. Extensions of time in session, time-saving procedural changes, some staff increases, a new committee system, etc. have made it possible to process an increasing number of bills—which for all practical purposes means government bills.[21] To put it bluntly, one might even argue that the government forced Folketinget to adjust to an increasing workload. As a matter of fact, the purpose of previous reforms often boils down to the question of how to handle the large number of bills proposed by the government.[22] Even the specialized committees established by Folketinget present some advantages from the government point of view, because they not only control and influence the government, they also provide the government with opportunities to explain its policies and to enlist support from those members of Folketinget who presumably possess special influence with colleagues in their party groups with respect to the policy domains in which they are specializing. The government can also use the committees to give out confidential information.

The situation is of course very different if evaluated on the basis of the strong parliament model. To the reformer, the long-term development shows a decline of parliament vis-a-vis the government despite some adjustment and reform. As a matter of course, reforms are proposed precisely to strengthen Folketinget, which it is considered too weak and too inadequately equipped to perform its proper functions.

Thinking in terms of political parties, one must conclude that the dominant legislative elite, which is still very strong even though several new parties have been represented in Folketinget since 1973,[23] on the whole is satisfied with the adjustments made and reforms passed, while the newer parties and perhaps also a minority among the back-benchers of the older parties (especially the younger members) would like to go much further toward adoption of the strong parliament model.

The Government-cum-Folketing Model

Some scholars will probably question the expediency of the two models used in the analysis on the ground that it is misleading to talk about the Folketinget and the government as if they were two separate institutions—which they are not. The Folketinget determines the composition of the government and party leaders move back and forth between government and nongovernment benches according to electoral successes, defeats, and the results of interparty bargaining about cabinet formations. No government can stay in office if a manifest parliamentary majority does not want it to. Also we noticed that Folketinget to some extent participates in legislative commissions and in the administration of legislation. If one adopts this perspective it is more appropriate to talk about the government and Folketinget as if they were a single political institution or at least two instruments playing the same concerts with political parties as conductors. This approach does have some merits and a few comments are thus in order.

First of all, if Folketinget and the government are viewed as two closely interrelated components of the same policy-making structure, it is not surprising that those parties which frequently occupy cabinet posts [24] or which have reason to believe that they will enter the government in a not-too-distant future (or perhaps just cooperate on a more or less permanent basis with another government party without formally joining the cabinet) might not want Folketinget to assume a more active and influential role: it could mean difficulties in getting government legislation passed if Folketinget insisted on conducting its own independent investigations and if opposition parties were able to draft their own bills in a legally and technically competent manner.

More important is a second point which suggests itself if the government and Folketinget are viewed as two jointly acting institutions. This is the question of whether the government is strong in other ways than vis-à-vis Folketinget, or better, whether the political leadership of the country has developed sufficient resources to cope with challenges created by societal development in this century.

Concerning overall planning in particular, there seems to be problems with the way in which the political-administrative machinery has worked so far. A most respected report published in 1973 revealed a serious lack of coordination among departments and it pointed to the fact that the working methods of the government had never been subjected to thorough scrutiny in order to determine their suitability for solving contemporary problems.[25] Thus the crucial question is whether the *government itself* has adjusted adequately to societal change. Some of the most conspicuous changes affecting the government as a political body are the growth of the administrative bureaucracy since the nineteenth century [26] and the development of strong, nationwide interest organizations throughout all sectors of society. The question of government adaptation cannot be answered without a systematic longitudinal analysis parallel to the one about legislative adjustment. This, however, is beyond the scope of the present chapter. Suffice it just to mention that the political leadership at cabinet level still numbers less than twenty people without any politically appointed assistants at all. Formally, the top political leaders control the administrative system, and in principle they are superior to all nongovernmental groups and organizations, but whether these are also empirical facts is quite another question.

Summary

A longitudinal approach shows a conspicuous expansion of government activity since the nineteenth century. The Danish parliament was instituted to limit the power of the government by way of sharing legislative and budgetary powers. To persistently perform these functions in a changing society Folketinget had to adjust to increasing demand and workload pressure. The members became full-time, salaried legislators; they adjusted rules and procedures to save time; to some extent they increased the small staff of officials; they made some money available to the party groups; and, not least, they specialized. Additional reforms created new structures and procedures which facilitated and improved the performance of Folketinget's functions, including control of the government at the supranational European Community level. Whether these adjustments, reforms, and innovations are adequate or not depends upon the role envisaged for a parliament in a cabinet-responsibility system of government. According to the "strong parliament" model of the reformers, they are definitely inadequate, while they are adequate, by and large, if evaluated by the "strong government" model of the establishment. Since early in the twentieth century Folketinget has determined the party composition of cabinets such that fusion of power rather than separation of power characterizes the relationship between the government and the Folketinget. If, for that reason, a "government cum Folketing" approach is used, the problem becomes whether the government itself is a strong institution, i.e., whether the political leadership has succeeded in coping with problems of modern society, which is not all that sure, but outside the scope of this chapter.

Notes

1. Most recently Jean Blondel in *Comparative Legislatures* (Englewood Cliffs, N.J.: Prentice-Hall, 1973) has stressed this aspect of the functions of classical legislatures.

2. Further information in Erik Damgaard, "Stability and Change in the Danish Party System over Half a Century," *Scandinavian Political Studies* 9 (1974): 103–125. For party political developments since 1973," *Scandinavian Political Studies* 9 (1974): 197–204 and "The General Election in Denmark, January 1975: Toward a New Structure of the Party System?" *Scandinavian Political Studies* 10 (1975): 211–216.

3. Data from Svend Aage Hansen, *Økonomisk vækst i Danmark*, vol. I and II (Copenhagen: Akademisk Forlag, 1972, 1974) and *Perspektivplan-redegørelse 1972–1987* (Copenhagen: Statens Trykningskontor, 1973) p. 186.

4. *Perspektivplan-redegørelse*, pp. 392f.

5. Blondel, *Comparative Legislatures*, p. 13.

6. The author is currently doing research on the Danish parliament which he hoped to report on more extensively at a later date.

7. Erik Rasmussen, *Komparativ Politik II*, (Copenhagen: Gyldendal, 1972) p. 158.

8. The results of the last three elections are: (not including four members elected on Greenland and the Faroe Islands)

	1971		1973		1975	
Party	% of Votes	Seats	% of Votes	Seats	% of Votes	Seats
Social Democrats	37.3	70	25.6	46	29.9	53
Radical Liberals	14.4	27	11.2	20	7.1	13
Conservatives	16.7	31	9.2	16	5.5	10
Liberals	15.6	30	12.3	22	23.3	42
Socialist People	9.1	17	6.0	11	5.0	9
Communists	1.4	0	3.6	6	4.2	7
Justice Party	1.7	0	2.9	5	1.8	0
Christian People	2.0	0	4.0	7	5.3	9
Left Socialists	1.6	0	1.5	0	2.1	4
Progress Party	—	—	15.9	28	13.6	24
Center Democrats	—	—	7.8	14	2.2	4
Others	0.2	0	—	—	—	—
Total	100.0	175	100.0	175	100.0	175

9. Kristian Hvidt, "Politiker—hverv eller erhverv," *Økonomi og Politik* 46, 4 (1972): 357–374.

10. For general discussion of committee functions, see Malcolm Shaw and John D. Lees, "Committees in Legislatures and the Political System" (paper presented at the IX World Congress of IPSA, Montreal, August 1973) pp. 45–55.

11. Shaw and Lees, "Committees in Legislatures" p. 45.

12. P. Munch, "Hvorledes arbejder Rigsdagen," *Den Danske Rigsdag*, vol. IV (Copenhagen: J. H. Schultz, 1949), pp. 201f.

13. Erik Damgaard, "Party Coalitions in Danish Law-Making 1953–1970," *European Journal of Political Research* 1 (1973): 35–66.

14. "Betænkning og indstilling om ændring af forretningsorden for folketinget" (Afgivet af udvalget for forretningsorden den 31. august, 1972).

15. "*Betænkning og indstilling om ændring af forretningsorden for folketinget*" (Afgivet af udvalget for forretningsordenen den 16. maj, 1973), cf. the debate in Folketinget, 23 May 1973, *Folketingets Forhandlinger 1972/73*, col. 6674–6739.

16. "*Betænkning afgivet af forfatningskommissionen af 1946*" (Copenhagen: J. H. Schultz, 1953) p. 37.

17. Described more extensively in Svend Auken, Jacob Buksti, and Carsten Lehmann Sørensen, "Danmark i EF: Tilpasningsmønstre i danske politiske og administrative processer som følge af EF-medlemskabet", *Nordisk Administrativt Tidsskrift*, 1974, pp. 239–286, and in John Fitzmaurice and Erik Damgaard, "National Parliaments and European Community Policy-Making: The Case of Denmark" (paper presented at meeting of the IPSA Research Committee on European Integration, Luxembourg, 22–24 May 1975.

18. Gerhard Loewenberg (ed.), *Modern Parliaments. Change or Decline?* (Chicago: Aldine Atherton, 1971); Abdo I. Baaklini, "Legislatures in Contemporary Societies: An Overview" (paper presented at second international conference *on legislative development*, Albany, N.Y., 20–24 January 1975).

19. Material used for this purpose is *Folketinget og Samfundsudviklingen*, published by Selskabet for samfundsdebat (Copenhagen: 1972, reprinted 1974) and *Forslag til folketingsbeslutning om gennemgang af Folketingets arbejdsformer m.v.* (Folketingstidende 1973/74, tillæg A, col. 2735–2746).

20. The civil servants agree with this, *Folketingstidende 1972/73*, tillæg B, col. 1996–1999.

21. Cf. Erik Damgaard, "Party Coalitions in Danish Law-Making 1953–70, p. 39.

22. Cf. *Folkentingstidende 1972/73*, tillæg B, col. 1969ff.

23. Party compositions of the Folketinget since 1971 are listed in note 8.

24. Cabinet coalitions in the twentieth century are reviewed in Erik Damgaard, "The Parliamentary Basis of Danish Governments: The Patterns of Coalition Formation," *Scandinavian Political Studies* 4 (1969): 30–57.

25. *Perspektivplan-redegørelse 1972–1987* (Copenhagen: Statens Trykningskontor, 1973) pp. 427–442, 600–618, 659–665.

26. Erik Damgaard, "The Political Role on Nonpolitical Bureaucrats in Denmark," in Mattei Dogan (ed.) *The Mandarins of Western Europe* (Beverly Hills, CA. Sage Publications, 1975) pp. 275–292.

Innovations and Reforms in the Indian Parliament

R. B. JAIN

In the last two decades, many legislatures in the world, fearing their eclipse by the rapidly increasing executive power, have been concerned with "on-going modernization efforts" to reinvigorate themselves so they can exercise adequate checks on the executive authority. There has been a serious reappraisal of their operations, procedures, and structures in the context of the new roles they were expected to play in their societies. This has resulted in their adoption of various devices to improve the performance of their legislative functions and make them more effective as control mechanisms. The Indian Parliament has also adopted various innovations to accomplish its role as an organ of legislative control and direction. This paper studies the innovations and reforms made in the Indian parliamentary procedures during the period of the first four Parliaments (1952–70) with a view toward analyzing their impact on the effectiveness of the legislative branch of the government.

Shifting Emphasis in the Role of India's Parliament

Over the last twenty-five years the Parliament's role has been frequently changing. The emergence of the welfare-state concept and the consequent increase in socioeconomic problems needing solutions have, more than anything else, contributed to the increased range and scope of state activities. This has necessitated a corresponding expansion of the administrative machinery, which has upset the balance between the representative institutions and the executive and posed special problems for the maintenance of democratic control by the legislature. The range and magnitude of governmental activities in modern times has shifted the Parliament's role to that of oversight of administration.

The role of the first three Parliaments in India (elected in 1952, 1957, and 1962) was limited to a hesitant acquiescence to executive policy proposals. The 1967 Parliament, born of the traumatic 1962 war with China, was a very different body to the previous two. The 1967 Parliament broke loose from Erskine May's parliamentary practice, shattering the genteel cover this had placed over the discontent, then seething, in the country. The so-called "Zero-Hour," the frequency of "Adjournment Debates," the slow progress of "question-hour" (to a dwindling average of no more than four questions in an hour), and regular outbursts of uproar on the floor of the House were products of that period. It was quite some time before the parliamentarians inside, and the elite outside, realized that these by themselves do not put the parliamentary system at risk. The press, emerging out of the extraneous difficulties outside, was beginning to influence the idioms of Indian parliamentary practice. The outcome was not wholly unwelcome. The 1967 Parliament developed in a direction that made happenings there more important than the decisions taken outside. It reversed the situation which had made parliamentary reactions predictable.

The situation is, however, fast changing. With the economic crisis increasingly impinging on parliamentary proceedings and the loss of authority by men in power charged with graft, the forensic ability of the small but hostile opposition groups has, in the first half of 1975, turned Parliament into a forum of daily inquisitions reflecting the public mood. Parliament was utilized to hurl charges of corruption. "Parliamentary proceedings were brought to a standstill almost every day, settling at naught not only parliamentary rules and procedures but all codes of decency and orderly behaviours." [1] The situation has, however, changed and in the changed context, the Parliament has emerged as a critic and evaluator of the administration's policies. It oversees and criticizes government legislative and administrative activity, while preserving at the same time administrative flexibility and direction.

Improving the Efficiency of Parliament: The Indian Innovations

How far has the Indian parliamentary system responded to such changed conditions? It is commonly believed that the parliamentary procedures in India are a replica of the procedures of the British House of Commons. The Indian Parliament is certainly an adaptation of the British institution, and although in matters of broad principle there is a similarity between the two systems, there are appreciable differences in the details and actual working. Indian parliamentary procedures have by and large kept pace with changing circumstances and have embodied innovations and practices designed to meet the requirements of the changing role of the Parliament. Many such changes introduced during the last two decades have sought to strengthen the Parliament from within. In broad terms these were made so as to secure effective utilization of available time, effective use of the committee system, better oversight and control of administration, improved effectiveness of individual members, and establishment of certain institutional innovations for effecting continuous improvements in the parliamentary processes. The balance of this chapter attempts to examine the extent to which these objectives have been realized through the introduction of various procedural and structural innovations in the Indian Parliament.

In order to utilize the available time effectively, the Indian Parliament has introduced two specific devices. It conducts business according to a precise timetable, with the help of a Business Advisory Committee and it saves time lost in various divisions in the House through the use of automatic voting device.

The Business Advisory Committee

As table 1 shows, the parliamentary program is generally very crowded, making it necessary to plan the business of the

House within the time allotted for discussion. Business Advisory Committees have, therefore, been constituted in both houses of Parliament to advise on the allocation of time for the discussion of various items of government business.

The committee was first constituted in the Lok Sabha (the lower house) on 14 July 1952. Such a committee was also constituted in the Rajya Sabha (the upper house) in 1953. In the Lok Sabha the committee consists of fifteen members, including the speaker, who is its chairman. The deputy speaker is also one of its members. The unique feature of the committee is that its membership consists of the leaders of various political parties and representatives of all sections in the House.

The committee is nominated at the commencement of a new House after a general election and thereafter from time to time. No specific term of office is laid down in the rules, but like all other parliamentary committees, it holds office until a new committee is nominated. Casual vacancies are filled by nomination of new members for the unexpired term of the committee. The committee generally meets at the beginning of the session and thereafter from time to time as may be necessary.

The committee's function is to recommend time that should be allotted for the discussion of the stage or stages of such government legislation and other business as the speaker, in consultation with the leader of the House, may direct for reference to the committee. In practice, however, all items of government business for consideration by the House are now referred to the committee for allocation of time. In suitable cases, the committee has the power to indicate in the proposed timetable the different hours at which various stages of a bill or other government business shall be completed. Where the subject matter of two or more items of business so warrants, the committee recommends combined discussion of those items in the House. Like other parliamentary committees, the committee also works through its subcommittees when a matter needs to be considered in detail. Since 1960 a standing subcommittee of the committee has been in operation.

The decisions the committee reaches are always unanimous in character and representative of the collective view of the House. The committee presents its report to the House, which by convention is adopted by the House unanimously on a motion moved by the minister of parliamentary affairs. After acceptance, the motion takes effect as an order of the House.[2]

The Impact of the Business Advisory Committee. The Business Advisory Committee has met 234 times and presented a total of 220 reports since its inception in 1952 until the dissolution of the Fourth Lok Sabha in 1970. An average meeting of the committee lasts from half an hour to an hour's duration once a week during sessions of the Parliament. In the absence of any precise available data about the time the committee may have spent on its deliberations, it may be assumed that a maximum of 234 hours might have been spent by the fifteen members of the Lok Sabha in planning the work of the Parliament spreading over to 14,197 hours during the first four Lok Sabhas (1952–70). The time was allocated by the fifteen members of the Lok Sabha (representing a mere 2.85 percent of the total membership of 525) outside the normal hours of the meetings of the Lok Sabha. The time spent by the committee in its deliberations is merely 1.65 percent of the total time allocated. In pure quantitative terms, therefore, the impact of the Business Advisory Committee has been quite satisfactory insofar as it has helped to plan the timetable of the Parliament in a precise and systematic manner.

In respect of the number of bills and number of other items of business, for which the time has been allotted by the Business Advisory Committee during the sixteen sessions of the Third Lok Sabha, the Business Advisory Committee was able to find time for 198 bills and 183 other items, i.e., various types of discussions, motions, reports, railways and general budgets, president's address, and other business requiring a total of 3,733 hours.

On the qualitative side, the success of the committee lies in its flexibility. Whenever there is lack of unanimity on the time limit for a measure, the committee generally agrees upon the minimum acceptable to everybody and authorizes the speaker to increase the time if, after considering the trend of discussions in the House, he feels that more time should be provided for a particular business. Rules also provide that even where a specific allotment of time has been made by the House on the rec-

Table 1

Time Taken on Various Legislative Business

	First Parliament	Second Parliament	Third Parliament	Fourth Parliament
Average Annual duration of sitting (1951–1970)	788.1 hours in comparison to 337.2 hours between the years 1929–1950.			
N of Sittings	677	567	578	469
N of Hours (time taken)	3784 hrs	3651 hrs	3733 hrs	3029 hrs & 24 mts
Average duration of a sitting	5 hrs & 25 mts	6 hrs & 26 mts	6 hrs & 27 mts	6 hrs & 15 mts
Legislative Business (excluding budget)	48.8%	28.2%	23.0%	22.08%
Budget Discussion (including replies)	18.5%	901 hrs & 49 mts 23.89%	25.0%	19.13%
Questions	14.6%	15.1%	564 hrs & 41 mts 15.1%	15.94%
Resolutions	6.3%	5.5%	5.9%	6.45%
Motions	7.1%	13.7%	13.2%	9.22%
Discussion on President's Addresses	n.a.	97 hrs & 8 mts	105 hrs & 1 mt 2.9%	69 hrs & 36 mts 3.3%
N of Bills passed	370	260	290	216

n.a.—data not available.

ommendations of the committee, the speaker may, after consulting the leader of the House and the committee, ask the House to revise its earlier decision if, in his opinion, it is necessary to give more time for the discussion of a particular subject.

This has set a precise timetable for the proceedings of the House and has provided a relief to everybody from the great stress and tension which used to be noticeable before the advent of the Business Advisory Committee. There used to be uncertainty about the business of the House. The speaker was called upon to determine in each case when a debate should end, unless it ended by itself by natural exhaustion. Now one can reasonably foresee when an item of business will terminate. Under the present procedure, it is the House which determines the length of a debate and this saves the speaker from any blame.

Above all, the committee helps the government to plan in advance the disposal of its business. It is now known fairly early in a session what measures will get through during the session within the time available and how their priority should be determined. This also ensures proper arrangement of business between the two Houses. The political parties also know what time will be available for them, and they plan in advance what number of members should be put up and in what order. Members can also plan their engagements in advance. There is proper allocation of time between important and ordinary items of business.[3] Questions regarding extension of Lok Sabha sessions and fixing of House sittings on days when it would not normally sit are first considered by the committee.

The committee has at times *suo motu* recommended that the government bring forward a particular subject for discussion in the House and also recommended the allocation of time for such discussion. It was at the initiative of the committee that discussions were held on certain subjects of current and topical interest, *viz.*, peaceful uses of atomic energy,[4] economic policy of the government, agrarian policy of the government, press commission report, and GATT.[5] This is a clear indication that the committee has at times performed a valuable service in preventing the government's efforts to let many current and topical issues go without any discussion on the floor of the House, particularly when such cases exposed government weakness in handling a particular issue or exploded allegedly corrupt executive practice or misdeed.

It is, however, claimed that the working of the committee has not been without a drawback. In the earlier days, when the time of the House was not so regulated, it afforded opportunities to the House members to prepare speeches in advance and exploit their oratory skills to influence the other members as well as the public at large. The tenor of debate and discussions, as many veterans of the Parliament recall, used to be of quite a high standard. However, because of the precise regulation of parliamentary time by the Business Advisory Committee, it is now not possible for the House to let the members speak for an unduly long time. Consequently, the members have ceased to prepare speeches in advance with the result that the standard of debate and discussions is said to have declined in recent years. Against this criticism, it can be asserted that members now get increased opportunities to speak and, therefore, discussion in the House is more broad-based and representative than before. Moreover curtailment of time can sharpen members' arguments, for having only limited time at their disposal to speak, they wish to make the best use of their opportunity. In any case, the utility of the Business Advisory Committee cannot be undermined by such an assumption. The only thing that might happen is that certain important issues on which the opposition might not be very vocal may not be adequately discussed on the ground that the time had already been regulated by the Business Advisory Committee.

The Automatic Vote Recorder

Before 1956, when the Automatic Vote Recorder System was installed in the Indian Parliament, the usual method for division was through the Ayes and Noes lobby system followed in the British House of Commons and some other legislatures. In India the automatic recorder has helped the Parliament save considerable time. The former lobby system took on an average ten to fifteen minutes for counting a division. With the new system the members not only are able to cast their votes from their seats without going into the lobbies, but the whole process from the declaration of the ringing of the usual division bells to the declaration of the results has been reduced to an average of four minutes.[6] It has also enabled the members to record secret voting.

The Effective Use of the Committee System

In a parliamentary system of government, the executive is directly responsible to the elected representatives of the people. To avoid waste of members' time and for more effective scrutiny and control of governmental activities, the British legislature adopted the practice of appointing committees of the Houses of Parliament to go into the details and to carry out preparatory work for the use of the deliberative body. The Indian Parliament has incorporated the British practice of constituting committees for the effective discharge of its responsibilities.

The committees in the Indian Parliament can be divided into three categories: those concerning members and housekeeping activities (Committee on Privileges, Committee on Office of Profit, Committee on Absence of Members from the sitting of the House, Joint Committee on Salaries and Allowances, Library Committee, Rules Committee, House Committee and the Business Advisory Committee), those which are primarily concerned with the enactment of legislation (the various Select Committees of the Lok Sabha which are constituted to consider the proposed legislation in the House, and the Committee on Private Members' Bills and Resolutions), and those which operate in a particular sphere of government's work, but have the basic function of scrutinizing and controlling governmental actions (the three financial committees—the Public Accounts Committee, the Estimates Committee, and the Committee on Public Undertakings [which was constituted in 1964 following the success of its British counterpart in exercising control over nationalised industries], the Committee on Subordinate Legislation, the Committee on Petitions, the Committee on Government Assurances, and the new Committee on the Welfare of Scheduled Castes and Scheduled Tribes).

The Indian procedure can claim pioneering work with respect of the last two committees, the first of which is designed to follow up directions given by the House from time to time and to ensure that various assurances, promises, undertakings given on the floor of the House have in fact been carried out. The second—the Committee on Scheduled Castes and Scheduled Tribes—is a special functional committee of the Parliament, which has the responsibility of safeguarding minority rights.

The committees perform a variety of activities and a major part of the legislative function is accomplished through them.

Despite the fact that the committee system in India is still in rudimentary form and is not as sophisticated or specialized as the US congressional committee system, the available facts and figures indicate that it has on the whole not worked badly. Except for the three financial committees, the committees in Indian legislatures do not have adequate or professionally qualified staff. Their procedures of testimonial consultation are highly restricted. The committees do not have the requisite measure of continuity and for one reason or another their members are not inclined to specialize in particular subjects. The injunction against members publishing evidence tendered to them before it is laid before the legislature is yet another example of the Committee System in India clinging to a tradition which has lost much of its meaning.[7] Even the three financial committees suffer from a serious lack of staff help.

There is therefore a need for a stronger committee system, which would not only give content to the concept of parliamentary accountability, but would also contribute substantially to a gradual solution of the "twin problems of the alienation of the backbenchers and disorders on the floor of the House." Apart from those who find a place in the parliamentary power structure either as ministers or as officeholders of the various parties, there is a very small number of assertive and articulate members who claim the limelight. The rest are relegated to the position of spectators and their interest in the proceedings soon gives way to a sense of frustration and futility. A committee system endowed with vitality and vested with an effective role in the process of democratic government would give the backbenchers "a sense of participation and a sense of belonging, and he would be less prone to fits of temper or to a wholesale repudiation of the system. It would lead to the socialization of the bulk of the members at least where their iconoclasm is not impalpably ideological. It would also make for improved information management in Parliament and ensure a more effective system of deliberation and decision-making." [8] However, short of reorganizing the committee system on the US pattern, some of the important committees in Indian Parliament have certainly adopted innovations which make them more effective.

Action-Taken Reports

The committee system in India, although built on the broad principles of the British system, embodies some new concepts which are not found in Britain. For example, the financial committees of the Indian Parliament have introduced adequate measures to ensure that their recommendations are given due consideration by the government, and where these are not implemented, the committees are apprised promptly of the reasons. As a rule, the ministry concerned is required to send replies to the recommendations contained in a report of a financial committee within three months from the date on which the report is presented to the House. A statement showing action taken or proposed to be taken by the government on the recommendations of the committee is compiled by the secretariat of the concerned committee. This statement enables the committee to know the extent to which its recommendations have been implemented by the government. The replies of the ministry are examined by the concerned committee and its comments thereon are set out in an "Action-Taken Report," which is presented to the House. Replies received from government to the recommendations in respect of which final replies were awaited at the time of presentation of the report to the House are laid on the table without further processing or comments by the committee. In this way, the progress in the implementation of the recommendations as well as any unresolved differences between the committees and government are brought to the notice of the House.

An analysis of some of the Action-Taken Reports of the various financial committees demonstrates the effectiveness of this system. The percentage of recommendations accepted by the government with respect to the Committee of Public Undertakings varies from 36 to 91 percent. For the Estimates Committee they are 50 to 100 percent. While the figures do not adequately indicate the quality of the committee recommendations, they do show that most receive the government's careful attention and are rejected only after due consideration. The procedure provides ample scope for constant interaction and discussion of the controversial issues between legislators and administrators. This implies that the committees exercise adequate influence over the administrative process; unless they are fully convinced that a particular recommendation is either not practicable or leads to some further complications, discussion of the recommendation continues. Thus the financial committees carry out a close and meaningful scrutiny of replies received from government indicating action taken by them. This systematic follow-up has helped impress the executive with the necessity of taking action on committee reports both in letter and spirit.

The Action-Taken Reports have another purpose. Despite the great demand by the members of Parliament, the reports of the financial committees are not, as a rule, discussed on the floor of the House. The danger is that if discussion on a financial report is allowed, it may lead to avoidable controversy and even split the committee members along party lines, thus jeopardizing a tradition built up by these committees over the years of judging all issues objectively and on intrinsic merit. On rare occasions a discussion may be allowed in the House, but it has to be a subject of wide public importance, and it has to take place after the committee has examined the goverment's action-taken notes and given its final Action-Taken Report, highlighting any areas of divergence between its recommendations and the government's stand.

The one disturbing aspect, however, is the time lapse between the submission of a committee's 'Initial-Report' containing its original recommendations and the Action-Taken Report on such recommendations. For example the Committee on Public Undertaking must wait a minimum of two to three years before it can bring out the Action-Taken Report on its recommendations made earlier. By the time recommendations are carried out, circumstances may have changed making the recommendations undesirable or removing the cause for their suggestion. On the whole, however, the Action-Taken Report system of the financial committees in India tends to have a salutary effect on the administration inasmuch as it makes it conscious of its responsibilities towards parliamentary directives.

Oversight of the Administration: Some Procedural Innovations

In overseeing the administrative process, the Indian Parliament has provided certain new devices not generally available in older parliaments. A significant contribution was the establighment of two scrutiny committees, the Committee on Government Assurances and the Committee on Scheduled Castes and Scheduled Tribes. The former is meant to follow up directions given by the House to ensure that these are in fact being carried out, and the latter is supposed to safeguard the rights of the socially backward and depressed classes whose amelioration is guaranteed in the Constitution. Two other innovations are the Calling-Attention Notices, which enable a member to draw the government's attention to any matter of urgent public importance, and the Short-Duration Discussion, which makes it possible to have a discussion in the House on a matter of urgent public importance for a short period.

The Committee on Government Assurances

This standing committee watches, on behalf of Lok Sabha, the implementation of various promises and assurances that ministers have given on the floor of the House. The creation of this Committee on 1 December 1953 was in fulfillment of a strongly felt need to devise some effective mechanism which would ensure that the government did not use such assurances to evade criticism by the members.[9] During the Third Lok Sabha, 3,327 out of 3,560, or 93.5 percent, assurances were implemented. In the Fourth Lok Sabha, while there has been a threefold rise in the number of assurances given, the corresponding drop in the number implemented in comparison to the Third Lok Sabha is only 15.3 percent.

Impact of the Committee's Performance. The committee has been gaining increased popularity, which is evident from the growing number of representations being received by it from organizations and individuals relating to the nonfulfillment of specific assurances given in the House. The committee examines such representations and, if necessary, hears the views of the parties

Table 2

Committee on Government Assurances

Lok Sabha	N of Sittings	N of Reports Presented	N of Assurances Given	N of Assurances Fulfilled	% of Assurances Fulfilled to Total Given
First	n.a.	n.a.	5,000	4,559	91.18
Second	23	2	4,323	4,108	95
Third	29	4	3,560	3,327	93.56
Fourth	61	10	11,000	8,602	78.2
			23,883	20,576	89.47

concerned before making suitable recommendations as to the remedial measures.

Serving as an important link between the government and the Parliament, the committee enables individual citizens and organizations to participate more actively in Parliament's consideration of issues directly affecting the public. Since the committee is composed of members of different parties, it has also been helpful in promoting a corporate sense among members and has contributed to the consideration of matters purely on merit and in a nonpartisan manner. It is mainly for this reason that the committee's deliberations and conclusions have been objective and its recommendations unanimous.[10] The committee's success in the Lok Sabha has prompted the establishment of a similar separate committee in the upper house of the Parliament, the Rajya Sabha, where it has now been in operation since 1973.

Committee on the Welfare of Scheduled Castes and Scheduled Tribes

The Scheduled Castes and Scheduled Tribes (Backward Classes) comprise more than 21 percent of the Indian population. The framers of the Indian Constitution had envisaged the necessity of an independent machinery to continuously investigate all matters relating to the safeguards provided for the Scheduled Castes and Scheduled Tribes under the Constitution and report to the president upon the working of these safeguards. Under Article 338 of the Constitution, a special officer (commissioner for Scheduled Castes and Scheduled Tribes) is appointed to perform this function. The first commissioner was appointed in November 1950. Each year he submits to Parliament an annual report of his work in protecting the interests of these communities.

The new Parliamentary committee, called the Committee on the Welfare of Scheduled Castes and Scheduled Tribes (CSCST), was established by the government in November 1960 with thirty members; twenty from Lok Sabha and ten from Rajya Sabha, elected in accordance with the system of proportional representation by means of single transferable vote. The Committee has a two-year term. The first Committee started functioning on 18 December 1968. The functions of the committee are:

> to consider the reports submitted by the Commissioner for Scheduled Castes and Scheduled Tribes under Art. 338(2) of the Constitution and to report to both the Houses as to the measures that should be taken concerning their welfare and the Welfare programs and the action taken by the Union Government in respect of matters within the purview of the Union Government including the Administration of the Union Territories;
>
> to examine the measures taken by the Union Government to secure the representation of the Scheduled Castes and the Scheduled Tribes in services and posts under its control (including appointments in public sector undertakings, statutory and semi-Government Bodies and in the Union Territories), having regard to the provisions of Article 335;
>
> to examine such of the matters as may seem fit to the Committee or are specifically referred to it by the House or the Speaker.[11]

Impact of the Committee's Work on the Executive. A study of this committee during 1968–71 has expressed satisfaction over its effective performance.[12] The committee has taken particular care to seek information or clarification from the government as to the action taken on the commissioner's recommendations, with particular reference to the subjects selected by the committee for examination. The committee has not hesitated to take the executive to task whenever there has been any government failing to implement any of its statutory recommendations. This is the only committee besides the financial committees which submits Action-Taken Reports on the implementation of its reports. Thus the committee not only pursues the recommendations of the commissioner, but it also makes its own suggestions for the amelioration of the conditions of Scheduled Castes and Scheduled Tribes. In the committee the commissioner has found a strong champion of the backward community, which the executive cannot easily brush aside. From the very beginning, the committee has been conscious that the commissioner, as the special officer of the president, should have an independent status. On various occasions the committee has made recommendations relating to the reorganization of the commissioner's office and his procedures of work.[13]

Calling-Attention Notices: Necessity and Implications

Rule 198 of the Rules of Procedure and Conduct of Business in Lok Sabha provides that a member may call the attention of a minister to any matter of urgent public importance and the minister may make a brief statement or ask for time to make a statement at a later hour or date. A Calling-Attention Notice gives members an opportunity to criticize the government directly or indirectly and to bring to the surface the failure or inadequate action of the government on an important matter. The speaker admits or selects a notice purely on the importance and urgency of the matter raised.[14]

Members of Parliament have been making increased use of Calling-Attention Notices to air their grievances. The number of hours spent by the Lok Sabha on this activity has been increasing consistently (from 21 hours and 39 minutes in the Second Lok Sabha to 112 hours and 40 minutes in the Third, to 143 hours and 67 minutes in the Fourth, and to 182 hours and 17 minutes in the first eleven sessions of the Fifth Lok Sabha). Time spent on this activity is almost three or four times that spent on adjournment motions, which indicates that this device has increasingly replaced adjournment motions. Practically speaking, adjournment motions are never carried through to a point of censure due to the government's majority in the Parliament. The device has been profitably used by members to question the government on matters of public importance and to force them to reply, while not driving them to resignation.

The subjects on which ministers have made statements have covered matters like disturbances in any part of India, incursions of foreign armed forces in India, migration of refugees from Pakistan, violation of air space by enemy aircraft, strikes involving railways, ports, harbors, air companies, the position of Indians overseas, the plight of Indians in Burma, and others.

The fall in the number of motions for adjournment and the increasing number of Calling-Attention Notices has demonstrated that the procedure has been satisfactory. According to a well-known observer, three factors have contributed to this success: the decisions are taken instantly, and urgent and important matters are brought before the House the same day; if conditions warrant, more than one such matter is brought on the same day; the members who have given notice of the matter are each allowed to ask one question.[15] The procedure has enabled Parliament to keep the government on its toes and to call for their explanation as soon as a vital matter of importance to the public has taken place; it has also enabled the government to state the facts or its decisions or to deal effectively with the matter with knowledge and the feeling that it has the support of the House.[16] Although no specific conclusions are recorded, the atmosphere is such that each member is free to interpret the short discussion in his own light and to come to his own conclusions.

Discussions on Matters of Urgent Public Importance for Short Duration

In order to provide opportunities for members to discuss matters of importance, a convention was established in Lok Sabha in March 1953 whereby members could raise discussions for a short duration without a formal motion or vote thereon. This was later incorporated in the Rules of Procedure and Conduct of Business in Lok Sabha.

A member desirous of raising discussion on a matter of

urgent public importance for short duration has to give notice in writing to the secretary-general, specifying clearly and precisely the points on which he wishes discussion to be raised. The notice must be accompanied by an explanatory note stating reasons for raising discussion on the matter in question and has to be supported by the signatures of at least two other members.[17] Only one matter can be raised for discussion in a notice.

The speaker may call for such other information from the member who has given the notice and also from the minister concerned as he may consider necessary. If the speaker is satisfied that the matter is of sufficient importance, he admits the notice. If an early opportunity is otherwise available for discussion of the matter in question, the speaker may disallow the notice.[18] Normally, discussion on matters of urgent public importance for short duration is taken up on Tuesdays and Thursdays. In exceptional circumstances, it may be taken up on any other day.

After a notice is admitted and a date fixed for discussion, the item is included in the List of Business for that date in the name of the member who gives the notice and who initiates the discussion and makes a short statement. Members who have previously intimated their intention to the speaker to take part in the discussion and the minister concerned all give brief statements.[19] The member who has raised the discussion has no right to reply. There is no formal motion before the House, nor is there any voting. The purpose of the discussion is to enable members who possess knowledge about the matter to apprise the House of it.

The number of such discussions has been increasing since the Fourth Lok Sabha. Subjects range over a very wide variety of matters from questions of foreign policy to economic policy, law-and-order situations, railway accidents, strikes by Air India pilots, repatriation of criminals from abroad, fall in production, and even the sports policy of the government. All of these matters could at any time have formed the subject of adjournment debates, but they were successfully discussed through this device and passions subsided.

Although in a sense the device serves the same purpose as an adjournment motion, it is different in some ways. A motion involving a decision of the House is not drawn up, and there is no decision of the House thereon. A subject or a motion calling for discussion only is put down for discussion, members place before the House their points of view, and the government makes a reply. The respective points of view having thus been stated, the air is cleared and no definite decision is recorded. Consequently there is no question of censure of the government. This procedure has been further strengthened with a provision that such a notice can be put in the Parliamentary Bulletin as soon as it is admitted by the speaker and before the government finds time to test the support of other members of the House thereon. Such notices are circulated under the heading No-Day-Yet-Named Motions. Those members who wish to support these notices append their names to them and such names are noted from time to time in the Parliamentary Bulletin for the information of the members. When a large or a considerable number of members support a particular motion, the government must find time for discussion.

Improving the Individual Member's Effectiveness

Another direction where the Indian Parliament has taken significant strides is in its efforts to improve the performance of its individual members. The role of the legislator has been radically transformed due to the proliferation of governmental activities. Since many of the executive bodies are nowadays engaged in functions of industrial, commercial, scientific, or technological nature, it is necessary that the legislators should possess adequate information about the working of these institutions and other allied matters. In the absence of authentic and reliable information and data, a member's scrutiny and supervision of governmental departments and institutions can hardly be effective. A well-informed legislator is the backbone of a good government and can alone stimulate new ideas and provoke fresh thinking and thereby contribute to elevating the standard of debate in the House. The busy parliamentary life, however, leaves the modern legislator with little time to undertake independent or in-depth studies of complex political and economic problems. The legislator's problem is thus twofold.

First he lacks time to read through the mass of available literature or to undertake independent studies. And second, he needs to have an objective and independent analysis of various problems and issues.

Research and Information Service in the Indian Parliament

Realizing the need for an independent research and information organization to provide for such assistance to the legislators, the Parliament has greatly strengthened its Library and Research organization.[20] The Legislative Reference Service in India has been in existence since 1950, but its organization had not crystalized properly on account of continuous experimentation. The present library, reference, research, and information functions in the Indian Parliament are organized into three services, namely, the Library Service, the Research and Information Service, and the Documentation Service. Apart from analyzing and documenting all the useful data from the literature produced by governmental and other agencies from the point of view of the peculiar needs of the legislators, the Research and Information Service provides information to members, both on demand as well as on its own initiative. Assistance to members includes on-the-spot answers to their inquiries and the supplying of quick references from authentic sources and published documents, collections of factual data, statistics etc. The service also does extensive study of reference works, preparation of bibliographies on important legislative measures coming up before Parliament, production of brochures and information bulletins on current national and international affairs, and research notes on current economic, legal, or social problems likely to be discussed in the two Houses of Parliament.

Members of Parliament desirous of obtaining detailed information on any subject are required to send a formal requisition in a prescribed form to the Research and Information Service, indicating precisely the points on which the information is required and the date and time by which they would like to have it. This information is then collected and supplied to them.

References from the Members. The number of references received from members of both Houses of Parliament has shown a continuous upward trend, although the statistics may not stand any comparison with the number of references received and processed in the US Library of Congress or the libraries of some major Commonwealth countries. However, this certainly reveals the growing popularity of the reference service amongst the members and the fact that they do make use of this facility.

During the term of the Second Parliament, as many as 1,300 written references and 940 spot references were received and attended to. The spot references included inquiries made orally by members at the counters. At times, these oral inquiries are even more important than the written ones. During the Third Parliament (1962–67), the number of written references rose to 1,913 and spot references to 1,650. The number of references registered a phenomenal increase during the four years of the Fourth Lok Sabha (1962–70), the House having been dissolved a year ahead of schedule. As many as 2,925 written references and 3,000 spot references were attended to by the reference staff. In 1971 the total number of references is said to have exceeded the figures of previous years, but exact figures are not readily available.[21]

The range of members' inquiries, like that in the US and other countries, varies from the routine—like the total railway mileage in India, zonewise and statewise; total aid received under PL 480 program; figures of external assistance received from various countries—all involving collection and copying out of figures from published documents or getting the information from concerned ministries or departments over the telephone or through written request, to the preparation of comprehensive research notes on subjects like the effect on India's trade of Britain's entry into FCM, regional imbalances, unemployment problems, water scarcity problem, rural electrification, and defection of MLAs from one political party to another.[22]

Briefs and Research Assistance for Conferences and Committees. For the past decade or so, the Research and Information Service has been preparing well-documented, original research notes and briefs on subjects scheduled for discussion at the annual Commonwealth Parliamentary Conferences and Conferences of the Inter-Parliamentary Union. While in the US Congress and some major Commonwealth parliaments committees depend for their secretarial and research work mainly on the Congressional Research Service, the committees of the Indian Parliament have, from their very inception, evolved secretariats of their own. Although separate branches attached to each committee, staffed by committee officers and committee assistants, attend to all the work relating to arrangements for meetings and study tours, preparation of minutes and tour reports, drafting of questionnaires and analysis of material received from ministries, sifting and editing of the evidence and drafting of reports, nevertheless the Research and Information Service does come to the aid of all the parliamentary committees in various research and information gathering assignments. The extent of service rendered can fairly be compared to the assistance available in other countries, excepting the United States. The very same service also provides the secretarial as well as the research assistance to the parliamentary committees that are appointed to consider the Five-Year Plan Drafts.

However limited the resources or undeveloped the economy of a country, if it can afford a legislature, it must provide the necessary legislative reference service facilities to the legislature and the legislators, so as to enable them to perform their functions properly and effectively. Any economy on this service is shortsighted. An adequate legislative reference service is, in fact, the backbone of the "grand inquest of the nation" and, as such, the sheet anchor of democracy. It must not fail the parliamentarian and must keep pace with his growing needs and the complex responsibilities in the modern world. The danger inherent in such a service is the growth of a powerful legislative bureaucracy which may erode the position of the legislator himself, and in a parliamentary system of power distribution it may come into conflict with the executive departments or ministries. However, the legislators owe it to themselves to develop their expertise and professionalism. "No amount of Legislative Reference Service briefing or expert assistance or other facilities could ever substitute legislators of better calibre and quality." [23]

Orientation of Members

The democratic system of government rests on the assumption that the average individual in the society is politically conscious and is intelligent enough to understand its problems and to exercise his right of vote in a rational and responsible manner. A good deal of political education is thus a necessity concomitant of a healthy democracy. In many countries this function is performed by political parties. However, the parties in India have not been performing this role in a satisfactory and a concerted manner with the result that even the people's representatives—the legislators—do not, at times, seem to be well equipped in the "tenets, tools, and operational mechanics of parliamentary institutions." The social and economic background of the legislators in the Parliament and State Assemblies has been fast changing. The Fourth General Election (1967) brought about far-reaching changes in the socioeconomic background and the occupational pattern of the legislators, both at the Union and the State levels. The political elite in India is gradually getting ruralized. There has been, in recent years, a substantial decline of legislators from the intelligentsia. Brought up in traditional and humble environments, most current legislators come to the Assembly for the first time and are not fully, or even casually, acquainted with the rules and procedures of the House, nor are they aware of the various conventions, regulations, mannerisms, and the formalities of a legislature. To enable them to overcome these deficiencies and to alleviate their confusion, it is desirable that new members should be given some training in the basic procedures of their job and the rules of the House in which they sit.

Realizing this gap in some members' political education and the virtual nonexistence of any institutionalized attempt on the part of Parliament to teach members the fundamentals of their profession, the Institute of Constitutional and Parliamentary Studies, a nonofficial organization established at New Delhi in 1966, worked out a comprehensive plan and launched experimental orientation seminars for legislators all over the country. A zonal seminar scheme, bringing together a fixed number of legislators from areas contiguous to each other in a particular place mutually agreed upon by the presiding officer of the House of the participating States and Union Territories, was initiated to cover the 520 members of the Lok Sabha and 250 members of the Rajya Sabha at the Union level, and nearly 3,500 legislators in the various States and the Union territories. Despite the heterogeneous groups participating from different states and drawn from all shades of political parties, a happy sense of unity and institutional solidarity, and a feeling of togetherness seemed to prevail throughout these seminars, which is said to have resulted in certain spontaneous consensus on several controversial issues.[24]

Apart from the six seminars for the State legislators, the Institute of Constitutional and Parliamentary Studies also organized, in 1971, an orientation course for the new members of the Fifth Lok Sabha. Unfortunately, the members did not show much enthusiasm and the response was very disheartening.

Institutional Innovations for Continuous Improvements

The Indian governmental system, being federal in character, has within its framework the legislatures of the Union government and twenty-one State legislatures. They all employ a parliamentary system of government. The existence of such a large number of legislative bodies, composed of people of heterogeneous background and character who operate in different political, economic, and social environments, necessitates the establishment of a common forum for discussion of certain general problems in order to bring about some uniformity in legislative procedures throughout the country and to effect continuous improvements in the parliamentary processes. Parliamentarians from the different parts of the country must have a forum where they can meet to discuss and find a solution to their common problems, and where also some sort of cross-fertilization of ideas can take place between the older and the younger parliamentarians. These problems can be, and no doubt are, discussed at intergovernmental conferences, but those discussions are not so frank and free as they can be in a conclave of legislators.[25] In India such forums exist in the periodic conferences of the presiding officers of the Union Parliament and State assemblies, of the secretaries of the Union and State assemblies, of the chairmen of various committees of the Union and State legislatures. While the activities of these conferences are not well known, as the proceedings are kept confidential and are not meant for public consumption, the Inaugural Address of the President of the Conference of Presiding Officers does receive wide publicity and sometimes becomes a subject of heated controversy.[26]

Summary

To cope with the pecularities of Indian politics and to meet the emerging needs of a society in rapid transition, the Indian legislature has, in the last quarter century, undertaken a number of structural and procedural reforms. These reforms concerned innovations to insure the effective utilization of time, such as the establishment of a Business Advisory Committee and the introduction of the Automatic Vote Recorder. Other reforms concerned improvement of the committee system and included the establishment of the Action-Taken Reports procedure and the provision of professional staff help. Other innovations were aimed at improving the legislature's ability to oversee the administration—here we have the creation of the Committee on Government Assurances and another committee on Scheduled Castes and Scheduled Tribes and the institutionalization of two procedural innovations, the Calling-Attention Notices and the Short-Duration Discussion. Other reforms were concerned with improving the effectiveness of individual members of Parliament. These included the provision of a research and information service and orientation for new members of Parliament. Finally, some innovations were concerned with establishing certain institutional capabilities for effecting continuous improvements in parliamentary processes, such as periodic conferences for presiding officers, secretaries, and chairmen of the various committees of the Union and State parliaments.

Notes

1. See "Congress Working Committee Resolution, July 15, 1975," as reported in *The Indian Express*, 16 July 1975.

2. India, Lok Sabha Secretariat, *First Parliament (1952–1957): A Souvenir* (New Delhi, 1957), p. 95.

3. M. N. Kaul, "Parliamentary Procedures Since Independence" in *First Parliament Souvenir*, no. 3, p. 32.

4. India, Lok Sabha, Business Advisory Committee, *Minutes*, First Lok Sabha, 22 April 1954. Also see M. N. Kaul and S. L. Shakdher, *Practice and Procedures of Parliaments* New Delhi n.p. 1972 p. 660ff.

5. India, Lok Sabha, Business Advisory Committe, *22nd Report*, I Lok Sabha (1952–57).

6. See India, Lok Sabha, *Automatic Vote Recording Equipment in Lok Sabha Chamber* (New Delhi, 15 February 1967).

7. L. M. Singhvi, "Key Role of Standing Committees—Agenda for Reform" in the Institute of Constitutional and Parliamentary Studies, *Parliamentary Committees in India* (New Delhi, 1973), p. 2.

8. *Ibid*, p. 2.

9. S. L. Shakdher, "Committee on Government Assurance in Parliament of India" in *The Parliamentarian* (London) 55, 2 (April 1974): 72–77.

10. *Ibid*, p. 76.

11. See *Journal of Parliamentary Information* 15 (1969): 50–51.

12. See for details, B. K. Mukherji, "Machinery for Implementation of the Constitutional Safeguards for Scheduled Castes and Scheduled Tribes—I and II" in *Journal of Parliamentary Information* 17, 3 and 4 (July and October 1971).

13. *Ibid.*, no. 4 (October 1971), pp. 42–43.

14. Durga Das, "Parliament and the Press," in *Journal of Parliamentary Information* (New Delhi) 15 (April 1969): 16–17.

15. S. L. Shakdher, "Calling Attention Notices" in *Indian Journal of Public Administration* (New Delhi) 10 (1964): 212.

16. *Ibid.*

17. Lok Sabha, *Rules of Procedure and Conduct of Business in Lok Sabha*, Rule 193.

18. *Ibid.*, Rule 194.

19. *Ibid.*, Rule 195.

20. For details of the growth of the parliamentary library, see A. L. Seth, "Parliament Library in India" in *The Parliamentarian* 51 (July 1970): 21–23.

21. See A. N. Kaul, "Legislative Reference Service in Indian Parliament" in *Journal of Constitutional and Parliamentary Studies* 7, 3 (July-September 1973): 63.

22. *Ibid.*

23. This section of the paper is mainly based on the article by Subhash C. Kashyap, "Orientation Seminars for Legislators" in *The Parliamentarian* 51, 2 (April 1970): 81–86. The quotation is from Subhash C. Kashyap, "Information Management for Members of Parliament," *Journal of Constitutional Law and Parliamentary Studies.* 7:1973:116.

24. *Ibid.*

25. Kaul and Shakdher, *op cit*, p. 918.

26. For example, in the latest conference of the presiding officers, held at Shillong in the first week of November 1974, a controversy arose about the Chairman Dr. G. S. Dhillon's (speaker, Lok Sabha) reported support of one-party government in India while addressing a Rotary Club meeting. This became a subject for heated debate in the

current session (Winter 1974) of the Parliament. Similarly, his reported remarks against the deputy speaker (Professor G. Swell) prompted the latter to boycott the conference on account of "near famine" conditions existing in the State of Meghalaya, where the conference was taking place. See his statement in *The Hindustan Times* (New Delhi), 9 November 1974.

Legislative Reforms in Lebanon

ABDO I. BAAKLINI

Within the past few years Lebanon has been undergoing a series of political crises that are shaking the very foundations of its existence. While these crises are to a large degree due to forces external to the Lebanese political scene, nonetheless, certain internal conditions have acted as catalysts in bringing the country to a full-fledged civil war. Under the pressure of the Arab-Israeli conflict and its political, economic, and military ramifications, including the emergence of the Palestinian Liberation Organization as a major military and political force in Lebanon, and as a result of the emergence of many Arab oil-producing countries as major international political and economic actors, Lebanese internal equilibrium, which had been meticulously worked out during the past half a century, has been shattered. The Palestinian struggle against Israel from within Lebanese territory and the continuous Israeli incursions into Lebanon to stop Palestinian resistance led to the explosion of a series of issues that have, until recently, been politically mediated and contained. The political conflict in recent years has taken a violent turn, pitting Christians against Muslims, rich against poor, and rightists against leftists. In this struggle there is scarcely a political institution that has not been scorched. Political parties, for some time thought to be a substitute for the "sectarian" political institutions in existence, were forced to take sides, the army was discredited as a pro-Christian force, and the presidency, a preserve for the Maronite Christians, was sidestepped as unrepresentative of the whole population. Ironically one institution, which has been since its inception under continuous criticism and ridicule for its unrepresentativeness, idleness, traditionalism, mosaic, archaic, and contradictory composition, emerged as the only viable institution. It is here that the various crises are being mediated and where the attributes of any new political order, if and when it emerges, are being worked out. The Lebanese Chamber of Deputies has emerged as the only peaceful arena for settling disputes and political differences. Even the various combatants in the civil war are concerned with adopting strategies that will maximize their representation at the Chamber of Deputies once the violent conflict ends. Thus the phalangist Christian rightist party is fighting not to eliminate the Muslim or leftist parties, a task that it fully realizes is absurd. It is fighting with an eye to the next parliamentary election, when it hopes to cash in on its image as the defender of the Christians. Other groups are also following strategies to insure their representation in the forthcoming legislature, where most day-to-day political bargains are expected to take place. In other words the extraordinary, violent politics predominant in Lebanon at this stage is a temporary phase that will soon give way to the normal politics that will be played within the constraints of the legislative institution. Whatever the results of the present conflict, the legislature is the arena where the future rules of the game are being worked out and where the political game will be played out.

This makes the issue of legislative reforms both academically and practically relevant. After a brief overview of Lebanon's legislative institution, this chapter will discuss Lebanese legislative reforms under these headings: macro system reforms, procedural reforms, and structural reforms.

Legislatures in the Lebanese Political System: Historical Development

The Chamber of Deputies has long been a central institution in the Lebanese political system. Its power and importance has steadily been institutionalized over the years. Its origin dates back as early as 1842 with the fall of the Shihabi emirate, which initiated the end of the feudal system. With the establishment of the Double Kaimakamate [1] and, more significantly, the establishment of the Mutassarifieh [2] system in 1861, the importance of the institution that came to include representatives of various political and sectarian communities in Lebanon was on the rise. The indirectly elected Central Administrative Council eventually gave rise to the modern Lebanese Chamber of Deputies. After the declaration in 1920 of greater Lebanon under the French mandate, the Central Administrative Council, which had earlier been disbanded, was replaced by what the French called the Administrative Committee, and later by the Representative Council. The Representative Council, acting as a constitutional assembly, was finally to draft the Lebanese Constitution in 1926. Since then, with only a few interruptions under the French mandate, the 1926 constitution and its subsequent constitutional amendments [3] has provided the basis for the political institutions of the country. The legislature came to be viewed as a conflict-resolution mechanism where representatives of the various communities constituting Lebanon would voice their preferences on policy matters.

The constitution of 1926, its subsequent amendments, and the National Pact of 1943 [4] laid out the institutional structure of present-day Lebanese politics. Today Lebanon has a unicameral legislature. The three major political officers in the country are, by convention, distributed among the main religious sects. The president of the Republic (the chief executive), who is selected by the Chamber for a nonrenewable six-year term, is a Maronite Christian. The president of the Chamber of Deputies, elected yearly by the Chamber as the official spokesman of the legislative branch, is a Shia Muslim. The prime minister, who is designated by the president of the Republic, is a Sunni Muslim. The Chamber is popularly elected for a period of four years. As in all parliamentary systems, a cabinet in Lebanon cannot assume power before it secures a vote of confidence from the Chamber. Thus the three major political officers have a very close working relationship.

The internal rules of the Chamber provide that the Chamber shall be administered by a bureau composed of a president, vice-president, two secretaries, and three questeurs [5] elected annually at the first meeting of the second regular session of the

Table 1

Presidents of the Lebanese Chamber of Deputies (1943–1974)

Name	Religion	Period Presided
Habib Abu Shahla	Greek Orthodox	1945–1946
Ahmad al Assa'd	Shia Muslim	1951–1953
Adel Oseiran	Shia Muslim	1953–1959
Sabri Hamadeh	Shia Muslim	1943–1945, 1946–1951, 1959–1963, 1965–1967, 1968–1970
Kamel al Assa'd	Shia Muslim	1964, one session of 1968, one session of 1970 1971–1974

Chamber in October of each year. The bureau, acting through its president, is the formal administrative authority in the Chamber.[6] The president, however, has evolved as the main figure.[7] although he is elected annually, there has been a large degree of continuity among the holders of the office, which only five persons have held since Lebanon achieved its independence in 1943. One of the five (who presided only one year) was a Greek Orthodox; the remaining four were Muslim Shia.

As table 1 indicates, the figure who dominated the presidency of the Chamber after independence was Sabri Hamadeh. Only during the Presidency of Camille Shamun (1951–1958) was Hamadeh clearly excluded from power.

Hamadeh's presidency of the Lebanese Chamber of Deputies was characterized by the high degree of informality with which he applied the rules and regulations governing the legislative process. Through his close and intimate association with the chief executives of his time—Presidents Bishara al Khouri, 1943–1952; Fuad Shihab, 1958–1964; and Charles Helou, 1964–1970—Hamadeh was able to pursue his prime interest, facilitating the work of the government. Procedures and processes were adjusted to fit the needs of a Chamber with no single majority party or permanent power center. Rather than rewriting written procedures, he bent them to fit political realities. As for the organization and staffing of the Chamber, Hamdeh left it to proliferate pragmatically. Through his exclusive power to appoint the legislative staff Hamadeh recruited a number of loyal supporters to fill the established positions. Most jobs went to his kin and members of his constituency.

Apparently this situation was allowed to continue for two reasons. First, the Shia sect to which Hamadeh belonged was clearly underrepresented in the goverment civil service, and joining the legislative staff, which was not limited by entry requirements or special qualifications, was one method of correcting this. More basic, however, was the low importance attached to organizational and structural development by the legislators themselves. In a small country like Lebanon intimate knowledge of issues and personalities discouraged members of the Chamber from seeking administrative or professional staff help. Intimate personal relationships with constituencies, executive agencies, and departments militated against any priority for competent legislative staff. Members of the Chamber conceived of themselves as professionals and experts-at-large on matters pertaining to their work. If and when the need for expert opinion arose, members of the Chamber had easy access to personal friends, (relatives), their personal staff (most prominent Lebanese members of the Chamber have been lawyers by profession and have had access to their office staff), the press, and quite frequently to the executive departments concerned. Legislative staff was limited to running personal errands for members of the Chamber and to performing the routine clerical work of the Chamber's sessions.

While Hamadeh failed to develop a viable legislative staff organization, he nonetheless made significant contributions in other aspects. His greatest achievement was in hammering out a symbiotic relationship between the Chamber and the executive. This relationship has been a basic contributing factor to the Chamber's survival.

Before Adel Oseiran took over the leadership of the Chamber in 1953, Ahmad Al Assa'd, the father of the present Chamber leader, Kamel Al Assa'd, served as president for two years.

During his leadership the Chamber was for the first time provided with an organizational regulation defining the structure of the administration and the positions needed.[8] The filling of these positions was left to Oseiran. When President Shamun came to power in 1952 at the head of a popular uprising ousting Bishara al Khouri, much sentiment in favor of a strong legislative institution was heard.[9] Oseiran, a graduate of the American University of Beirut and a representative of the new forces, was elected as president of the Chamber.

Until 1953 the Chamber had been run in accordance with rules drawn up in 1930. Under Oseiran's leadership these rules were overhauled in 1953. The 1953 revisions added three questeurs to the bureau of the Chamber; defined explicitly the Chamber president's area of jurisdiction and that of the various bureau members; defined and reorganized the Chamber's committees, taking into consideration the subject matter of proposed legislation; and increased the power of that individual member of the Chamber by abolishing articles that restricted his actions on the floor. Legislative processes and work procedures were clarified and simplified.[10]

Under Oseiran's leadership a number of young college graduates were encouraged to join the staff of the Chamber, however, Hamadeh's political appointees maintained their jobs. Political allegiance to the president of the Chamber or to influential legislative leaders remained an important criteria for appointment to the legislative staff.

By the early 1960s the concern with and need for legislative reform took a different turn. Until then the close relationship between the legislature and the government bureaucracy discouraged the separate organizational development of the Chamber. Members had easy access to the bureaucracy and were able to act like an ombudsman between their constituencies and the various government agencies.[11] The call for legislative reforms was limited to macropolitical-structural changes—abolishing sectarianism, instituting reform in the electoral laws [12] and the political parties, and reforming the parties' relationship to the legislature. Kamel al Assa'd's term in office in 1964, 1968, and 1970–1974 saw the emergence of a new approach toward developing the Chamber. Under the impact of Shihabism, with its stress on developing and depoliticizing the bureaucracy, the Chamber, especially its prominent political leaders, sensed that Shihab's administrative reform measures [13] and his reliance on a group of young technocrats had strained the relationship that existed between the executive and the legislature. Shihab's military background predisposed him unfavorably toward politicians in general. Legislators saw in him and his regime a threat to political life as known in Lebanon.[14] Several attempts were made by the political institutions of the country (especially the Chamber and the cabinet) to reassert themselves as the center of political action.[15] In the summer of 1970 the Chamber scored a victory by turning down the Shihabi candidate and electing Suleiman Franjieh, a member of the Chamber, as the new president of the Republic. With Franjieh's election, the advocates of a strong legislature became prominent. Saeb Salam became prime minister and Kamel al Assa'd the president of the Chamber.

Macro System Reforms

Macro system reforms centered around three basic issues: sectarianism, the relationship of the legislature to political parties, and finally the relationship of the legislature to the executive.

Sectarianism

As early as 1926 the legislative institution in Lebanon was under attack for favoring the Christian segment of the population. Under the French mandate the Christians were heavily favored, first by the fact that presidents of the republic were always Christian, and second because they had the majority of seats in the Chamber. What had been considered a provisional arrangement to be rectified as soon as the mandate was over became a permanent arrangement to which the Muslim and the Christian leadership became committed by the National Pact. Muslim and secularist resistance to this informal arrangement continued. The Muslims felt that they were underrepresented and the secularists [16] felt that the arrangement perpetuated sectarianism as a permanent feature of the Lebanese political sys-

Table 2

Distribution of Parliamentary Seats by Sects
1947–1972

	Sect	1947	1951	1953	1957	1960–72[1]
Christians	Maronite	18	23	13	20	30
	Greek Orthodox	6	8	5	7	11
	Greek Catholic	3	5	3	4	6
	Armenian Orthodox	2	3	2	3	4
	Minorities	1	3	1	2	3
Muslims	Sunni	11	16	9	14	20
	Shia	10	14	8	12	19
	Druze	4	5	3	4	6
	Total	55	77	44	66	99

[1] Since 1960 there have been three elections—in 1964, 1968, and 1972. The sectarian distribution remained the same as in 1960.

tem and therefore prevented the emergence of a secular, national, democratic state.

Since independence seats in the Lebanese Chamber of Deputies have been distributed among the various religious sects in ratio of six Christian seats to five Muslim seats. Table 2 shows the distribution of parliamentary seats among the various sects between 1947–1972.

While the Muslim reformers insisted that the Christian-Muslim ratio should be adjusted to reflect the true numerical strength of each sect, the secular reformers urged the entire abolition of sectarian distribution, thus making it possible for every citizen to compete for any seat regardless of his or her religion.

A permanent feature of Lebanese electoral laws since independence has been the list system. Each district, with the possible exception of the districts created in accordance with the 1953 electoral laws, has more than one seat to be filled. The 1960 electoral law, for example, divides Lebanon into twenty-six electoral districts. Only one of those districts (the city of Saida) is made into a single-member district. The remaining twenty-five districts are multiple-member districts ranging in size from two seats, as in Batroun and Bshari, to eight, as in the first district of Beirut and Shuf. The multiple-member districts

Table 3

Districts and Sectarian Distribution since 1960

Sect	District	Sectarian Distribution of Seats	Total N of Seats
Totally Maronite	Kisrawan	4M	4
	Zgharta	3M	3
	Bshari	2M	2
	Batroun	2M	2
Totally Shia	Bint Jbeil	2Sh	2
	Sour	3Sh	3
	Nabatiya	3Sh	3
Totally Sunni	Saida	1S	1
	Villages of Tripoli	2S	2
Totally Greek Orthodox	Koura	2GO	2
Mixed Christians	Matn	3M, 1GO, 1AO	5
	Jezzin	2M, 1GO	3
	Beirut First	1M, 1GO, 1GC, 1P, 1AC, 3AO	8
Mixed Christians-Muslim	Saida-Zahrani	1Sh, 1GC	2
	Marjeoun	2Sh, 1GO, 1S	4
	Shuf	3M, 2S, 2D, 1GC	8
	Aley	2M, 2D, 1GO	5
	Baa'bda	3M, 1D, 1Sh	5
	Jbeil	2M, 1Sh	3
	Zahle	1M, 1S, 1Sh, 1GO, 1GC	5
	Rachaya-West Biqa'	1S, 1Sh, 1GO	3
	Baalbeck-hermel	1S, 4Sh, 1M, 1GC	7
	Beirut Second	4S, 1GO	5
	Beirut Third	1S, 1Sh, 1Mi	3
	Tripoli	2S, 1M, 1GO	4
	Akkar	2S, 1M, 1GO	4

M = Maronite; GO = Greek Orthodox; GC = Greek Catholic; S = Sunni; Sh = Shia; D = Druze; AO = Armenian Orthodox; AC = Armenian Catholic; Mi = Minority; P = Protestant

vary not only in size but also in terms of sectarian and ethnic composition, as indicated in table 3.

In multiple-member districts where the voters are asked to choose among contestants who belong to the same sect, the competition is intrasectarian. The issues are normally local and center around local leaders. Alliances are in terms of what strength each candidate brings to the list. Normally a list includes a representative of a very strong and influential family or a candidate who can secure a certain geographical area within the district. Thus a list in Zgharta will invariably have a representative of the Franjieh, the Dweihi, or the Muawad family. In the Koura district a successful list will need a representative of the Ghusn or the Boulus family. In Matn, in addition to sectarian and political considerations, a successful list needs to have a representative of the coastal towns, the middle ridge, and the upper highlands. Thus geographical, sectarian, family, and political considerations enter into the formulations of lists. In no case are these alliances permanent or ideological; in many they crystallize at the last moment before the election only to break apart as soon as the election is over. The main uniting force is desire to win the election. In mixed areas where candidates from more than one sect compete, competing lists are composed of candidates from the sects who are entitled to seats in that area. Thus the competing alliances in Baa'bda will be between two or more lists, each composed of three Maronites, one Druze, and one Shia.

Candidates who are unable to join a list or to formulate a list of their own may compete for a particular seat independently. Voters, regardless of their sects, have the right to elect a whole list, or to choose their candidates from more than one list or to choose independents. In other words they are not bound to choose any one single list. They can choose as many candidates as the number of seats in that district, provided they observe the sectarian distribution. Thus a voter in the Baa'bda district, regardless of his sect, may choose any five candidates running in the district provided they include three Maronites, one Druze, and one Shia. He cannot choose more than five candidates, nor can he alter the sectarian distribution by, for example, voting for two Druzes instead of one. He is, however, entitled to choose one candidate for a particular seat and leave the other seats vacant. This means that while the sectarian distribution of seats in a particular district is specified by the electoral law, the voter is free to formulate his own list in accordance with his preferences. He is not restricted by political party or formal alliances among candidates. This places the voter in a strong position vis-à-vis the party or the list maker. For an alliance to be successful the preferences of the voters have to be respected or else they do not vote for the whole list.

Although running on a list is no guarantee that a candidate will win, running independently is almost a sure way to lose, as the figures on table 4 indicate.

Table 4

Independent Candidates and Incidence of Success

Year	1960	1964	1968	1972
N individual candidates	123	66	78	137
N successful candidates	4		2	2

Of the ninety-nine Chamber members less than 2 percent have been elected independently. The remaining 98 percent have been candidates who have run on one list or another. Table 5 indicates the number of lists that have managed to have all their members elected during four parliamentary elections. With the exception of the 1964 election, when the Shihab regime played an active part in eliminating the opposition and in forging alliances, approximately 50 percent of the deputies have been elected as members of completely successful lists. The remaining deputies managed to be elected, as independents, from various competing lists. This is a very clear indication of voter independence. It is not uncommon to find that in a district of five seats two may have been elected from one list and the other three elected from another list.

Table 5

Lists With All Candidates Elected
in Four Parliamentary Elections

Year	1960	1964	1968	1972
N lists	15	20	13	17
N deputies	48	65	44	56

Voter independence, however, poses certain problems for political parties and independent political leaders. Political parties cannot insure that their members will vote for a whole list regardless of the alliance it represents. Ideological political parties like the Baa'th party and the Syrian Social Nationalist Party are even more hampered. If their candidates are to have any chance of winning an election, they must join a list. But to join a list involves cooperation compromise with local leaders and the forces that these parties consider to be "traditional," "feudal," or "reactionary." If they do cooperate, they face the prospect of insubordination and possible defection among their party regulars. If they do not, they are certain to lose the election and possibly leave their followers frustrated with both the system and the party. This is why the only political parties that have been able to send representatives to parliament are the nondoctrinaire, compromising political parties that manage to accept political divisions in society as natural and healthy.

The Legislature and Political Parties

Secular and doctrinaire political parties have been the severest critics of Lebanon's sectarian electoral system. They have argued that the list system was invented to perpetuate sectarianism and traditional leadership and to prevent the emergence of national secular parties that cut across the sectarian lines. They advocate an electoral system that abolishes the sectarian distribution and the list system in favor of a system based on proportional representation, where only candidates who are nominated by political parties are allowed to run for election. A legislature whose members belong to political parties, it is argued, whould be in a better position to deal with contemporary issues than a legislature where two-thirds of its members, as table 6 shows, belong to no political party and act in an independent capacity.

While the opponents of the present electoral system agree that it should change, they are divided with regard to the system that should replace it. Table 7 summarizes the position of the leading political actors' preference with regard to the electoral system to come.

Table 6

Parliamentary Membership of Parties in Lebanon[1] 1951–1972

Party	1951	1953	1957	1960	1964	1968	1972
Syrian Social Nationalist Party			1				
Ba'ath (Arab Renaissance Socialist Party)							1[2]
Arab Nasserite Coalition							1[2]
Dashnak (Armenian Party)	2	2	3	4	4	3	2
Najjada				1		1	
Progressive Socialist Party	3	2–4	3	6	6	5	4
National Action Movement					1	1	1
National Appeal	Membership flexible and indeterminate						
National Organization				1			
Kataeb (Phalange)	3	1	1	6	4	9	7
Constitutional Union	Flexible and indeterminate			5–8	5	4	
National Bloc	2	3	4	6	2	5	3
National Liberals	Party nonexistent			4–5	6	8	7
Democratic Socialist Party							3[2]
Democratic Party							1[2]
Total	10	8–10	12	32–37	28	36	30
Total Members in Chamber	77	44	66	99	99	99	99
Percent of members in political parties	13	24	18	35	28	36	30

Source: Ralph E. Crow. "Religious Sectarianism in the Lebanese Political System," *Journal of Politics*, 24 (August 1962), p. 284. Michael Suleiman. *Political Parties in Lebanon*. (Ithaca, NY: Cornell University Press 1967), p. 265.

[1] The following parties were unable to elect any members to the parliament: Lebanese Communist Party; Muslim Brethren; Ibad-ar-Rahman (The Worshipper of God); Muslim Group; Tahreer; Hunchak (Armenian Party); Ramgavar Azadagow (Armenian Party).

[2] The election of 1972 brought to the parliament representatives of three parties that were never represented before and the creation of a new party, the Democratic Socialist Party, headed by Kamel al-Assa'd.

The Legislature and the Executive

Since independence the presidents of Lebanon have been Maronite Christians. Muslim elements of the population as well as secularist political parties have argued that the presidency should be open to all citizens and that instead of the president being selected by the Parliament, he should submit to a vote by the whole population. Supporters of the present system have argued that a Christian president in a Lebanon situated in an all-Muslim Arab world is desirable, since it gives the Christian

Table 7

Attitudes of Political Parties in Lebanon With Regard to the Electoral Law[1]

	Name of Political Party													
	National Appeal	Progressive Socialist Party	Najjada	National Action	Democratic Party	National Bloc	Kataeb	Syrian Social Nationalist Party	Lebanese Communist Party	Union of Nasirite Forces	Ba'ath Party (Syria Br.)	Ba'ath Party (Iraq Br.)	Syrian Social Nationalist Party (Abdul Masih Br.)	Nasirite Organization
Against sectarianism in politics	x	x	x	x	x	x	x	x	x	x	x	x	[2]	x
Advocates complete elimination of sectarianism from electoral laws					x			x					[2]	
Advocates gradual elimination of sectarianism from electoral laws	x	x	x			x	x		x	x			[2]	
Strengthening the role of political parties in election	x	x	x	x	x	x	x	x	x	x	x	x	[2]	x
Proportional representation based partly on political party; partly on sects			x				x						[2]	
Proportional representation based partly on political parties; partly on independent members								x	x	x			[2]	

For large constituency								x					2	
For small constituency (2–4 seats)				x		x					x		2	x
For single member constituency, if sectarianism is abolished	x									x		x	2	
For enlarging the number of deputies[3]	x	x						x	x	x	x	x	2	x
Deputies assuming ministerial posts[4]	x									x			2	
Lowering the voting age to 18 yrs old	x	x	x[5]	x	x	x	x	x	x	x	x	x	2	x
For the issuance of special I.D. cards for eligible voters[6]	x	x	x	x	x	x	x	x	x	x	x	x	2	x
Establishment of special tribunal judges to verify electoral result[7]	x					x	x	x			x	x	2	
Proportional representation by party only		x			x								2	
For adjusting sectarianism distribution[8]			x										2	

[1] The attitudes of these parties were expressed by the parties in a series of articles published by *Al-Nahar* between 30 May 1972 and 23 June 1972.

[2] Keep things as they are. It is useless unless people change.

[3] Present number of deputies in the chamber is 99. Most want to enlarge it to 121.

[4] At present a deputy could and often does become a cabinet minister. The change calls for cabinet ministers to be from outside, subject to vote of confidence by the Chamber.

[5] The Najjada wants the age for eligible voters to be lowered to twenty years.

[6] Presently voting takes place in accordance with lists prepared by bureau of vital statistics. The new change calls for the issuance of special I.D. for eligible voters in order to eliminate fraud in the lists.

[7] At present the Chamber acting through one of its committees, acts on complaints regarding electoral frauds. The suggested change calls for the establishment of a special appeal court of independent judges to perform that function.

[8] Present sectarian distribution calls for a six to five, Christian-Muslim ratio in the Chamber. The Najjada proposal calls for a six to six ratio, since the demographic distribution of population in Lebanon, according to Najjada has changed in favor of the Muslims.

Table 8

Presidents of Lebanon 1943–1976

Years	Name of President	Sect
1943–1952	Bishara al-Khouri	Maronite
1952–1958	Camille Shamun	Maronite
1958–1964	Fuad Shihab	Maronite
1964–1970	Charles Helou	Maronite
1970–1976	Suleiman Franjieh	Maronite

a sense of participation in Arab affairs. It can also serve as a bridge in dealing with the Christian West and in maintaining stability inside Lebanon.

Proponents of strong legislature have severely criticized one aspect of the relationship between the legislature and the president. Under the present constitution, the president has the right, after obtaining the cabinet's approval, to dissolve the Chamber and call for a new election. Although the new legislature cannot be dissolved for the same reason, critics argue that there is nothing to prevent the president from dissolving the legislature as many times as he wishes, offering in each time a different reason. It is also argued that the mere threat of dissolution gives the president an extraordinary power to control a legislature. The majority of the members do not belong to political parties and are consequently afraid to face another electoral campaign, for it requires substantial monetary resources, which the candidate should be prepared to provide from his personal resources.

Supporters of the present system have argued that notwithstanding the present constitutional power of the president, he is bound to act as an arbitrator among the various groups in the legislature. It would be helpful to remember that the executive in Lebanon refers to two separate institutions: the president of the Republic and the cabinet, headed by a prime minister. The president is elected by the Chamber for a period of six years, while the prime minister is appointed by the president and can only serve as prime minister after receiving a vote of confidence from the Chamber. In accordance with the National Pact, the president must be a Maronite and the prime minister a Sunni

Muslim. Both the constitution and the political culture and norms within the Chamber have equipped the president to serve as an arbitrator and not as a partisan. Presidents who have tried to play an openly partisan role have jeopardized their political influence.

Playing an arbitrator's role, especially in the absence of majority political parties in the Chamber, is both a presidential power source and limitation. Since the president cannot immediately renew his term in office, he need not be subservient to a Chamber that might decide his reelection. The Constitution has provided him with several powers, all of which, however, can be exercised only with the approval of the cabinet and with the signature of the prime minister. The president acting in the Council of Ministers can dissolve the Chamber and call for a general election. He can postpone the convening of the Chamber for a month, or he can ask the Chamber to convene in a special session. He has the right to nominate the prime minister and the cabinet members. Finally he can veto a bill passed by the Chamber, and his veto can only be overridden by a two-thirds majority.

From a constitutional perspective, the president's powers appear to be extensive, especially if one assumes that he controls his cabinet as presidents of the United States control theirs. In fact the president's powers are limited by a number of considerations.

The fact that he can exercise his power only in council, a provision intended to protect him from political responsibility and to enable him to play the role of arbitrator similar to the crown in Britain, puts the cabinet in a very strategic position. Since the cabinet is headed by a Sunni Muslim, who is usually a leader in his own right, and since the cabinet has to represent all the significant political trends in the Chamber if it is to receive a vote of confidence, the cooperation of the cabinet in endorsing presidential decisions cannot be taken for granted. Thus the cabinet, in a sense, can be conceived as an executive committee of the Chamber assigned to work with the president in carrying out the policies adopted by the Chamber. Presidents who have tried to go their own way regardless of the political feeling in the Chamber have found themselves isolated.

Bishara al-Khouri, in spite of his popularity as a national hero in 1943, found himself isolated in 1952, when parliamentary leaders supported by popular pressure asked for his resignation. In less than a month he tried to formulate two cabinets but failed. In the final analysis none of the Sunni Muslim leaders would serve as prime ministers under him. This led him to appoint Fuad Shihab, a Maronite, as a prime minister. Shihab's short term in office was a caretaker government that oversaw al-Khouri's resignation and the election of Shamun. Thus the president's ability to control his cabinet depends on his ability to satisfy the political forces in the Chamber that support the cabinet; otherwise the Chamber can withdraw its confidence. The cabinet in this perspective acts more as a check on the president's power rather than an aid to his office.

Another factor that has contributed to the president's arbitrator role is the absence of majority political parties. To be elected, the president has to depend on the support not only of his political party but of independents as well. Since the majority of deputies in the Chamber are independents, they usually elect a president who is not a party member. With the exception of Bishara al-Khouri, who was founder and president of the Constitutional Union, none of the presidents since independence have belonged to a political party. Even Shamun, who was politically active in the Constitutional Union, was not a member when elected in 1952. He established his party, the National Liberals, after he completed his term as president in 1958. What has been said about presidents is also applicable to prime ministers. In the absence of majority political parties, prime ministers tend to be selected from among the independents with strong local support from their constituencies.

In formulating their cabinets, presidents usually consult with the various parliamentary groups. Before a cabinet is announced, the president meets with every political group, the independent members, and the parliamentary groups to ask them about their candidate for the prime minister and what sort of cabinet they would like to see formulated. Once the process of consultation is completed and the cabinet is announced, the vote of confidence becomes a formality, since by that time supporters and opponents have already been identified. Presidents who have attempted to formulate cabinets against the wish of the majority in the Chamber were forced to retreat. This process of consultations, in which the president of the Chamber plays a major role, continues after the cabinet is formulated. Through his close touch with the Chamber, the president can advise the prime minister to resign because his support is failing within the Chamber. Thus the observation that no cabinet has failed to receive a vote of confidence is explained not by the Chamber's impotence, as some have concluded,[17] but rather by the open communication and consultation between the Chamber and the president, which allows preferences to be voiced outside the formality of roll-call voting.

In the absence of majority parties in the Chamber, the power of dissolving the Chamber and calling for a new election is a rather ineffective instrument. Even if he could find a cabinet to agree to the dissolution, the president stands little to gain. Since he is nonpartisan, he cannot expect his political party to win the election. Because members of the Chamber are closely related to their constituencies, a president from a different constituency, with no political party, and in many cases from a different religion has little chance of influencing the voters' choice. This is why few presidents have resorted to this method as a means of increasing their political support. In fact when Shihab in 1960 and Helou in 1969 were faced with a political impasse, they threatened to resign rather than dissolve the Chamber.

The president's powers to reward are as limited as his powers to punish. The Civil Service is less his creation than the cabinet's. Although the president theoretically heads bureaucracy, the latter enjoys almost total immunity from dismissal. Once a civil servant is appointed, he cannot be dismissed unless he commits a flagrant violation. Only under extraordinary circumstances and with the explicit approval and authorization of the Chamber and the cabinet can the president dismiss a civil servant from his job. Even when the president has been empowered to dismiss an employee, his action has usually been required endless negotiations with the cabinet, the Chamber, and other prominent leaders of opinion. In the final analysis the aggrieved employee is entitled to appeal his case to the Council of State, which can overrule the decision. Through this immunity the bureaucracy in Lebanon, even at the top levels, consists of a motley array of all political shades.

Appointments to high-level jobs are as much removed from the president's exclusive control as dismissal. A multiplicity of factors must be taken into account when dealing with each single case. Sectarianism and regionalism are important variables, as are the interests of cabinet members, legislative leaders, and other leaders. Thus what is normally a source of strength to the chief executive, appointments and dismissals, turns out to be only marginally under the Lebanese president's control. Higher civil servants appointed under former administrations tend to continue in their jobs, thus creating a cadre of "trustee" bureaucrats.

While the absence of majority political parties in the Chamber restrains executive power, it can simultaneously be a source of strength. The president can act as a broker among the various interests. Presidents who manage to maintain an image of objectivity, fairness, and nonpartisanship do negotiate compromises between various interest groups. The budget is usually the result of such negotiation and compromise. Thus, contrary to the overpowering leviathan image of the president dominant in the literature on Lebanon, the president operates under severe constitutional and political limitations. The president, the cabinet, and the Chamber are so closely intermeshed with each other that it is conceptually sounder to view their relationship as a set of three concentric circles rather than as separate dichotomous institutions.

Procedural Reforms

Legislatures have usually been accused of reacting too slowly to the rapid changes characteristic of developing societies. Too concerned about their prerogatives and privileges, legislators find themselves unable to cope with needed legislation. The cumbersome nature of the legislative process with its tedious methods of procrastination and its proclivity for statism does not equip legislatures with a mechanism to initiate or even to respond promptly to needed changes. Legislative institutions which fail to develop a reasonably quick response mechanism to change find themselves superseded by a strong executive supported by a mobilizing political party, an army, or a bureaucracy.

The Chamber of Deputies in Lebanon, in spite of the frequent accusation of its critics that it is a copy of the parliament under the Third Republic in France, developed-sophisticated mechanisms to cope with change and at the same time to maintain itself at the center of decision-making. Two methods will be discussed: the ways bills are introduced and delegated legislation.

Methods of Bill Introduction

Proposed legislation, whether initiated by the government or by individual members, can take any of three routes in the Chamber. In the regular procedure proposed legislation is deposited at the office of the president of the Chamber, who with the help of the bureau decides on forwarding it to the appropriate committee for consideration. Theoretically the committee must report back to the Chamber within forty days, but they are entitled to ask the president for a time extension if the need arises. If a committee fails to report within the prescribed time, the Chamber, acting through the president, can force a recall of the proposed bill. This procedure, however, is rarely used.

The second route is the "urgent" method. Here the proposed legislation must be accompanied by an explanatory statement justifying the need for urgency. The president forwards the proposed bill to the appropriate committee, which has to give this bill priority over regular bills. The committee must present its recommendations to the Chamber within one week. If the Chamber fails to act (accept, amend, reject, or return) on the proposed bill within forty days, the president of the Republic, with the approval of the Council of Ministers, then has the right to promulgate the proposal as law.

The third route is the "double urgent" method. Bills presented under the double urgent method cannot exceed one article and require a statement of justification for their urgency. Such bills bypass the committees and are taken up directly on the floor.

Legislation through the urgent and the double urgent methods has long been a controversial among the members of the Chamber. While all those engaged in the controversy realize that circumstances may require the government to use the urgent methods, they object to the frequency with which the executive, particularly Shihab, has done so. The concern has centered on the subject matter of urgent legislation and the procedure that the Chamber must follow in dealing with it.

Advocates of increased legislative power argue that the constitution clearly states that certain areas of legislation cannot become law except if clearly acted upon by the Chamber. These areas, they argue, cannot be presented under the urgent or the double urgent methods. The areas include: levying of new taxes, the amendment or abolishing taxes, budget proposals, proposed emergency appropriations exceeding £15,000 ($5,000), contracting a loan, and granting franchises and monopoly rights.[18] Bills in these areas must be presented under the regular provision.

And while admitting the government's need for the urgent method of proposing legislation, proponents of increased legislative power feel that the following procedures should be instituted in considering urgent bills. The method should only be used when there are special extenuating circumstances, and the Chamber should decide whether to accept or reject the urgency status of a bill.[19] If it rejects the urgency of a bill, then that bill should follow the regular procedure.

Moreover, the forty-day period should be applicable only during the regular session of the Chamber. If it is to be applied during extraordinary sessions, then the proposed urgent bills should be included in the original agenda of the extraordinary session at the time the Chamber is asked to convene. In addition the forty-day period should start when the whole text of the proposed bill and the accompanying justification have been distributed to all the members of the Chamber in session. Action by the Chamber does not simply mean approval but includes amendment, rejection, or even denial of the bill's urgency. The prevailing practice of calculating the forty-day period either from the time the bill is deposited at the bureau of the Chamber or when it is forwarded to the committee without being considered in its entirety by the Chamber should be abandoned. If members of the Chamber are to be responsible for acting or failing to act upon a proposed bill, then, the reformists suggest, they should know its full content and not simply its subject matter. Then and only then can the executive promulgate the bill as law.[20]

This group of reformists goes on to suggest that each deputy should be entitled to ask the president of the Chamber, through a justified written proposal, that a vote be taken with regard to the urgency of a proposed bill even after the urgency provision has already been granted by the Chamber. The proposals for determining the urgency of the bill should be put to a vote at the beginning of the first session, and if the urgency status is denied then that bill should follow the regular procedure. To avoid situations where a committee may neglect its work, this group proposes that committees be required to study urgent bills before the rest of regular legislation. If a committee fails to present its recommendations within a specific time (between seven and twenty days) the president of the Chamber should have the right to recall the proposed bill and put it up for floor debate and action. Furthermore, in preparing the agenda of the session, the president of the Chamber should include the urgently proposed bills and present them to the floor before the other regular business.

In recent years some of these recommendations have been adopted. Furthermore, extensive use of the urgent method has subsided. Table 9 shows the distribution of bills by methods introduced and the percentage approved in each category from 1953 to June 1972.

In analyzing table 9, we notice that 52 percent of the bills have been introduced through the regular method with 53 percent of them obtaining Chamber approval. The remaining 47 percent have been rejected, postponed, referred back to the committee, or not reported at all from the committees; this indicates the controversial nature and importance of the bills introduced by the regular method. The number of urgent bills has not exceeded 29 percent of the total introduced. Of the urgent bills, 38 percent were approved by the Chamber, 33 percent were passed by executive decree, and 29 percent were

Table 9[1]

Proposed Bills in Accordance With Method of Introduction and Percentage Approved in Each Category 1953–1972

Method of Introduction	Total N Bills	Percentage of Total	N Bills Approved by Chamber	Percentage Bills Approved
Regular	2149	52	1137	53
Urgent	1209	29	461	38
			398[2]	33 71
Double Urgent	799	19	508	64
			26[2]	3 67
Total	4157	100		

[1] The data was collected by the author from the official register of the Chamber in the summer of 1972.

[2] Approved by executive decree.

either rejected, postponed, withdrawn by the government, or referred to committee under the regular method. In a separate study it was found that the overwhelming majority of bills passed by decree were either minor bills or bills that had been with the Chamber several months after the expiration of the forty-day period.[21] It was also found that Chamber unwillingness to deal with urgent bills even after they had been under its consideration for several months after the forty-day period is only partially due to lack of professional staff support. The Chamber prefers to have the executive promulgate such bills by decree and thus be held responsible in case of failure. There is no doubt, however, that an aggressive executive with some support in the Chamber, as was the case with President Shihab between 1960–1964, could turn this instrument into a major tool of usurping power from the legislature. Thus far the urgent method has been largely employed to introduce legislation in areas where there is maximum consensus or in areas where the legislature has been reluctant to move with the necessary speed.

Legislation introduced through the double urgent method is usually consensus legislation and is similar to legislation introduced on the Consent Calendar of the House of Representatives in the US Congress.[22] This is why about 64 percent of the bills introduced through this method are approved by the Chamber. The remaining 36 percent are either rejected, postponed, or referred back to committee to be studied under the urgent or the regular methods. Only 3 percent have been passed by an executive decree after being reintroduced under the urgent method.

Delegated Legislative Power

Under certain exceptional circumstances, like the 1952 overthrow of Bishara al-Khouri, the 1958 civil war, or the 1967 Six Day War, the Chamber of Deputies may delegate to the cabinet the right to legislate in specified areas for a limited period of time. This is a device to meet emergency needs in circumstances that render the time-consuming legislative process inoperative.

Critics of this device, including both politicians and social scientists, have argued that if used excessively it could undermine the legislative power of the legislature. A review of the way this power can be used and the instances in which it was used point to different conclusions. To start with, the power can be obtained only in exceptional emergency conditions for a limited time after the approval of the Chamber. Moreover this power is delegated to a cabinet composed of members who usually represent the major political forces in the Chamber. Delegation of such a power renders the cabinet's role similar to that played by the Rules Committee of the House of Representatives in the US Congress; it allows the political leadership in the Chamber to reach a quick compromise in a Chamber where no majority party exists.

Furthermore, the Chamber as a whole has two chances to review the proposed legislation of the cabinet. When the cabinet asks for the power of delegated legislation, it approves the general principles of the proposed legislation as submitted by the cabinet in its statement to the Chamber; and when the time in which the cabinet was authorized to legislate expires, the Chamber can review whatever legislative decrees the government has passed. The Chamber can reject, amend, or approve the legislative decrees as it sees fit. It is therefore unlikely for a

Table 10

Delegated Legislation, Duration, and Subject Matter Since Independence 1953–1972

Duration	Subject Matter
1952 (6 Months)	Reorganization of the Administration. Socioeconomic legislation. Political legislation.
1954 (3 Months)	To amend legislation prepared in 1952.
1958 (6 Months)	Administrative reorganization. Socioeconomic legislation and political legislation.
1965 (3 Months)	Administrative reorganization. Socioeconomic legislation and political legislation.
1967 (2 Months)	Financial economic legislation and national security. Internal and public order.

Source: Compiled by the author.

cabinet that represents a coalition of the major political forces in the Chamber to undertake legislation that is in defiance of what the majority of the Chamber wants, especially when it is in the power of the Chamber to reverse whatever legislation has been enacted by a simple majority.

Since independence the Chamber has delegated its legislative power to the cabinet five times for a limited period of time, but in very broadly defined areas, as table 10 shows.

While delegated legislation has enabled the system to face urgent needs, it has not prevented the Chamber from being the final authority in the legislative field. Once an emergency situation has passed, many legislative decrees have either been amended or repealed. Much of the basic legislation enacted through legislative decrees, if not revoked altogether, has been amended either to remove weaknesses not anticipated at the time of enactment or to reflect the legislators' preferences. An analysis of active Lebanese laws in 1968 reveals that the overall bulk of major legislation, particularly political matters, has been enacted by the Chamber. Table 11 shows the laws that were operative in 1968 and the method by which they were enacted. Over 65 percent were enacted by the Chamber through the regular method, while 14.4 percent and 19.8 percent were enacted by legislative decree and decree laws, respectively.[23]

Table 11

Active Legislation Between 1943–1968 By Methods Issued and Regime
(1968 collection of laws)

Method Used	al Khouri 1943–1952 N	Shamun 1952–1958 N	Shihab 1958–1964 N	Helou 1964–1968 N	Total	%
Law	103	83	84	126	396	65.8
Legislative Decree		6	63	18	87	14.4
Decree Law	25	23	37	34	119	19.8
Total	128	112	184	178	602	100.0

Source: Compiled by the author.

It is significant to note that the number of decree laws and legislative decrees passed during al-Khouri's and Shamun's presidencies were much lower than decree laws and legislative decrees passed by Shihab alone. Two reasons account for this. The first is Shihab's military background, which made him impatient with the legislative process and distrustful of politicians. He therefore made extensive use of the urgent method and the delegated legislative power given to him right after the 1958 civil war. The second reason is that as time passes, the Chamber tends to amend or abrogate legislation passed under the urgent method or as delegated legislation. In other words, the likelihood of legislative decrees or decree laws surviving for any length of time unamended is less than for a law enacted through legislation in the Chamber.

By way of examination of the type of enactment method used, the laws existing in 1968 have been divided into eight categories and classified according to the method by which they were enacted. Table 12 shows the distribution: legislation enacted through legislative decree and decree law has been used most frequently in administrative and government reorganization, followed by economics, health and social welfare, defense, and education. In political legislation, such as nationality and individual rights, foreign affairs, and local government, most legislation was enacted by the Chamber through the regular method.

As a further means of examining the importance of legislation enacted by each method, the 1968 active laws have been di-

Table 12

Active Legislation By Subject Matter and Methods Passed
(1968 collection of laws)

Types of Legislation	Law	Legislative Decree	Decree Law	Total
Administration and Government Organization	108	45	48	201
Nationality and Individual Rights	54	4	6	64
Foreign Affairs	28	3		31
Defense	30		16	46
Economics	127	13	43	183
Health and Social Welfare	22	14	2	38
Education	14	5	2	21
Local Government	13	3	2	18
Total	396	87	119	602

Source: Compiled by the author.

vided into three categories: important, intermediate, and minor legislation. The combination of factors used to classify the laws into each category were: time span of the law, funds and number of people involved, and political implication of the law. Table 13 shows the distribution obtained from this classification. Of the legislation enacted by the Chamber, over 51 percent was important, more than 19 percent was intermediate and 28.5 percent was minor, while only 17.2 percent of the legislative decrees and 14.3 of decree laws could be classified as important. Forty-six percent of the legislative decrees and 58.8 percent of the decree laws were minor laws. It is therefore safe to conclude that while delegated legislative power is an appropriate safety valve allowing the political institutions in the country enough flexibility to respond quickly to emergencies, in the long run the bulk of major legislation is enacted by the Chamber under the regular method.

Table 13

Methods Issued and Importance of Legislation
(1968 collection of laws)

Method Issued	Total N	Important N	Important %	Intermediate N	Intermediate %	Minor N	Minor %
Law	396	205	51.8	78	19.7	113	28.5
Legislative Decree	87	15	17.2	32	36.8	40	46.0
Decree Law	119	17	14.3	32	26.9	70	58.8

Source: Computed by the author.

Organizational Reforms

Organizational reforms refer to those proposals aimed at providing the legislature with appropriate structures and competent personnel to enable it to perform its functions within the present constitutional setup.

The Committee System

As is the case in all its political structures, committee composition reflects an emphasis on consensus politics. Although committee members are elected annually by the whole Chamber, a large degree of membership continuity exists. Usually the composition of each committee is informally agreed upon by the various bloc and parliamentary leaders before the election. Assignment to committees usually takes into account geographical and political distribution, individual preference of the member, and expertise in the subject matter. With the exception of a few prestigious committees like Finance and Budget, Foreign Relations, Administration and Justice, Defense, and Public Works, competition to join a committee is very low. As a matter of fact as table 14 shows, there are more committee seats than members in the Chamber.

In addition the Chamber has a special select committee to adjudicate disputes and complaints connected with electoral results. In other words, the bureau of the Chamber, the Committee of Internal Order of the Chamber, and the Committee of

Table 14

Standing Committees of the Chamber

Name of Committee	Number of Members
Finance and Budget	17
Administration and Justice	15
Public Works	15
Foreign Affairs	15
Labor and Social Affairs	12
Public Education	12
Agriculture	12
National Economy	12
National Defense	10
Public Health	10
National Planning	10
Post, Telephone, and Telegraph	10
Internal Order of the Chamber	8
Total 13	158

Electoral Adjudication are all intended to insure the internal autonomy of the Chamber in running its own affairs, adopting its rules and procedures, and adjudicating the electoral claims of its members.

Since cabinet members cannot be committee members and since the size of the cabinet is usually about fifteen, the number of deputies eligible to join committees is no more than eighty-three. The internal regulations of the Chamber require a member to belong to at least one committee and to no more than two. (The Committee of Internal Order is excluded from this regulation.) Since many of the leaders of political parties or parliamentary blocs, prospective prime ministers, and presidents of the Chamber choose to join only one committee (in some cases no committee at all), it has become the practice in recent years to ask some members to join more than two committees.

Unlike the case in the US Congress, joining a committee is not a sign of political power, but a sign of sacrifice and willingness of the deputy to work hard. This is due to several reasons. Work on a committee does not involve any monetary remuneration; it has to be done in the absence of any staff help except for a secretary who acts in a clerical capacity; but most significantly is the low importance attached to decisions reached at the committee level.

Under a system where executive-legislative coordination takes place at more than one level, where the president of the Chamber is very powerful, where committees lack technical and professional help, where political parties are not in a dominant position, and where the legislative process itself militates against a strong committee, the committee's role in decision-making becomes insignificant. Differences over proposed legislation are ironed out before a bill reaches the committee. Through supporters either in the bureaucracy or in the cabinet, interested parties try to influence the content of legislation at the time it is being prepared by the bureaucracy or when it is being deliberated upon by the Council of Ministers. The fact that most bills (about 80 percent) which are reported by the committee are approved either unanimously (60 percent) or by a majority (20 percent) of the Chamber does not indicate a strong committee system.[24] Committees, composed on the same model as the cabinet with representatives of all major segments of the Chamber, tend to act through consensus rather than through majority-minority votes. Any member of the Chamber can attend a committee meeting and participate in all the deliberations short of having the right to vote.

The fact that the president of the Chamber enjoys great powers in assigning bills, determining priorities, and setting up agendas for the parliamentary session leaves the committees tied to him regarding what bills to consider and in what order. Also the right of the government to present proposed legislation under the double urgent method can remove a bill from committee discussion and put it directly on the floor. Even under the provisions of urgent legislation, the committee has only one week to act on the bill before it must be forwarded to the floor. Furthermore the Chamber has the right to recall a bill from a committee, assign it to another committee, or take it directly to the floor. Added to these technical limitations is the intimate relationship which exists between a committee chairman, the president of the Chamber, and the prime minister or the minister concerned. Finally, since final action on bills is taken on the floor and in the absence of organized majority parties, the committee seeks to recommend what is generally acceptable rather than what its chairman wants. (A committee chairman gains power through his ability to gear his actions to the satisfaction of the largest number possible of his colleagues.)

All proposals for committee reform center around increasing the power of the committee by providing it with professional staff and the prolonging of the committee term from one year to four years, making it coterminous with the term of the legislature. Similar proposals have been advocated with regard to the president of the Chamber. The difficulties in adopting such proposals stem from the sectarian and political composition of the legislature. Since the president of the Chamber is always a Shia Muslim, non-Shia members are not enthusiastic about strengthening that office and prefer to keep it open to their influence through the yearly election. Furthermore, extending the term of the president and the committee members requires a constitutional amendment, an act that many Christian deputies are fearful to undertake since it may open the door to other amendments, such as amending the powers of the presidency.

With regard to providing the committees with professional staff, many independent members fear that such a course of action would strengthen the power of the chairman and in the absence of organized political parties would put him beyond the control of the individual members. Furthermore, it is argued that the present one-year term keeps a measure of flexibility to meet political exigencies that are often reflected in recurrent cabinet turnovers enabling the members of parliament to become cabinet members.

Competent Legislative Staff

The organizational confusion and staff inefficiency and incompetency of the Lebanese Chamber of Deputies have long been a subject of criticism by the press and the rank-and-file deputies. While unqualified staff members managed to stay around and keep their positions, those who were qualified snapped up the first opportunity to move to an executive position. Lacking job security and a clear personnel policy, the fortune of the Chamber's staff had to depend on political favoritism. The reforms adopted in the summer of 1971 came as an answer to these problems. They provided the legislative staff with a coherent and clear personnel policy, which defined job qualifications, recruitment procedures, promotions, transfers, dismissals, and salary scales. All new entrants to the legislative staff, except those who belonged to the top two grades, were required to pass a competitive examination. Employees already working in the Chamber were required to pass a qualifying examination before they could continue to hold their jobs. The jurisdiction as well as the job description of each position was clearly defined. Almost the same personnel laws that applied to the executive civil service were adopted for the legislative staff.

The reforms recognized the need for professional staff to help the president of the Chamber in certain specific fields, and all professional staff were to be under his direct supervision. The reform fell short, however, of providing any professional staff to work directly with legislative committees. Opposition to the provision of professional staff to committees was based on the belief that since the Chamber works in close association with the government, it has easy access to the professional staff available in the various government agencies for information, opinion, or advice. If expert advice is needed, the president of the Chamber may contract for the services of outside professionals for a temporary period.

Although permanent professional staff attached to committees were not deemed necessary, all who are to occupy positions in Category III are required to have a university degree in law or in some other field of specialty. Many of the positions in Category II (about sixteen) are also required to hold university degrees, although appointment is not subject to competitive examination. Each parliamentary committee has been assigned a secretary who holds a university degree in law or another specialty. The clerical and secretarial work is to be carried out by centrally organized units (see table 15).

Clearly, the new organization, while specifying the limits within which the president can operate with regard to the Chamber's staff, has strengthened his position, for he has full control of a bureaucracy of about 135 members, excluding the

Table 15

The New Organizational Chart for the Lebanese Chamber of Deputies

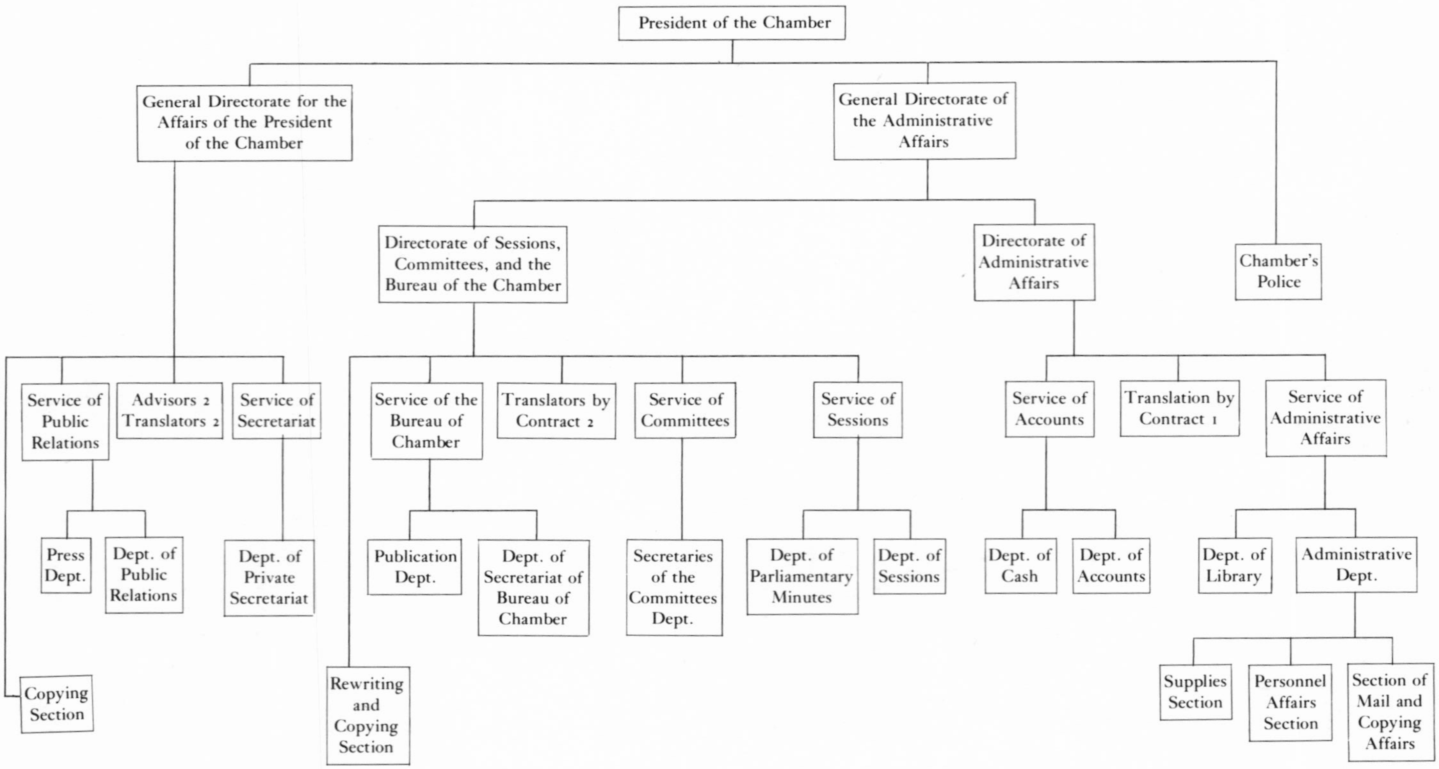

police force, which is about 75 in number. The president of the Chamber has been provided with a special General Directorate, secretariats, translators, advisors, a public relations man, and a press advisor; all of these will work to augment the power of the speaker and, consequently, the Chamber. In 1973 the Lebanese legislature passed a resolution to establish a Research and Studies Directorate to work under the supervision of the president of the Chamber. The implementation of this resolution is still under way.

Postscript

The recent civil war in Lebanon gave an urgency to some of the legislative reforms suggested in this chapter. It also gave rise to new calls for additional legislative reforms.

Of all the political institutions in Lebanon, the Chamber of Deputies emerged as the core around which political solutions to the Lebanese bloody war are likely to be developed.

Two central positions were made clear throughout this war. The first had to do with redistribution of the Chamber's seats among the various groups in the country and the second was to redefine the relationship between the legislature and the executive.

As to the redistribution of the Chamber's seats, the proposals ranged from outright abolition of sectarianism as advocated by the Front of the Nationalist and Leftist parties under the leadership of Kamal Jumblat, to a centrist position calling for the need to increase the share of the Moslem section of the population, especially the Shia sect, and the gradual abolishing of political sectarianism. The Christian right, while admitting the need for minor adjustment in seat distribution, maintained the necessity of a sectarian division of political power.

With regard to the relationship between the legislature and the President, the major reform proposals called for the strengthening of the legislature by giving it the right to elect the Prime Minister and the ministers. This is contrary to the existing constitutional provisions which give the President of the Republic the power to nominate and accept the resignation of the Cabinet; and the Chamber the right to grant or withdraw votes of confidence from the Cabinet. Advocates of this constitutional amendment argue that this suggested reform will free the Prime Minister (who is always a Moslem Sunni) and make him responsible and accountable only to the Chamber.

Other suggested legislative reforms call for the separation of membership in the Chamber from membership in the Cabinet so that the Chamber may be free and independent to exercise its function of control and oversight.

Finally, it has been suggested that as a means to strengthen the legislature the Constitution should be amended so that the President of the Republic may no longer be empowered to dissolve the Chamber of Deputies in case of conflict.

It should be pointed out that all of these suggested reforms, if and when they are enacted, will be enacted with the professed goal of strenthening the Chamber and weakening the Presidency which was undermined and distrusted during the war. Whether these reforms, if enacted, will achieve their purported objectives is not a foregone conclusion. It is also erroneous to conclude that the presidency had been permanently weakened and irreparably damaged. The political future of the Lebanese political institutions will, for some time at least, be tied to actions, intentions and goals of the Syrian-Arab troops (the deterrent force) that are presently keeping law and order in Lebanon.

Author's Note

This chapter is based on research done in connection with the author's latest book entitled, *Legislative and Political Development: Lebanon 1842–1972* (Durham, NC: Duke University Press 1976) especially Chapters 5 and 6.

Notes

1. Mount Lebanon was divided into two districts; one ruled by a Christian, the other by a Druze. See Kamal Salibi, *The Modern History of Lebanon* (New York: Frederick A. Praeger, 1965), pp. 53–79.

2. Kamal Salibi, *Modern History of Lebanaon*, pp. 106–119.

3. Since it was adopted in 1926 the Lebanese Constitution has been amended six times by the legislature and one time by an executive decree.

4. The National Pact is a compromise agreement among the Muslims and Christians in Lebanon regarding the distribution of power among Lebanese national entities.

5. Article 2 of the Internal Rules of the Chamber in Lebanese Political Science Association (ed.) *Collection of Basic Documents Relating to the Political System in Lebanon* (Beirut: Sader Press, 1968).

6. As one of its standing committees the Chamber yearly elects eight deputies to form the Committee on Internal Rules, which has the responsibility to consider, interpret, and deliberate on procedural matters.

7. See Antoine Arej, *Assultat al Ama* (Lebanon: The Public Authorities), (Beirut: Badran Press, 1963), p. 116.

8. See Decree No. 66 taken by Ahmad al Assa'd dated 19 March 1953 in archives of the Lebanese Chamber of Deputies.

9. The Socialist National Front, to which President Shamun belonged and which was credited with ousting President al Khouri from power in 1952, included as part of its reform platform the strengthening of individual and public liberties guaranteed in the Constitution, womens' sufferage, and limiting the power of the president to fit the parliamentary form of government. For details see Anwar al Khatib, *Constitutional Collection*, Vol. II (Beirut: Cadmus Press, 1970), pp. 544–548 (in Arabic).

10. The new Internal Rules have 118 articles instead of 228.

11. Arnold Hottinger, "Zu'ama' in Historical Perspective" in Leonard Binder, ed., *Politics in Lebanon* (New York: John Wiley and Sons, Inc., 1966), p. 85 and 105.

12. Since independence in 1943 Lebanon has had six electoral laws promulgated. See Lebanese Political Science Association, *Collection of Basic Documents Relating to the Political System in Lebanon* (Beirut: Sader Press, 1968), in Arabic.

13. Particularly Legislative Decree 112 of 1959 concerning the personnel system in Lebanon and the establishment of a Civil Service Board. For details on this subject, see Iskandar E. Bashir, *Planned Administrative Change in Lebanaon*, (Beirut: American University of Beirut, n.d.); Adnan G. Iskandar, *Bureaucracy in Lebanon*, (Beirut: American University of Beirut, 1964); Abdo Baaklini, "The Civil Service Board in Lebanon," (MA thesis, American University of Beirut, 1963).

14. See interview with Prime Minister Saeb Salam, *Al Nahar*, 28 June 1971; interview with Raymond Eddeh, *Al Nahar*, 5 July 1971. For Salam's and Eddeh's accusation against Shihabism and the military interference in politics, see the *Parliamentary Record* of 1968, sessions 29 May and 6 August 1968.

15. An interview with Prime Minister Saeb Salam published in *Al Nahar*, 15 August 1971. Raymond Eddeh proposed three laws to limit the power of the army; all were approved in 1971.

16. The term secularists refers to national and leftist political parties such as the Syrian Social Nationalist Party and the Lebanese Communist Party.

17. R. E. Crow, "Parliament in the Lebanese Political System," in A. Kornberg and L. Musolf (eds.) *Legislatures in Developmental Perspectives.* (Durham, NC: Duke University Press, 1970), pp. 297–299.

18. See articles 81, 82, 83, 85, 88, and 89 of the Lebanese Constitution.

19. Articles 86 and 89 of Internal Rules of the Chamber.

20. *Parliamentary Life*, 1972, pp. 50–92.

21. The nature of legislation passed by the Chamber of Deputies in Lebanon since independence is the subject of a forthcoming study by the author.

22. L. Rieselbach, *Congressional Politics*, (New York: McGraw-Hill, 1973), p. 118.

23. Decree laws are those bills introduced by the urgent methods and are promulgated by the executive after forty days in the Chamber with no action. Legislative decrees are those enacted by the executive in accordance with delegated legislative power.

24. R. E. Crow, "Parliament in the Lebanese Political System," p. 295.

Index

[redacted]